The Trueblood Professors' Seminar

Accounting and Auditing Case Studies

DISCUSSION LEADER'S GUIDE

*The Touche Ross Foundation
and
The American Accounting Association*

With the exception of reproduction by colleges and universities for classroom use,
all rights reserved, and no portion hereof may be reproduced without the written consent
of the holder of this copyright.
Copyright© 1983, The Touche Ross Foundation
Library of Congress Catalog Number: 83-50669
ISBN: 0-86359-045-2

Table of Contents

Case No.	Title	Page No.
	Preface	
	Henry C. Korff	iv
	Foreword	
	Thomas J. Burns	vi
1.	Whose Audit Report Is It Anyway?	2
2.	Big GAAP/Little GAAP	7
3.	Special Reports	12
4.	Off-Balance-Sheet Financing	21
5.	Debt vs. Equity	28
6.	Shareholder Accounting	33
7.	Employee-Stockholder Transactions	39
8.	Troubled Debt Restructuring	46
9.	Purchase Accounting — Reporting Results	53
10.	Purchase Accounting — A Bargain Purchase	60
11.	Pooling of Interests Accounting — Intent	67
12.	Interim Accounting — Deferral of Costs	73
13.	Uncertainties — Accounting and/or Reporting	80
14.	Liquidity Problems	87
15.	Accounting for Hindsight	96
16.	Contingencies	103
17.	Profit Recognition	108
18.	Cost of Goods Sold — and Otherwise Disposed of	112
19.	Accounting for Doubtful Real Estate Loans	119
20.	Depreciation	126
21.	Audit Planning	133
22.	Auditing — Confirmations	138
23.	Prior Period Adjustments	144
24.	Historical Cost Accounting	149
25.	Letter of Representations	159
26.	New Client Acceptance	167
27.	Attorney/Auditor Responsibility	174
28.	Auditing Commission Payments	183
	Appendices	
	AAA Representatives Attending Trueblood Professors' Seminars	191
	Trueblood Professors' Seminars Touche Ross & Co. Faculty	192

Preface

Touche Ross & Co. began the professors' seminar program in 1966. The first session addressed the subject of computer auditing, and interestingly, computer auditing continues to be a profession-wide critical topic seventeen years later. The star performers of the first program were Touche partner Greg Boni (now deceased), who gave a nearly spellbinding lecture on "A Conceptual Analysis of Auditing"; Boni was a genius of a man who had also been the thesis advisor to Tom Porter, the second instructor, who was then a Ph.D. candidate at Columbia University, and is now a partner in the Seattle office. The third member of the faculty was Dennis Mulvihill, who had received his Ph.D. from the University of Pittsburgh and is now a partner in the Melville, Long Island office. Three computer auditing seminars for professors were held. All subsequent seminars, with one or two exceptions, have dealt with current accounting and auditing topics. Since the initial programs, nearly a thousand professors from more than 300 schools have participated in these programs.

We may have never held a seminar for professors were it not for the support of Robert Beyer, who was then Managing Partner of the firm. It was he who agreed to experiment with the program and approved the budgets necessary to cover all the expenses. (Robert Beyer is also responsible for the CMA Gold Medal given for the highest grades on the Certified Management Accountant examination.)

From the beginning, the program has received high praise and the professors who have participated urged us to put together the case material used in the program and make it available for classroom work. The reason for this publication is to honor that request.

The programs have had two important ingredients: the case material and the discussion leaders. The cases are prepared by a gifted group of partners working on our National Accounting and Auditing staff. Their objective is to capture the essence of a client problem, usually in a few paragraphs, design the description to stimulate group discussion, and disguise the situation enough so as to protect client confidentiality. Even with good case material, programs might fall short if it were not for the skills of the discussion leaders.

The first seminar cases were designed by Hans J. Shield, an Austrian-educated member of our National Accounting and Auditing staff who worked for Robert M. Trueblood. Donald J. Bevis, who served as Managing Partner of Touche Ross, Bailey & Smart and was subsequently appointed a member of the Accounting Principles Board for a number of years, also designed cases and led discussions. Those professors who attended these initial programs still remind me of the favorable impression they retain of our sharing with them the most challenging and interesting professional issues facing our firm and our clients. The Seminar format has always required two discussion leaders, a National Accounting and Auditing staff partner and a line partner from the field, who on a daily basis works with implementation issues in the client environment. Robert J. Sack, who is now a partner in the Cleveland office, deserves special mention. Sack is undoubtedly the most outstanding discussion leader in the accounting profession. Those who have attended the program give testimony to this through the hundreds of complimentary letters we have received concerning Bob's great skill.

Upon the death of Robert M. Trueblood, Chairman of the Board of Touche Ross & Co., Managing Partner Russell E. Palmer suggested that we recognize the contributions Trueblood made to the firm and to the profession in some appropriate way. After considering several alternatives, I proposed that we share the professors' seminars with the American Accounting Association and name them the Trueblood Professors' Seminar. The trustees of the Touche Ross Foundation concurred and the President of the Touche Ross Foundation, Gerald Polansky — a member of the Board of Directors of Touche Ross & Co. — and Robert M. Anthony — the President of the American Accounting Association — and I prepared an agreement in which we made a three-year commitment to the American Accounting Association to have the professors' program as a part of the professional development activities of AAA. The original three-year commitment has been extended twice. Polansky headed up a pledge campaign to honor Trueblood, and the funds contributed by individual partners were used to finance the first eighteen seminars. Subsequently, Touche Ross & Co. has contributed to the Foundation the necessary funds for the seminars. Without the help of Russell E. Palmer, our Managing Partner at the time, the program could not have been continued.

In more recent years, the National Accounting and Auditing staff, under the direction of Donald Georgen and Robert Kay and with support from Robert Sack, Michael Bohan and Raymond Perry, prepared much of the case material which was used both in our own partner and manager training programs and subsequently shared with professors attending the seminar programs.

As a result of "sharing" the program with the AAA, Touche Ross & Co. also transferred to AAA the responsibility for determining the selection procedures to be used in inviting participants to the program. Lists of schools have been compiled and selection is made on a random basis. Individual professor participants are chosen by accounting department chairpersons. Previously the Foundation had selected and invited professors to attend based upon recommendations from our local offices.

The cases contained in this publication represent the work of a number of Touche partners, but recognition must go to Mike Bohan, Bob Sack, Bob Kay, and especially to Tom Wall, a Touche partner in the San Francisco office, who worked hard writing, editing, redrafting, and doing all those things necessary to put the discussion leader's material together.

The seminar program continues with support from our present Managing Partner, David Moxley, and the National Director of Accounting and Auditing, Stanley Russell.

It is Touche's goal to have our professor friends and students use the cases in the college classroom in a way which will enhance the development of future professional accountants. The material has been designed so that one volume of cases, instructor guidelines and reference material, will be available for professors of accounting, and a separate volume, containing the cases and selected reference material, will be available to students of accounting. While the material is copyrighted, professors are free to duplicate the material for classroom usage. The case material may not be used in books, manuals, articles or other publications.

In recognition of the many professors who have supported the program through their AAA committee work and the partners of Touche who have made the programs so successful, we have included their names in the appendices.

Special mention should also be made of AAA President Yuji Ijiri of Carnegie-Mellon University, President-elect Harold Q. Langenderfer of the University of North Carolina, and Professor Samuel Frumer of Indiana University, who offered encouragement to publish the cases in cooperation with the American Accounting Association. Special thanks are also extended to Paul L. Gerhardt, Executive Director of the AAA, Janet G. Nuñez, Publications Director, and to Carol Galante, the Assistant Secretary/Treasurer of the Touche Ross Foundation.

Henry C. Korff
Secretary/Treasurer
The Touche Ross Foundation

Foreword

The American Accounting Association, in cooperation with The Touche Ross Foundation, is most happy to make available to its members and other accounting educators a compilation of the outstanding cases presented at the Trueblood Seminars.

Since 1975 the Trueblood Seminars have been held three times annually in honor of Robert M. Trueblood, former Chairman of the Board of Touche Ross. Nearly a thousand professors from among more than 300 institutions have attended these seminars. Each seminar, administered by an Association committee and Touche Ross partners, has focused on 16 to 25 cases dealing with accounting and auditing issues, which have been developed from Touche Ross practice offices and which are presented by Touche Ross discussion leaders at an annual out-of-pocket cost to Touche Ross now approaching $100,000. The high quality of these cases has been judged as being of exceptional merit, even by professors such as myself who have not participated in a seminar but who have been provided with copies of some of these cases by attending colleagues or former students.

Now all of us are given the opportunity to have access to this unique source of educational material with the publication of these two volumes.

Thomas J. Burns
Professor and
Director of Education

The Trueblood Professors' Seminars

Accounting and Auditing
Case Studies

Discussion Leader's Guide

Whose Audit Report Is It Anyway?

You and your audit team examined the financial statements of Peoples County Farm Cooperative for the year ended December 31, 1980. Your audit report, dated February 18, 1981, was qualified significantly. Your middle paragraph explained that the cooperative had suffered significant losses in the past two years, had invested in certain ventures that were not working out, had not collected substantial past-due advances to members, and had not allocated significant cumulative losses to individual members.

In September, 1981, the cooperative issued a proxy in connection with a proposed merger with another cooperative. You were not aware of the proposed merger — it came to your attention when the client sent you a courtesy copy of the proxy. The proxy was prepared by the client's administrative officer with the help of client's legal counsel.

Most of the 1980 financial statements were included in the offering circular. A number of the more important footnotes were omitted — and so was your report. The proxy explains that the statements were audited by a major firm but does not mention your firm's name. It summarizes your qualified opinion and states that a full, audited annual report is available for inspection upon request.

A little piqued, you called the administrative officer and asked him why he omitted your report and the other financial data and disclosures. He explained that your report and the omitted disclosures were cumbersome and technical and would be difficult for the readers to understand as they were not educated in financial matters. "Besides," he went on, "neither your report nor those footnotes were necessary for the proxy. Our attorneys told us what we had to include to be legal and we included only those things they told us to include. Also, if I had included your report, you'd have been very upset that we didn't give you permission to redo the audit as of today. And we've already paid for one audit this year!"

WHAT SHOULD YOU DO NOW THAT YOU ARE AWARE
OF THE MERGER PROXY?

DISCUSSION LEADER'S GUIDE

Whose Audit Report Is It Anyway?

Objectives of the Case

This case focuses on the question of the right of clients to use, and control the use of, auditors' reports. In particular, the case deals with the unauthorized alteration or summarization of the report, and with the general reference to the fact that the statements were audited (without identification of the auditor) and to the implication that the statements presented are the ones that were audited when in fact that is not so. Upon completion of this case study the students should have an understanding of the obligation of auditors to deal with possible unauthorized use of their reports. In addition, the case study could lead to discussion of the question of the need for "auditors of record" or continuous auditor contact with client affairs.

Applicable Professional Pronouncements

Statement on Auditing Standards No. 1, Section 530 — Dating of the Independent Auditor's Report

Statement on Auditing Standards No. 37 — Filings Under Federal Securities Statutes

Business Assumptions and Other Data

Auditors and others are responsible under the 1933 Securities Act (Section 11) for untrue statements of material facts in registration statements. Their liability under that section could be viewed as more onerous than liability under the 1934 Act or under civil litigation or other similar proceedings. In recognition of this sterner provision in the 1933 Act, registration statements are required to have currently dated auditors' consents (by Section 7) before they are allowed to become effective. And, until recently, that was about the only control auditors had over their opinions that might be used in documents furnished shareholders.

A few years ago, amid the flurry of mergers and acquisitions, auditors and the Securities and Exchange Commission became painfully aware that a number of proxies contained auditors' reports included without knowledge of such auditors (to the end that the auditors had no opportunity to extend their procedures to consider "subsequent events," i.e., those between the date of the report and the date of the proxy). This shortfall was corrected by requiring a currently dated type of consent from the auditors, in substance similar to the requirements of the 1933 Act.

That is about where legally required control by auditors over subsequent use of their reports ends. Some other Securities and Exchange Commission filings can, and do, still contain auditors' reports without their knowledge, and thus without any possibility of their review of subsequent events. Two of the more common filings with such deficiencies are Form 8-K (usually in situations containing reproduced or photocopied financial statements and auditors' reports of companies being purchased by the filing company) and amendments to tax shelter offerings (usually in situations where additional units of the same shelter are being made available for public purchases).

While some measure of control, as noted above, is afforded auditors of publicly held companies, corresponding controls in other than SEC-reporting companies is severely limited — at times, nonexistent, as in the case at hand. The situation is changing, but gradually. For example, public offerings of municipal bonds in years past were typically made without audited financial statements. Then some offerings started to contain information about as shown in this case, and some began to contain full financials and complete auditors' reports. As the latter stage approached, underwriters began to insist on a comfort letter, currently dated, from the auditors, thus giving the auditors a chance to review subsequent events. Another force adding impetus is the bond rating house, which typically will now rate only bonds of those municipalities whose financial statements are audited. Still, neither the law nor professional auditing literature requires a currently dated consent, comfort letter, or the like for use of an auditor's report in a municipal offering document.

Except for Section 561 of SAS 1, and SAS 37, current auditing literature sets forth no requirement that auditors control the use of their reports after the dates of issuance. SAS 1 gives procedures to be followed by auditors who, subsequent to the date of their reports on audited financial statements, become aware that facts have existed as of that date which might have affected their reports. Statement 37 deals with procedures to be followed by auditors who consent to the inclusion of their report in a registration statement filed under the '33 Act.

The requirement for review of subsequent events under the 1933 Act is, in substance, an exception — the only exception — to Section 530 of Statement on Auditing Standards No. 1, which provides that "the auditor has no responsibility to make any inquiry or carry out any auditing procedures for the period after the date of his report, unless the auditor becomes aware that facts may have existed at the date of his report which might have affected his report had he then been aware of such facts." The language is clear that an auditor has no responsibility to make further investigation or inquiries as to events which have occurred during the period between the original report date and the date of release of a reissued report.

The profession skirted the issue at hand when it issued Statement on Auditing Standards No. 8, "Other Information in Documents Containing Audited Financial Statements," but it essentially limited the applicability of that statement to annual reports, which the proxy is not. Further, it limited the required procedures essentially to a reading of the other information to identify inconsistencies between that information and the financials, which is somewhat different from the auditor's concern here, which is the possibility of subsequent events requiring further handling. The students could discuss the advantages and disadvantages of extending Statement on Auditing Standards No. 8 from annual reports to cover all documents and, further, to require something more than identification of inconsistencies.

Limited as legal and professional requirements may be regarding reproduced financial statements and auditors' reports, they are prolific compared to the rules regarding summarization — or emasculation, in the Peoples case.

Case 1: Whose Audit Report Is It Anyway? 5

Discussion

The students may gain perspective from an early-on discussion of the purpose of a subsequent review by auditors. For filings under the 1933 Act, the purpose is clear: "To sustain the burden of proof that he has made a 'reasonable investigation' . . . , the auditor should extend his procedures with respect to subsequent events from the date of his report up to the effective date or as close thereto as is reasonable and practicable in the circumstances." But, can the legal requirement for a "reasonable investigation" be said to be equally applicable to security offerings outside the 1933 Act, to proxy solicitations, and other documents submitted to shareholders and prospective shareholders to influence their action, one way or the other, regarding issuance of additional securities? Points of view will differ, obviously, and certainly no easy answer exists. As noted previously, without benefit of any law or professional requirement, some progress toward the affirmative is being made, as in the municipal bond market. A strong possibility exists that review of subsequent events will either remain status quo or be expanded in relation to future court findings for or against auditors in situations such as this one.

It is hard to see how auditors could have much responsibility for subsequent review if they have no control over subsequent use of their reports or, as in this case, reference to their reports. When auditors release their reports they have no further control over their use. Professional literature is clear on that, except for 1933 Act filings. Yet, the public and the courts may not necessarily agree with that stated position.

The students ought to discuss the reasonableness of public assertion or court findings of auditor responsibility in cases outside the 1933 Act. They should understand how difficult it is for auditors to stay continuously involved in their clients' activities and to be continually updating their audits. But, on the other hand, it should be clear to the students that the public is ill-served by a situation where auditors audit financial statements and then effectively "wash their hands" of further responsibility; some would advocate the profession must look for ways to change the traditional role so that auditors examine the business rather than the financial statements. One means, as suggested by many, is the "auditor of record" approach which would have auditors involved more or less continuously in all public communications to shareholders, prospective shareholders, and others.

The students could have fun discussing the possibility that important footnotes were left out or that the client may have erred in its summarization of the auditor's opinion, but ultimately the class discussion must come back to focus on the auditor's responsibility for subsequent events.

The crux of concern undoubtedly arises from two principal issues: (1) from the extended delay of seven months between the audit report date and the re-use of the report in the proxy, and (2) from the modifications made to the financial statements and to the auditor's report. Presumably, had the proxy been issued concurrently, or within a short period, the students would consider that the auditor would have less concern; had the proxy faithfully reproduced the financials and the auditor's report, the students would again see less concern for the auditor. A discussion of these two possible variations and their effects should bring the case into sharp focus.

Similarly, the students might discuss their position had the fact, instead, been that of including the same modified statements and footnotes but with absolutely no reference either to the fact that they had been audited or to the fact that the audit report was available for inspection upon request. The omission of certain statements and important footnotes is still as grievous and, presumably, could lead to claims against auditors should the financials presented be construed as misleading.

The students might also discuss whether their solution would be affected by the belief that, in good faith, the auditors were not informed on a timely basis. Perhaps, management and its counsel lacked business sophistication that would say, "This is something we had better involve our auditors in." In this case, there is a hint that good faith may have been lacking. The client seemed more concerned with cost than with doing the "right thing" — that is, notifying the auditors on a timely basis and getting their view of what they considered was necessary in the circumstances.

No matter how indignant auditors may be over being bypassed, given the circumstances of this case, they probably have no legal action against the client.

The Solution

The auditors promptly resigned in this case. (They might not have done so under different circumstances and had they not shared a belief that the client was not dealing with them in good faith.) The auditors did not feel that they could legally ask that the proxy be recalled and reissued, or even ask that the client distribute full financial statements with the complete auditor's report. They did, however, ask for the opportunity to go in and do some review of subsequent events (at their own expense). There was some risk in that, of course; they were obviously faced with an antagonistic client relationship. And, it would not be a stretch of the imagination to see the client withholding vital information from the auditors. Also, by making that inquiry, the auditors could be seen as accepting a responsibility which might otherwise only have been implied. Nonetheless, they felt they had an obligation to make appropriate inquiries (though they were not required to do so by professional literature) regarding events during the elapsed seven months. In this instance no adverse developments were found.

Big GAAP/Little GAAP

During the audit of the Country Bank, one of your associates noticed another client's financial statements in the loan files. That client, Forthwright Co., is a small local manufacturer whose financial statements have never been audited. Your associate seemed to recall your having mentioned some financial difficulties at Forthwright, but her reading of the statements leaves no impression of financial difficulties.

The statements in the bank's files were compiled statements that contained no footnote disclosures but did contain your firm's report. Your associate casually mentions to you that she saw your compilation report on Forthwright in the bank's loan files and says further, "They sure didn't suggest to me that Forthwright was in trouble — of course, there wasn't much in the way of disclosures because you left out all the footnotes." Not liking her inference, you counter that it was Forthwright and not you that omitted the footnotes and, further, that they had every right to do so according to Statement on Standards for Accounting and Review Services No. 1.

While you may have straightened out your associate as to what is what, you feel far from elated. You seem to recall Mr. Forthwright was adamant that he wanted all disclosures omitted even though you were suggesting that you put together statements with all of the generally accepted accounting principles-type disclosures you were aware of. Mr. Forthwright had said, "Most of those disclosures are silly. I sure don't need them to run my business, nor does my banker need them; he knows everything about my business. Besides I doubt if I'll even give them out, I just want a record for my files." So, you left off the disclosures.

Yet, you wonder. Mr. Forthwright may have changed his mind and given those statements to the bank (which he had every right to do), or the bank may have asked for them. You wonder, for example, if the banker is aware that if the Environmental Protection Agency has its way, expensive equipment to clean up chemical wastes will need to be installed over the next two years, and that would really strain Forthwright financially unless suitable financing could be arranged. Worse yet, the statements you compiled do not show a strained financial position now, but that is only because Forthwright sold a lot of its equipment at December 31 and leased it back in order to bolster its cash so as not to be in default on its working capital requirements under the bank loan agreement.

And you wonder now if you should have stuck to your guns and told Mr. Forthwright that if he did not use the disclosures appropriate to generally accepted accounting principles on his financial statements, he could find himself another boy. On the other hand, he could be right — the banker may know all of this.

You keep thinking, "Maybe I ought to do something; but, what?"

WHAT SHOULD YOU DO?

DISCUSSION LEADER'S GUIDE

Big GAAP/Little GAAP

Objectives of the Case

The broad issue is whether two standards of disclosure are appropriate for annual financial statements given to users outside a company, whether such difference in disclosure is based on size, public ownership, users' needs, or other criteria. Closely akin is whether standards should be required beyond those that appear to be necessary for specific users. Also at issue is whether accountants/auditors should associate their name with financial statements devoid of all disclosures, including some that might be relevant to the users. Further, who is in a position to decide what is and what is not relevant? And, at issue is the question of whether, and if so how, accountants/auditors can satisfy themselves that, to their knowledge, the omission of disclosures was not undertaken by clients with the intention of misleading those who might reasonably be expected to use such financial statements. The students should also explore the imponderables in trying to appropriately say what should be Big GAAP and what should be Little GAAP. At issue also is the responsibility of the accountant for compiled financial statements devoid of all disclosures both when the accountant is comfortable and, as here, uneasy about their absence. And on the question of responsibilities, the case should develop the student's perceptions of the credit grantor's responsibility in accepting a report that clearly states that omitted disclosures might influence the lender's (user's) conclusion.

The students may want to discuss the ethics involved where an auditor learns through a client's audit certain matters affecting another client of the same firm. Though such is not the objective of the case, it certainly introduces the possibility of interesting actions or constraints.

Applicable Professional Pronouncements

Statement on Standards for Accounting and Review Services No. 1, "Compilation and Review of Financial Statements"

Statement of Financial Accounting Standards No. 21, "Suspension of the Reporting of Earnings Per Share and Segment Information by Nonpublic Enterprises"

Handbook of Accounting and Auditing, Burton, Palmer, and Kay, pages 4-2 to 4 and 4-9 and 10 (nonauthoritative)

Business Assumptions and Other Data

The FASB and the AICPA unfortunately did not agree on the definition of nonpublic enterprise (or nonpublic entity). However, the disparity is of no consequence here — Forthwright meets both definitions.

Case 2: Big GAAP/Little GAAP

The students can be told that this is the present accountant's first engagement for Forthwright, and it is not exclusively a compilation engagement. The principal activity for the client was perceived to be assistance in preparation of tax returns and participation in tax planning and advice. The previous accountant had prepared unaudited financial statements without disclosures, but marked for management use only as was permitted professionally before the advent of Statement on Standards for Accounting and Review Service No. 1, which became effective around mid-1979. The problems discussed in this case were not present in the June 20, 1979, year-end statements reported on by the previous accountant.

Discussion

There are so many issues involved in this case that to try to cover them all would be just too much. Some of the issues are discussed briefly below; however, all of those issues may not be developed by the students. They will recognize at the outset that no such thing as a professionally correct answer exists. One auditor might do this; another, that; and a third, nothing. Yet they could all be right, or all be wrong, dependent on the person making the judgments as to right or wrong.

The students should discuss the dual standards of disclosure and accounting that might be appropriate professionally. Here we have a set of annual financial statements with no disclosures. Since mid-1979 that is all right — thus establishing a standard for nonpublic entities that differs from standards for public entities. Statement on Financial Accounting Standards No. 21 permits nonpublic enterprises to omit disclosure of earnings per share and segment data. Both of these variable standards hinge on public or nonpublic ownership, and, of course, are quite narrow in application. Other disclosure or accounting differences could hinge on size of company, industry, or something else. The differentiation need not be limited to ownership criteria. For example, the Securities and Exchange Commission makes a number of disclosure distinctions based on size alone, such as those requiring disclosure of interim earnings, and current value or changing price data when certain size tests are met. Similarly, distinctions in both disclosure and accounting requirements can be found.

On a broad scale people often lump these distinctions together under a catch-all phrase, "Big GAAP/Little GAAP." The issue has facets other than Big-Little, but that is a good discussion topic for the students. As early as the mid-1970s the American Institute of Certified Public Accountants was attempting to deal with Big GAAP/Little GAAP. The Financial Accounting Standards Board has since mounted its effort, but no authoritative guidance has come from either. Who is to say what is "Big" and what is "Little"? Who can set the standards and how can a sort be made between "Big" and "Little" for each of the hundreds of disclosure requirements?

One student may say "little" companies should be able to omit pension plan data, operating lease disclosures, most foreign translation disclosures, and research and development disclosures. Another student will have a different laundry list of disclosures and omissions appropriate for "little" companies.

The *Handbook of Accounting and Auditing*, Chapter 4, could be used by the students to further their understanding of the disclosure issue for "big" and "little" companies which "have come under pressure to expend considerable amounts in producing information that they feel is not relevant to users." The Handbook quotes from the 1979 Annual Report of Dan River, Inc., thusly:

> Some material in the Notes to the Consolidated Financial Statements . . . is complex and, in the opinion of management, unnecessary to an understanding of the company. Such material is included only because it is mandatory, primarily due to government regulations and, to a lesser extent, the requirements of the public accounting profession.

And the Handbook goes on to say, "There are no signs the expanding disclosure movement will halt."

The "big" SEC-reporting companies continue to be battered with disclosure requirements; some relief may come for "little" companies. Though such relief may develop, and most likely very slowly, apparently few if any companies in good conscience are advocating deletion of all disclosures — the Forthwright case.

The students should discuss what happened to suddenly produce a seal of approval for what had previously been banned — association of an accountant/auditor's name with financial statements distributed outside the client company without GAAP-type disclosures.

The old rule seemed to work — that is, unless a client "cheated" and, ignoring the legend saying "for internal use only," distributed the financials. The new rule produces precisely the problem faced by the accountant/auditor for Forthwright. Can the new rule be better than the old? At least students should discuss whether they would want their names associated with Forthwright's statements, sans all disclosures, with foreknowledge that they would be used for credit purposes. Some accountants would refuse, and do refuse, such an association, notwithstanding the admonition in their report that

> Management has elected to omit substantially all of the disclosures (and the statement of changes in financial position) required by generally accepted accounting principles. If the omitted disclosures were included in the financial statements, they might influence the user's conclusions about the company's financial position, results of operations, and changes in financial position. Accordingly, these financial statements are not designed for those who are not informed about such matters.

Presumably, Forthwright's accountant/auditor also would have refused association with his name had he not been under the impression that the statements were to be used "for internal use only." Can statements that omit all (or substantially all) disclosures ever convey the financial data of a company with sufficient clarity to be meaningful, and not misleading, for use by creditors, investors, and the like? Perhaps in a few isolated cases they clearly can. But in most of the cases, as with Forthwright, the answer is not so clear.

And, that point could lead the students to a discussion of what is the responsibility — if, indeed, any — of Forthwright's bankers to do something on their own after having read the accountant's caveat, above, that if they knew what might be missing from the statements their lending judgment might be influenced. The banker is more likely to be a plaintiff than a defendant should the statements be grossly "underdisclosed" and should losses to the bank result. The courts are yet to weigh what responsibility resides with the bank to do something further; so, as a minimum, accountants could be faced with sizable legal fees before that question is answered. The companion question is whether accountants/auditors can hide behind a caveat such as the above if they are aware of information

Case 2: Big GAAP/Little GAAP

that, were it known to outsiders, would most likely influence their lending or investment decision. To our knowledge, no case has been adjudicated under the Statement on Standards for Accounting and Review Services No. 1 omitted-disclosure caveat — and may never be. Students should consider carefully, however, if that is the kind of case in which they would want to be a defendant.

Along this line, the students also should discuss the meaning of the language of Statement on Standards of Accounting and Review Services No. 1 to the effect that the omission of substantially all disclosures was not, to the accountant's knowledge, undertaken by management "with the intention of misleading those who might reasonably be expected use to such financial statements"; and, more particularly, they should discuss how an accountant/auditor can reasonably make any judgment except that the omissions were made with the express intention of misleading the users. That intention may not be present in a given case, but, by definition, financials that omit significant disclosures are "misleading." So how can the accountant/auditor say the client did not intend to mislead when what the client is handing out is misleading on its face?

The Solution

As noted earlier, the solution is what is perceived by the individual. There is no "right" answer. The case is a composite of more than one case and thus the solution given is a representation of suitable action where such case is encountered. The accountant should not breach the confidentiality of the information his associate obtained while plowing through the bank's loan files and thus should not tell Mr. Forthwright that he is aware that the bank has a copy of the statements that the accountant understood would likely remain with the company. The accountant could say to his client that his firm is concerned about issuing these kinds of reports where all disclosures have been omitted, unless the omission pertains to mundane subjects such as the method of depreciation used because such reports could be obtained and used by lenders or investors to influence their investment decisions. Further, he could say his firm has decided that in the future where matters of substance should be disclosed the firm will require GAAP-type disclosures. And, still further, he could say that where lenders or investors have been furnished statements in which disclosures of substance were omitted, the firm is advising its clients to consider, along with their attorneys, the desirability of furnishing such information to the users.

The accountant/auditor should be concerned as to whether Mr. Forthwright's indication that he would probably not give out the statements was in fact an attempt to deceive. While the answer probably can never be determined, where the accountant/auditor has a nagging feeling that he has been tricked, the suggested advice above should be confirmed in writing. And, further, in this situation, the accountant may want to contemplate the advisability of continuing to service the client.

Special Reports

You have received a call from the president of Farm Land Investment Corporation (FLIC) asking you to undertake a special engagement. FLIC is a subsidiary of Farm Agri-Management Company, which specializes in the management of irrigated farm land for many diverse ownership interests. FLIC deals with outside investors, selling shares in Farm Agri-Management's projects.

The farm land in the current project is in 170 circular parcels of 130 acres, each of which is planted with grain and each of which is irrigated by a circular irrigator. Each parcel has been clearly segregated and has been sold to outside investors. Ownership, parcel by parcel, differs; the grain from all parcels is intermixed in common grain silos. The management company supervises the property and directly oversees the planting, irrigating, and harvesting, the latter of which is done by independent contractors. When the property is harvested, the tenant farmer recovers his cost and is paid a profit based on production. The management company obtains a commission for its supervisory services, and any remaining cash flow is returned to the investors. Generally, there is no remaining cash flow. The investors are relying on appreciation in the value of the farm land for return on their investment.

The president does not want you to audit the financial statements of the management company or the investment company. He would like you to examine the reasonableness (in quantitative terms) of the harvest allocated to each investor so that he can provide an annual accounting to the investors.

You expect that reporting on the reasonableness of the harvest would entail, among other things: reviewing grain harvest procedures, observing the harvest on a test basis, tracing observed truckloads of harvested grain to harvest records, confirming acreage with independent surveyors, agreeing quantities to records received from grain elevators, testing mathematical accuracy of grain harvest records, confirming quantities and qualities harvested with grain elevators, and confirming yields per acre with tenant farmers.

You are aware of the scope of Statement on Auditing Standards 14 and Statement on Auditing Standards 35 concerning special reports but you are not sure that they apply to reports of the nature described above.

HOW WILL YOU DECIDE WHETHER OR NOT TO TAKE
THIS ENGAGEMENT? IF YOU TAKE THE ENGAGEMENT,
WHAT MIGHT YOUR REPORT SAY?

Case 3-1

Case 3: Special Reports

DISCUSSION LEADER'S GUIDE

Special Reports

Objectives of the Case

The lifeblood of any auditing firm is its ability to obtain quality new work that is profitable. This case study should focus on the auditor's ability to accept this new work and, assuming acceptance, the auditor's responsibility for amounts reported. Assuming acceptance, a further objective is to focus on the type of work to perform and the type of report to be used.

Applicable Professional Pronouncements

Statement on Auditing Standards, Special Reports, AU 621(SAS 14)

Statement on Auditing Standards, Special Reports — Applying Agreed Upon Procedures to Specified Elements, Accounts or Items of a Financial Statement, AU 622 (SAS 35)

Business Assumptions and Other Data

The economics of investing in land units as shown by this case does not sound too exciting since it is based solely on appreciation of agricultural land. To invest in residential rental property in certain metropolitan areas simply for appreciation often makes good business sense. The economic risks can be far greater with agricultural land. The investors are passive investors and thus subject to the risks attendant to their absence in an industry that is heavily dependent on good management.

Of interest to the investor, and certainly to the auditor, is the control over misapplication of grain to individual investors and over misapplication of related receipts and costs. The case study does not discuss such controls. It is safe for the students to assume that at best the controls are adequate, but more likely, marginal or inadequate. Nor does the case tell whether the management company, its parent, or their principals or management, own some of the 170 parcels. It should be assumed that parcels are owned by related parties, and this fact heightens the economic risk to the investor and the audit risk to the auditor.

The students, in deciding whether to accept this new work, should be concerned that the president did not want either the management company or the investment company to be audited. The president said he was willing to make the records of those companies available to whoever reports on the grain allocation, but audits were unnecessary.

The students may raise the question as to how a report on allocation of grain to investors can be of any value. The important information to the investor is not just how much grain came from a particular parcel or was allocated from a group of parcels, but the revenues and costs related to each parcel. The latter items were not to be covered by the auditor's report at the direction of the president — he wanted a report only on bushels of grain allocated to each parcel.

The students can assume that a number of tenant farmers are involved, but not one for each parcel, and that the contract harvester is the same for all parcels; further, the auditor can have access to the harvester's records, but grudgingly.

Whether a separate report is issued for each investor or a single report showing an allocation to all investors probably will have little effect on the scope of the audit. The students should assume that separate reports will be issued. In this way one investor does not know how much better or worse are the yields per acre of his or her fellow investors.

Discussion

The first issue to discuss is whether to accept the engagement. We can assume that the engagement is acceptable on all the conventional grounds, including the related party relationship, with its potential for conflicts of interests. If the new work is not to be accepted, the students need not spend time discussing the type of report to be issued and attendant matters.

The principal concern would seem whether such work is within the area of competency and professional capacity of the auditors. In jest, perhaps, auditors are often called "bean counters." They are quick to defend that their role is much, much broader than that. Yet, the engagement offered seems little more than "bean counting," or bushel counting, perhaps followed by some allocation to investors. The students may recall that some admonitions, indirectly at least, against "bean counting" exist in present-day literature and in practice.

For example, in dealing with Letters for Underwriters (also a form of special report), the American Institute of Certified Public Accountants in Statement on Auditing Standards 38 (AU 631.39) has the following to say:

> The accountants should refrain from commenting on matters to which their competence as independent public accountants has little relevance. Accordingly, except as indicated in the next sentence, they should comment only with respect to information (a) that is expressed in dollars (or percentages derived from such dollar amounts) and has been obtained from accounting records that are subject to the internal controls of the company's accounting system or (b) that has been derived directly from such accounting records by analysis or computation. The accountants may also comment on quantitative information that has been obtained from an accounting record if the information is of a type that is subject to the same controls as the dollar amounts. Accountants should not comment on matters involving primarily the exercise of business judgment of management. For example, changes between periods in gross profit ratios or net income may be caused by factors that are not necessarily within the expertise of accountants. The accountants should not comment on matters merely because they happen to be present and are capable of reading, counting, measuring, or performing other functions that might be applicable. Examples of matters that, unless subjected to the internal controls of the formal accounting system (which is not ordinarily the case), should not be commented on by the accountants include square footage of facilities, number of employees (except as related to a given payroll period), and backlog information. The accountants should not comment on tables, statistics, and other financial information relating to an unaudited period unless they have made an examination of the client's financial statements for a period including or immediately prior to the unaudited period or have completed an examination for a later period, or unless they have otherwise obtained knowledge of the client's accounting and financial reporting practices and its system of internal accounting control. . . .

DLG 3-2

Case 3: Special Reports 15

While the above quote pertains to giving negative assurance, or comfort, the students may be hard-pressed to understand how an audit opinion can be given, for example, on the number of square feet or on the number of bushels if professional literature prohibits even giving comfort on such quantities.

The same Statement on Auditing Standards says that independent accountants can properly comment in their professional capacity only on matters to which their professional expertise is substantially relevant (paragraph .02). Again, the Statement on Auditing Standards is concerned with negative assurance, but the students might conclude that, by implication, it also seems appropriate for audit opinions as well. And, the students may say that, by analogy, the report on the engagement, if accepted, could not be a negative assurance-type report.

In practice, similar restraints are exercised by auditors as to what items to include in their comfort letter, or negative assurance letter, regarding such things as compliance with contractual agreements. The governing professional literature lacks the specificity of the above literature on Letters for Underwriters, but in practice auditors are very careful to confine their comfort to specific sections of the agreements that relate to matters of the same general character as above.

Whether number of bushels of grain appropriately can be an area of audit (or comfort) seems to be a pertinent question. By way of background, the demand for auditors' reports on other than financial statements has increased over the years. The types of special reports requested now are infinite in number, this case being only one example. The natural inclination of auditors is to say, "We can do it"; they have an earnest desire to help their clients and they have an earnest desire to make money for themselves. Thus, the pull is strong to take on a wide variety of assignments involving special reports. Since the subjects that could be reported on cover such a wide range, standardization is not possible, and auditors must rely on their own judgment, in many cases, as to their ability to undertake such assignments and as to the style of reporting that is appropriate.

The students may want to discuss whether "bushels of grain" is in fact a "specified element, account, or item of a financial statement." If it is, then Statement on Auditing Standards 14 says it can be audited and Statement on Auditing Standards 35 says agreed-upon procedures can be applied to it. If it is not, presumably it is beyond the pale, not to be reached by either audit procedures or agreed-upon procedures.

The Statements on Auditing Standards make quite a distinction between Special Report engagements where there is a limitation on scope (SAS 35) and those engagements where there are no restrictions (SAS 14). The students might ask whether this is the kind of engagement where the limited-procedures approach might be followed. The discussion should explore the difference between the two approaches, the difference between the reports to be provided, and the appropriateness of the limited procedures report in the FLIC situation.

The students may find discussion of the background of negative assurance and agreed-upon procedures helpful. The use of negative assurance has long plagued the profession, and its use seems to be creeping upward despite the profession's attempt to stem the tide. A few years ago the profession proposed to do away with all negative assurances except those for underwriters, but that proposal failed. Admittedly it is not a great form of reporting, but it serves the purpose in more cases than one. The students may find it interesting that negative assurance cannot be given in some cases without having audited the financial statements (as with compliance with contractual agreements); that negative assurance can be, but is not, given as a matter of practice in some cases unless an audit of the financials is made (as with letters for underwriters); and that negative assurance can be, and on occasion is, given in practice without having audited the financial statements (as with applying agreed-upon procedures to specified elements, accounts, or items of a financial statement). Perhaps such an inconsistent position can be rationalized; but a fundamental question is why any auditors would feel they could give comfort or negative assurance without an audit base.

In this case, for example, the "beans" could be counted and allocated and comfort given without an audit base; but would one really want to? And, if not, would one be comfortable giving a stronger "clean" opinion on the same data without an audit base just because he/she "audited" the data (but not the financial statements), and such audit could be identical to agreed-upon procedures if the audit procedures were in fact the ones "wanted" by the client?

As noted above, bushels of grain may not be an element or item of a financial statement in which case neither audit procedures nor agreed-upon procedures would apply. Further, the students may point out that, notwithstanding the above issue, agreed-upon procedures may be unusable because it is impractical to satisfy, in a substantive way, the requirement that the parties involved agree upon the procedures (AU 622.02).

The students may reasonably conclude that Statement on Auditing Standards 14, or at least that section which applies to reporting on parts of a financial statement, should apply in this situation. Reporting on an allocation of a grain harvest is not too much of a stretch beyond a report on royalty sales. The students may have some problem making this application, but they should be encouraged to read the Statement on Auditing Standards broadly. The range of special reports which a practitioner encounters is so large that no Statement on Auditing Standards could have been written that would specifically identify each application.

As the students debate whether they would accept the engagement, they should be encouraged to identify the criteria they will use in their decision to accept or reject. For example, they should insist:

- That the management company and the tenant farmers maintain records in sufficient detail so as to support the total quantity and the allocation to the individual investors.
- That the agreements with the investors, specifying how the allocation will be made, are clear and free from conflicting interpretations.
- That the auditors be engaged sufficiently early to perform the tests and the observations that they believe will be necessary to support their opinion.
- That the reports which will be sent to the investors will clearly spell out the procedures the auditors have performed in establishing their opinion.

If the students' decision runs toward audit rather than negative assurance, the students ought to discuss what procedures, if any, are needed in addition to those mentioned in the statement of the case. Certainly they would want to add something about internal control both at the management company and at the independent harvester. They may want to confirm with investors the terms of the agreements, at least insofar as the terms relate to

Case 3: Special Reports 17

bushels of grain. Testing the scales used might even make good audit sense. Other procedures undoubtedly will come under discussion and may be considered necessary.

The students need to get into the extent of procedures in case they are going to make an audit (as contrasted to agreed-upon procedures). If the harvest produces 3,000 truckloads of grain, will it be sufficient to follow one truckload from loading, to weighing, to unloading, and to recording? How is the auditor satisfied that 20 percent of the trucks, for example, are not unloading ten percent of their grain before reaching the scales and storage silos? The examination has to be extended; that much is clear. But how much? The American Institute of Certified Public Accountants, in Statement on Auditing Standards 14, seems to require such extension with these words:

> . . . In such an engagement, an auditor expresses his opinion on each of the specified elements, accounts, or items encompassed by his report; therefore, the measurement of materiality must be related to each individual element, account, or item examined rather than to the aggregate thereof or to the financial statements taken as a whole. Consequently, an examination of a specified element, account, or item for purposes of reporting thereon is usually more extensive than if the same information were being considered in conjunction with an examination of financial statements taken as a whole. Also, many financial statement elements are interrelated, for example, sales and receivables; inventory and payables; building and equipment, and depreciation. The auditor should satisfy himself that elements, accounts, or items that are interrelated with those on which he has been engaged to express an opinion have been considered in expressing his opinion.

The students may point out that independent economic interests of various parties operate in such a way as to be useful to the auditor. These interests are:

- The harvesting is done by an independent contractor — contractors are usually paid on a basis of total harvest. Consequently, they would like to make the harvest as large as possible. On the other hand,
- The FLIC does not want to pay for what they do not receive, so a useful mutual check appears to be established.
- The tenant farmer has a similar interest; that is, to get the production as high as possible because he gets paid based on production, whereas the management company does not want to pay for what it does not receive.

These fact situations set up certain tensions between the parties: in that each is trying to protect his own interests; they are in opposition to each other; the tension can be useful to an auditor.

As the students get ready to write their reports, they should be asked which of the generally accepted auditing standards apply. Obviously, the general standards apply whether an audit or agreed-upon procedures were done. It would seem reasonable that the field work standards would apply in their entirety in an audit and be limited to the first standard of field work in agreed-upon procedures (AU 622.03). The students should conclude that the third and fourth standards of reporting apply if an audit is made. The reporting standards would seem generally inapplicable to agreed-upon procedures and guidance as to report content would come from Statement on Auditing Standards 35 (AU 622.04).

Discussion of the responsibility of the auditors — whether they make an audit or apply agreed-upon procedures — seems most necessary. Even with audits of financial statements, the responsibility of the auditors is often uncertain and often misunderstood. Assuming the students opt for the audit approach and later developments reveal that grain credits to 50 of the 170 parcels were shorted by skimming 15 percent off the top, presumably the auditors would stand responsible — though that is not certain. Were the same thing to happen where the auditors had applied agreed-upon procedures, presumably no responsibility would be alleged, in the absence of gross negligence. Because that is reasonable, the agreed-upon procedures route seems to have an attraction over the audit: among many reasons, the auditor is working without an audit base, is working on records of companies standing in an agency relationship, not as principal, and is working with limited knowledge, at best, of the operations of internal control of the various agents of the investors.

The students should be asked to prepare a report which can be measured against the answer provided with this case. The key elements of a report on audit should be as indicated in Statement on Auditing Standards 14, namely:

- The scope paragraph should carefully identify the subject of the report — the grain harvest produced and allocated to the investor during a specified period.
- The scope paragraph should refer to generally accepted auditing standards, and should identify the key audit procedures performed.
- The report should refer to the agreement between the investor and FLIC (and any subsequent interpretations).
- If the investment agreement does not specify a basis for allocating the harvest, the basis should be included either as a footnote or as a separate paragraph in the report.
- The auditors' opinion should refer to a fair presentation of the harvest on the appropriately described basis. Note that the opinion should not refer to the reasonableness of the harvest.

The key elements of a report on agreed-upon procedures, as noted above, can be found in Statement on Auditing Standards 35 (AU 622.04).

The students may question the use of "present fairly" or "fair presentation" in any report on an audit such as this. Even though examples given of audit reports in Statement on Auditing Standards 14, paragraph 14, use the phrase "presents fairly" in relation to a specified element, account, or item, it is a fact that those examples relate to items expressed in dollars and subject, generally, to a company's internal control procedures. Not so in the case of FLIC — the item is expressed in physical quantities and is likely subject to an amorphous internal control arrangement, involving the tenant farmers, the harvester, and the management company. The students might go on to assert that even were the report item expressed in dollars and the internal controls of only one company involved, the report on audit still should not say "presents fairly," in spite of the examples. They may have in mind the position taken in *Montgomery's Auditing*, Ninth Edition, page 24, where the discussion goes:

> There have been efforts to expand the first reporting standard to require auditors to report on 'fairness' separately from generally accepted accounting principles. The reason for the movement is a belief in some quarters that it is possible to use generally accepted accounting principles in financial statements that do not present fairly and may in fact be misleading. Unfortunately, there has been some basis for that view in the past. Until the issue is clarified, audi-

Case 3: Special Reports

tors should adhere to the concept that fairness and generally accepted accounting principles are inseparable, even though that concept is not explicitly included in the formal standards. A principal reason is that 'fairness' is too loose a term to be practical or useful unless it is defined in a specific frame of reference, i.e., generally accepted accounting principles. (SAS 5, 1975, The Meaning of "Present Fairly . . . " seems not to clarify the point of concern above.)

And in the case of quantities of grain the phrase "generally accepted accounting principles" simply is not applicable.

The Solution

The engagement was accepted and a decision reached that an audit would be performed and an opinion given on the allocation of grain to the individual investors. An example of the report is attached.

The students should understand that the solution in the actual case was strictly a matter of the auditor's judgment. Other auditors may have refused the engagement on any number of bases, such as, audited data were not expressed in dollars; internal controls were those of three agents, not the principal, and probably could not be sufficiently identified; or the auditors believed the exposure too great as they were lacking an audit base in all three agents. Likewise, other auditors may have opted for the agreed-upon procedures approach and have furnished negative assurance, or comfort.

DISCUSSION LEADER'S GUIDE ATTACHMENT

Special Reports

Board of Directors
Farm Agri-Management Company

We have examined the schedule of grain harvested from Farm Land Investment Corporation Parcels Nos. 1 through 170 and the related allocation of grain to the individual Parcel No. _____ for the harvest season of 198x. Our examination was made in accordance with applicable generally accepted auditing standards and included procedures we considered appropriate in the circumstances, including, among others, the following:

Reviewed control procedures of Farm Agri-Management Company and Ace Harvesting Company over grain harvested, transported, weighed, and stored.

Reviewed grain harvesting procedures, observing the harvest on a test basis.

Traced observed truckloads of harvested grain to harvest records.

Confirmed acreage of Parcel No. _____ with independent surveyors.

Confirmed quantity of grain stored with grain elevator companies.

Agreed quantities to records received from grain elevator companies and obtained certified tests of accuracy of scales used by these companies.

Tested mathematical accuracy of grain harvest records.

Confirmed yield per acre with tenant farmers.

Confirmed with investors terms of their harvest agreements with Farm Land Investment Corporation relating to grain harvest and allocation of grain harvest to individual parcels.

In our opinion, the schedule referred to above presents fairly the grain harvested from Farm Land Investment Corporation Parcels Nos. 1 through 170 and further presents fairly the grain allocated to Parcel No. _____ for the harvest season of 198x on the basis specified in the harvest agreement between the investors of Parcel No. _____ and Farm Land Investment Corporation.

We have not examined the financial statements for any year for either Farm Agri-Management Corporation or Farm Land Investment Corporation.

Certified Public Accountants

Off-Balance-Sheet Financing

Glass Bottle Company has perfected a new process for manufacturing small plastic bottles at half the cost of any comparable product. Glass has been actively promoting its new process and the response has been enthusiastic.

One of Glass's potential customers, International Drugs, could use so many plastic bottles that Glass would need to build a plant specifically to fill its orders. Glass does not have much capital and wants International to finance the construction. International refuses to put up cash, but wants the bottles and is agreeable to almost any financing plan.

Initially, Glass offered to create a new subsidiary, Plastics, to build the plant, finance it with a 100 percent bank loan, and lease it to International for 30 years. Lease payments would be substantially equal to the payments on the bank loan, which would be collateralized by the plant and by the lease agreement. Glass would have a 30-year management contract to operate the plant, for a fee. The plan looked good, and it certainly was convenient. The bottle plant was to be built next to International's main manufacturing facility and a conveyor belt was to carry the bottles into International's packing room.

But a snag soon appeared. International's auditors said that under Financial Accounting Standards Board Statement No. 13 on leases, the Plastics lease would require capitalization and the related additional "debt" would put International into default on its debt/equity requirement. Their conclusion was based on the fact that the proposed lease provided for minimum lease payments with a present value in excess of 90 percent of the fair value of the leased property. And so, International asked Glass to try again.

Now Glass has a new plan. Once again a new subsidiary (Plastics) would construct and finance the plant. This time, however, International would not be required to sign a lease but would simply be required to sign a purchase agreement. Under the purchase agreement, International would express its intention to buy all of its bottles from Plastics, paying a unit price which at normal capacity would cover labor, material and overhead, the Glass operating fee, and the debt service requirement on the plant. That expected unit price is substantially lower than current market. Also, under the agreement, if International takes less than the normal production in any one year, and if the excess bottles are not sold at a high enough price on the open market, International is to make up any cash shortfall so that Plastics can make the payments on its debt and retain a profit to the extent of the management fee. The bank will be willing to loan the money for the plant, taking the plant and the purchase agreement as collateral.

Glass is pleased with the new plan. It will have the management fee from operating the plant and a guaranteed source of funds sufficient to service the obligation for the plant. International has an assured source of supply, without incurring any obligation. The bank has its loan and feels secure. Glass's only concern is that International's auditor might object at the last minute. Glass's controller explains, "They were going to make International capitalize that lease but surely they can't make International capitalize a purchase agreement. But just to be on the safe side, I'd like *you* to study this deal and tell me what you think. I'd like to be able to tell International that our auditors agree that this contract need not be recognized as an asset, or as a debt."

WHAT DO YOU THINK OF GLASS'S NEW PLAN?
DOES INTERNATIONAL HAVE AN ASSET AND A DEBT TO RECORD?

Case 4: Off-Balance-Sheet Financing

DISCUSSION LEADER'S GUIDE

Off-Balance-Sheet Financing

Objectives of the Case

This case illustrates the difficulties that can arise in accounting for the economic substance of a transaction within the current accounting framework. The economic substance appears to be the financing of the construction of a new plant. However, a broader view of the economic substance of the proposed transactions might be the financing of a source of supply of small plastic bottles. One's view of the substance of the transactions could in fact affect the ultimate answer; yet, it should be clear to the students that whatever is being financed, the applicable financing is wholly dependent upon International's financial support, in one form or another.

The case further should develop an understanding of the inability of accounting standards to cope with fluid arrangements such as are demonstrated here. Neither the specific Statement on "Accounting for Leases" nor the more general Statements on "Accounting for Contingencies," "Product Financing Arrangements," and "Disclosure of Long-Term Obligations" are sufficiently comprehensive to furnish all the answers needed to account for the ever-increasing off-balance-sheet financing schemes.

Also, the case should encourage the student to focus on the business aspects of each of the propositions to visualize whether in substance they are the same or different. The principal consideration seems to revolve around property rights — at inception, during, and at the end of the 30-year contracts. Some other considerations would be the proprietary rights to formulae, technical know-how, and processes, particularly at the end of the contracts; the status of the management arrangement at the end of each contract; and the ultimate economics of the operating contract (under the lease) compared to the comprehensive unit price of product (under the supply contract). Accounting solutions are evolving more and more toward economic substance rather than legal form, though "rule book" requirements of certain accounting standards continue to stifle the recognition of such substance.

And, as is so often true when alternative business arrangements are available, the accounting consequences at times have forced the selection of one business decision over another. The students perhaps should talk about this very real fact of life and its application here.

Applicable Professional Pronouncements

Statement of Financial Accounting Standards No. 13, "Accounting for Leases," paragraphs 1, 5, 6, 7, 10, 64

Statement of Financial Accounting Standards No. 5, "Accounting for Contingencies," paragraphs 8, 10

Statement of Financial Accounting Standards No. 47, "Disclosure of Long-Term Obligations," paragraphs 6, 7

Business Assumptions and Other Data

In general, there has been a trend, since the mid-1960s, to debt financing for many major business enterprises. This has resulted from weak equity markets and the relative tax benefits of debt as opposed to equity financing. However, there are limits; companies are generally constrained by indenture covenants that specify maximum debt to equity ratios. Creative financial officers and investment bankers try to avoid covenant constraints by financing "off balance sheet." Initially, leasing was the way, but the Accounting Principles Board, through Opinions 5, 7, 27, and 31, and the Financial Accounting Standards Board, through Statement No. 13, largely reduced the off-balance-sheet financing possibilities inherent in leasing.

Therefore, companies and investment bankers are developing new means to finance off balance sheet. Some of the methods are: nonconsolidated captive finance companies, leveraged joint ventures, and take-or-pay contracts (which seem to fit the proposed supply contract). Naturally, the Accounting Standards Executive Committee is addressing problems raised by known methods of off-balance-sheet financing. And the FASB has recently issued two Statements aimed at off-balance-sheet financing: No. 47, "Disclosure of Long-Term Financing," and No. 49, "Accounting for Product Financing Arrangements." However, as with SFAS No. 13, it seems likely that as soon as a precise set of rules is established, a new financing method will be developed that will avoid the precision of the rules.

In this case, the use of the subsidiary, Plastics, in both instances would be for business reasons and would not affect the answer to the accounting question.

It should be assumed that in both alternatives the plant and facilities would remain the sole property of Plastics with International having no property rights at the end of the 30-year terms specified. Were the property to revert to International at the end of the lease, the accounting would not have been altered from that required by SFAS No. 13. However, if it reverts to International under the supply contract, some change in accounting may be appropriate.

Also, it should be assumed that the proprietary rights to the new manufacturing process remain with Glass or Plastics at the end of 30 years under either arrangement. Whether receiving a fee for operating someone else's plant (under the lease) might result in the same ultimate economic benefits to Plastics (or costs to International) as running one's own plant (under the supply contract) would have a bearing on whether the contracts are substantively the same. For this case, assume that some differences naturally would result but the effect would be immaterial.

Discussion

Until March, 1981, authoritative accounting literature did not cover specifically the second proposed arrangement (the supply contract). SFAS No. 47, "Disclosure of Long-Term Liabilities," appears to go a long way toward supplying an answer to this case (which initially was prepared and presented in the late 1970s), but it leaves the door open: the Statement does not "suggest that disclosure is an appropriate substitute for accounting recognition if the substance of an arrangement is the acquisition of an asset and incurrence of a liability." The case has already stated that were the lease plan followed, the substance of the arrangement would be the acquisition of an asset (the plant) and the incurrence of a liability (the lease obligation). So, while guidance is now better regarding accounting for long-term supply contracts, the substance of the arrangement may still necessitate recording an obligation and a related asset. Further, the FASB has stated that present practice is inconsistent and that better answers will come after further progress is made on the conceptual framework for financial accounting and reporting. In addition, the Board indicated that SFAS No. 47 is only an interim measure pending determination of whether assets and liabilities should be recorded for such product purchase arrangements. Thus, the case continues to have relevance, and it also raises the intriguing question as to whether the lease, in substance, might not be a long-term obligation subject to SFAS No. 47 instead of SFAS No. 13. In fact, the FASB seemed to recognize that possibility when it stated, "Future minimum lease payments under leases that have those characteristics (meaning those specified for an unconditional purchase obligation) need not be disclosed in accordance with this statement if they are disclosed in accordance with FASB Statement No. 13 [section 4053], *Accounting for Leases*."

The case has stated that the property rights at the end of 30 years would be the same under either arrangement. And the same equality has been assumed for proprietary rights to technical know-how, processes, and the like. Further, acting as an agent or as a principal has been assumed to produce substantially the same economic beneifts over the 30 years.

Thus, with the aggregate economic results under the two plans being substantially the same, the vital question should be "what is it?" The fact that the transaction started out as a lease does not mean that any alternative arrangement will always be a lease. That is not a bad theory for an auditor to operate from, but it does not always stand up. Nor would it for the second proposition — a supply contract. For example, International might consider the disclosure requirements of SFAS No. 47 onerous, particularly the disclosure of the amounts to be purchased, and opt for still a third contract which, with application of some ingenuity, may be both in legal form and in substance a guarantee, and not a lease and not an unconditional purchase obligation.

Under the old plan, the accounting would seem rather straightforward. Given a signed lease, the rules and requirements of SFAS No. 13, "Accounting for Leases," seem to apply. SFAS No. 13 is based on the premise that a lease which transfers "substantially all the benefits and risks incident to ownership" should be accounted for as a purchase of an asset and an incurrence of a liability by the lessee and a sale by the lessor.

The new plan is structured to be not a lease but rather a purchase commitment with an additional contingent guarantee provision. Until the advent of SFAS No. 47, one would have been hard pressed to find an authoritative pronouncement that governed the transaction. One might at the earlier date have looked to SFAS No. 5 for guidance (and some accountants believe it still furnishes all the guidance that is needed) though it is not clear that a gain or loss contingency is involved. Perhaps a case could be made that "it is probable" a liability had been incurred and the amount "reasonably estimated." Minimum amounts might be estimated with ease. A loss contingency would seem involved only if the plant's output is not used, which seems unlikely. Accordingly, before March, 1981, the state of the art for product purchase commitments would seem to have applied. But the issues, then and now, are far from settled. A recent FASB Research Report (December 1980), "Recognition of Contractual Rights and Obligations" by Yuji Ijiri, deals with the accounting to follow in similar situations. It takes no position but points out possible alternatives, some of which are applied in practice. And, as noted, SFAS No. 47 has helped clear the air, though uncertainties still remain regarding its application.

One such uncertainty is the apparent inconsistency between the requirements of SFAS No. 13 and SFAS No. 47 as they relate to financing of facilities that will provide a contracted plastic item. It is fair to speculate that most companies and practitioners would advocate capitalization of the lease under the first plan where the plant became the property of International at the end of 30 years — this would seem correct under both SFAS No. 13 and SFAS No. 47. But what about the situation, as here, where the plant remains the property of Plastic? While SFAS No. 13 requires it to be capitalized, SFAS No. 47 would seem to require only disclosure, if in substance no asset has been acquired and no liability incurred.

All of which could lead to a discussion of "what asset has been acquired." Conceivably, the asset is the right to purchase all of Plastics' inventory at a price expected to be lower than market. How is this asset to be measured? The Financial Accounting Standards Board has indicated that it would be difficult to quantify benefits when they may not be assured of realization. Viewed from the benefits (asset) side, perhaps no asset exists that can be measured and recorded. Perhaps some students, however, will take the position that an asset exists, be it a receivable to be settled in plastic bottles or some other form of "prepayment." Or, from another direction, the students' discussion might also touch on the old adage that "good disclosure does not make up for bad accounting." Yet there is no evidence that the readers of the financial statements will be misled if this "debt" is not included in the balance sheet, but simply explained in a footnote. And yet the root of our concern about lease accounting has been that anything that is like debt should be accounted for and recorded on the right-hand side of the balance sheet.

The students will see another possible uncertainty in applying SFAS No. 47 in the requirement that the supply contract be negotiated as part of financing for the plastic bottle plant. It may strike them as strange that an accounting principle would produce different levels of disclosure under identical arrangements requiring identical payments where on the one hand the financing of the facilities was negotiated concurrently and on the other it was not. The dollars spent and the timing could be identical, but not so the disclosures required. However, the Financial Accounting Standards Board has limited the scope of SFAS No. 47 intentionally to only those unconditional purchase obligations that are associated with financing arrangements. So be it.

The students may also think it strange that an accounting principle would be written with an understanding that a company does not have to attempt to obtain the facts that, if known, could change the disclosure requirements. It is stated that the FASB had no intention of requiring a company to investigate whether a supplier used an unconditional purchase obligation to help secure financing. Such a principle leaves a golden opportunity for a purchaser to tell a supplier, "Here is my unconditional purchase obligation; use it for financing, if you wish; but just don't let me know about it." (Perhaps auditors for purchasers will close any open loops of that kind through their confirmation procedures.) A more even-handed approach should result if all companies were required by the Statement of Financial Accounting Standards to establish their position in relation to each criterion, rather than leave it on the basis "if you happen to know," do one thing; if not, another.

The discussion should explore the day-to-day practice of "testing the water" as to accounting consequences of proposed transactions and, where unpalatable, to management's changing the form, though not always the substance, of the transaction. Here the company took one shot that missed the accounting objective of the customer, then took its second shot, which may or may not succeed. And if not, one can well imagine a third,

Case 4: Off-Balance-Sheet Financing

fourth, and fifth shot at structuring a transaction until the desired accounting consequence is achieved. Is this business practice good or bad? Views of the students might be interesting. If bad (second-rate business decisions should not be made simply to achieve first-rate accounting results), what, if anything, can be done to discourage the practice?

Conceivably, the discussion will explore the possibility that the answer given by International's auditors was wrong, and even though the lease meets one capitalization criterion it is not a lease but an unconditional purchase obligation. The issuance of SFAS No. 47 certainly did not change the economic substance of the first arrangement — it was what it was and still is. However, SFAS No. 47 makes it easier to focus on the possibility that, in substance, the arrangement was never a leasing arrangement and thus was never subject to the Statement on lease accounting.

The Solution

Any solution must come, of course, from International's auditors. However, the auditors for Glass took the position that the economic substance of both planned transactions was the same and, further, that the arrangements were the equivalent of so-called take-or-pay contracts and thus covered by SFAS No. 47. That Statement would require disclosure only unless, in substance, an asset had been acquired and a liability incurred. The decision was that the executory contract (i.e., the agreement by International to pay a guaranteed minimum amount for product purchases) did not, in substance, result in a recordable asset or liability; thus, the specific disclosure required by SFAS No. 47 would be required here.

Debt vs. Equity

Hopeful, Inc., a privately held company, has been struggling for several years to bring a new product to fruition. They have spent a great deal of money on product development and on market research. The original stockholders' equity is gone and their resources for borrowed funds are exhausted as well. Management is confident that with another year's work their product will be ready to go, but they need operating funds for that one more year.

To find those funds, management has desperately been exploring all options. The banks have all said that the company is too highly leveraged now and they have refused to extend additional credit. The market for common stock of development companies is very depressed. And, the present stockholders will not agree to the sale of additional common stock because of the dilution that would entail.

The company's investment banker, however, has suggested a new scheme — that the company sell an issue of preferred stock in a private offering. With the additional equity provided, the company ought to be able to increase its bank borrowings. He has put together a preferred stock package which he thinks he can sell and which has been tailored to the company's expected cash flows. He proposes to sell a thousand shares of preferred stock at $50, with a $5 cumulative dividend, payable if earned. To be marketable, the stock must be redeemable in five years at the option of the holder at $65 a share.

Clearly, the company does not intend to pay any dividends in the immediate future. However, if the product development goes as they expect, they should be able to pay the accumulated dividends within three or four years and to pay dividends from that point on. If things do not turn out well, the holders of the preferred stock will have a call on assets of the company equal to their original investment plus a reasonable return. The preferred stockholders would be junior to the outstanding bank debt, but senior to the common stockholders.

When the treasurer discusses this plan with you, you can tell that he is delighted. He points out that it will be difficult to account for the dividends and/or the increase in the redemption value. He suggests that you and he plan to discuss those questions later on, after the offering has been sold. He asks you to study the proposed preferred stock program and tell him if there are any other questions that need to be resolved now. After some hesitation, you ask him whether the preferred stock is really equity. You ask whether the $50,000 should be classified as additional debt, rather than as additional equity. The treasurer's smile fades. He asks, "Why would you call preferred stock debt? I can get you all kinds of legal opinions saying that preferred stock is legal equity. I'll admit it has some strange terms, but debt is debt and equity is equity. What basis could you have to override the legal definition?"

HOW SHOULD HOPEFUL, INC., ACCOUNT FOR
THE PREFERRED STOCK ISSUE?

Case 5-1

Case 5: Debt vs. Equity

DISCUSSION LEADER'S GUIDE

Debt vs. Equity

Objectives of the Case

This case illuminates the problem of the proper classification of preferred stock that has many of the characteristics of debt, in particular, the question whether the inclusion of a mandatory redemption provision, or an option to redeem on the part of the stockholder, should cause the preferred stock to be classified as debt rather than equity. But there is an overall issue which the discussion should bring out — the students should understand the accounting profession's preoccupation with substance. Without regard to the legal form of the preferred stock, the accountant in this case asks whether the preferred stock should be treated as debt, because he believes that the substance of the company's commitment to the preferred stockholders is more like that of a debtor than an owner.

Applicable Professional Pronouncements

Accounting Principles Board Opinion No. 15, "Earnings Per Share," "Additional Disclosures — Capital Structure," paragraph 19

Financial Accounting Standards Board Statement No. 13, "Accounting for Certain Marketable Securities," definition of Equity Security, paragraph 7a

Securities and Exchange Commission Regulation S-X, Rule 5-02.28 regarding redeemable preferred stocks

Financial Accounting Standards Board Statement No. 47, "Disclosure of Long-Term Obligations," paragraph 10

Business Assumptions and Other Data

Since the mid-1970s publicly held companies have drawn more and more on preferred stock issues with characteristics akin to debt. The financial press, analysts, the Securities and Exchange Commission, and others have extolled the impropriety of carrying such stocks as equity. In the late 1970s the Securities and Exchange Commission changed its rules to require segregation of redeemable preferred stock from equity. No similar action has been taken by the AICPA or the FASB. If they had done so, the solution would have been simple — i.e., follow the applicable authoritative pronouncement.

This case is a classic of "what if" accounting. There have been preferred stocks with mandatory redemption features for many years, but typically the redemption date was many years off. Accountants were satisfied to treat those preferred stocks as equity because the redemption date was so far away that no one ever really thought that they would be redeemed. But smart investment bankers began to play "what if" — what if the redemption date were only 15 years away; 10 years away; and, as in this case, five years away? There is a substantive difference between a stock with a redemption 30 years from now and a stock with a redemption five years from now; but it is not clear that we know how to account for those two different issues.

Students should understand that this question is not simply academic. So long as the client can keep the preferred stock out of the debt caption, it can avoid violating its debt agreements — and it may even be able to leverage that preferred stock for additional debt. It is a fact of life that debt instruments which set ratios and similar criteria are often blind to questions of substance.

Over the years a number of articles have been written on the subject of balance sheet classification of such preferred stocks. The Accounting Standards Executive Committee in the mid-1970s identified the problem as one requiring authoritative action. FASB stated an intention to render its decision on the problem, but had not done so in any comprehensive or authoritative way as of late 1981. Proponents of classification as equity point to the legal characteristics which provide subordination of claims of preferred shareholders to those of creditors and which usually forego serious consequences of passed dividends as contrasted to consequences of passed interest payments. Proponents of nonequity (liability) accounting would hold that such preferred shares are in substance unconditional obligations to a fixed amount at fixed dates.

Discussion

Clearly the case can draw on the arguments within the profession about this matter, and the well-prepared student will immediately point to the Securities and Exchange Commission's release, which positions this kind of preferred stock somewhere between debt and equity. The students recognize, however, that the SEC's decision really resolves nothing; it forces the reader to decide whether the preferred is really equity or debt. The Commission's position is a practice compromise; it could be no more than Pilate washing his hands, or it could be a stopgap measure while patiently waiting for the FASB to resolve the issue.

The state of the art, at least for private companies, is that redeemable preferred stock is classified as an equity security. This is its legal definition and accounting for private companies follows this definition for most circumstances.

The facts of this case are troubling, in that Hopeful has been cut off from both the debt and the common equity markets, yet the investment banker believes he can sell, in a private placement, preferred stock with rather attractive and unusual features. It is unclear whether the $5 cumulative dividend, if in arrears, would be paid in addition to the redemption premium, but assuming that no dividends were paid or payable and redemption in five years occurred at $65 for $50, this would be an average return over five years of six percent per annum ($65 minus $50 divided by 5 divided by $50). If the dividend arrearage is considered, the yield is 16 percent per annum. Assuming the company ultimately has taxable income at a 50 percent rate, the cash payout on the preferred would be equal to the after-tax cash payout on an equal amount of debt at approximately a 30 percent rate. One would think straight debt might be arranged at such a rate; however, it is true that some companies cannot borrow in conventional channels at any interest rate.

The case also is troubling because the investment banker believes that by the sale of this unusual issue of preferred stock the company's equity position will be improved in a manner that would allow new bank borrowing. The cash drain inherent in this issue of preferred could not escape notice of the bankers, and it is doubtful that simply classifying the issue as equity would convince a banker that the company's financial position had im-

Case 5: Debt vs. Equity

proved. Thus, the question of proper classification may be of greater importance to accountants than to the bankers.

Paragraph 19 of Accounting Principles Board Opinion No. 15 on earnings per share discusses additional disclosures regarding the capital structure of a company when complex securities are in existence; however, it may be applied to the case at hand, and reads as follows:

> The use of complex securities complicates earnings per share calculation and makes additional disclosures necessary. The Board has concluded that financial statements should include a description, in summary form, sufficient to explain the pertinent rights and privileges of the various securities outstanding. Examples of information which should be disclosed are dividend and liquidation preferences, participation rights, call prices and dates, conversion or exercise prices or rates and pertinent dates . . . .

Therefore, disclosure about the unusual aspects of this issue of preferred would be a necessary minimum.

Statement of Financial Accounting Standards No. 21, "Accounting for Certain Marketable Securities," defines an equity security in paragraph 7:

> Equity security encompasses any instrument representing ownership shares (e.g., common, preferred, and other capital stock) or the right to acquire (e.g., warrants, rights, and call options) or dispose of (e.g., put options) ownership shares in an enterprise at fixed or determinable prices. The term does not encompass preferred stock that by its terms either must be redeemed by the issuing enterprise or is redeemable at the option of the investor . . . .

While the Board excludes mandatory redemption preferred stock from the category of equity security for investor accounting, it is unfortunate that the Board gives no guidance as to how such preferred stock may or should be classified in accounting by the issuer.

A further question arises as to any distinction between preferred stock which by its terms must be redeemed and preferred stock which by its terms may be redeemed at the option of the investor. The Securities and Exchange Commission says no distinction should be made and that preferred stocks with either redemption feature should not be included in Stockholders' Equity or combined in a total with other equity accounts. Although the SEC requirements do not establish generally accepted accounting principles, they typically must be followed by SEC reporting companies, and often find general acceptance in non-SEC reporting companies. In the absence of an authoritative release by the FASB, the Rule in Regulation S-X may furnish guidance in classification of preferred stock of a non-SEC reporting company. In general that rule provides, in part, that if preferred stock: (1) is mandatorily redeemable at a fixed or determinable price on a fixed or determinable date or dates, whether by operation of a sinking fund or otherwise; or (2) is redeemable at the option of the holder; or (3) has conditions for redemption which are not solely within the control of the issuer, such as stocks which must be redeemed out of future earnings, such stock should not be included under a general heading "Stockholders' Equity" or combined in a total with other stockholders' equity items. The Rule further requires certain disclosures on the balance sheet and in the footnotes.

In 1981, the FASB adopted disclosure requirements (SFAS No. 47) for redeemable preferred stock and adopted that portion of the SEC disclosure requirements calling for the mandatory redemptions. The students should recognize that such disclosure is mandatory for privately held companies commencing in mid-1981. However, such FASB disclosure requirements seem not to extend to conditionally redeemable preferred stocks (such as stocks which must be redeemed out of future earnings) or to stocks redeemable at the option of the holder; although these two categories are covered by SEC rules, as noted above.

The discussion thus far might lead students to ponder how such stocks should be classified when it is the intention of management to redeem, though the stock investment has no provision for mandatory redemption, or option to the holder, or contingent (based on earnings) redemption feature. Neither the Securities and Exchange Commission nor the Financial Accounting Standards Board has addressed this issue nor given any indication that it is doing so. Yet management's intentions can have a significant effect on balance sheet classifications, as, for example, where management's intention is to use a long-term debt commitment to refinance short-term debt (SFAS No. 6) or in cases of management's intention to dispose of a segment of a business (APB Opinion No. 30).

The students should also examine whether a change in classification would be a change in accounting and whether a reclassification to a "twilight zone" between liabilities and equity (the SEC method) is a meaningful accounting classification. A similar appropriate discussion would be whether there now exist two standards of reporting — one for publicly held companies and one for privately held companies. And, if so, whether such differentiation should be continued indefinitely. The students should avoid a hassle about how to accrue the mandatory redemption premium; it is safe to assume that it ought to be accrued over the first five years of the debt. But they ought to be asked to discuss how they would account for the dividend/premium accrual. Should it be included as interest expense and used in the determination of net income, or should it be charged in the equity section as a dividend? In most observed instances, dividends are deducted from retained earnings, leaving the balance sheet accounting in the nature of debt and the earnings statement accounting in the nature of dividends. It would seem that the dividend/premium accrual should be accounted for consistently with the balance sheet treatment of the principal balance. However, based on the SEC's release, the principal amount must be included in that half-way position between debt and equity. And, the dividend/premium accrual would be treated as a dividend and charged through the equity section. It will, of course, enter into the computation of earnings per common share. Whether that is the right answer or not, that is what is required presently, at least for publicly held companies.

The Solution

The company's management decided that the issue of preferred should be classified as equity, with full disclosure as to the nature of the issue and as to its redemption terms, which they could do because the company was not publicly held and was not required to follow the SEC Rule. As the company's auditor, you have no basis to insist that the stock be removed from the equity classification; however, you do have the responsibility to point out (1) the preferability of reclassification, (2) the attitude of the financial press, analysts, and others opposed to an equity classification, (3) the lack of comparability that will result from use of different standards of classification by public and nonpublic companies, and (4) the inevitable reclassification required should the company in the future offer securities of any kind to the public.

DLG 5-4

Shareholder Accounting

Fresh Wind had been owned equally by three individual shareholders. But, the three had some personal and business disagreements, and finally Mr. Three decided to get out. You and the company's attorney met with the three stockholders and worked out an arrangement whereby the company bought Three's stock, paying $200,000 in cash and giving an eight percent, $800,000, eight-year note, payable in equal annual installments.

One and Two then set out to find a new shareholder. After several months, they succeeded in interesting a prominent local citizen, Mr. Four. He is known in the community as an aggressive business leader and is reputed to have extensive real estate holdings. One and Two are happy to have him. He has agreed to become an equal shareholder, to sit on the board, and to lend his management skills when they are needed. He will not be a full-time participant in the business, but that may be just as well considering the previous conflicts between the three owner-operators.

Mr. Four appears to be a very wealthy man, but apparently he is "cash poor." In exchange for his stock, he has paid $50,000 in cash and has given a $950,000 balloon note (with eight percent interest) payable at the end of two years. Anticipating your concerns, One and Two asked Four for financial statements. He has given them a personal financial statement audited by another respectable firm. A few discreet inquiries among your business acquaintances verify that Mr. Four is indeed an intelligent businessman of considerable wealth.

You explain to One and Two that traditionally a stockholder receivable arising from sale of stock is shown as a reduction in equity and not as an asset. Mr. One, who is the financial man and responsible for relations with banks, is stunned. He says, "The purchase from Mr. Three was a credit transaction and we booked it as a reduction of equity and an addition to liabilities. Why can't the sale to Mr. Four be shown as an addition to our assets and our equity?" The company's attorney assures you that the transaction is totally legal under the state's corporation laws. The shares can be considered fully paid and nonassessable and the note is legally enforceable against Mr. Four by the corporation or its creditors. Mr. One argues, "It is a legal transaction and Mr. Four is certainly good for the money. We have a good asset and a good stockholder — I want the statements to reflect those facts."

HOW SHOULD THE STATEMENTS REFLECT MR. FOUR'S INVESTMENT?

DISCUSSION LEADER'S GUIDE

Shareholder Accounting

Objectives of the Case

The broad questions, of course, relate to the substance of the sale of stock from the treasury, principally on credit terms, and to enforceability. In a narrower sense, the discussion should focus on the problem of classifying an issue of capital stock. The case should also prompt the students to discuss the effects of SEC rules, regulations, and administrative interpretations on accounting followed by non-SEC reporting companies. The case may raise a discussion as to whether the accounting is, or should be, different dependent on whether the receivable is for a stock subscription or for an outright, legal sale of treasury stock.

Applicable Professional Pronouncements

Computing Earnings Per Share: Unofficial Accounting Interpretations of Accounting Principles Board Opinion No. 15, paragraph 83 (or AC ¶ U2011.28-1)

Welsch, Zlatkovich and White, *Intermediate Accounting*, "Subscription," paragraphs 644-645 (or similar section of other intermediate accounting textbooks)

Defliese, Johnson, MacLeod, *Montgomery's Auditing*, "Receivables," page 271

Statement on Auditing Standards No. 6, "Related Party Transactions"

Securities and Exchange Commission Regulation S-X, Rule 502.30 regarding subscriptions receivable and SEC Release Staff Accounting Bulletin No. 40, Topic 4E, regarding receivables resulting from stock sales

Burton, Palmer, and Kay, *Handbook of Accounting and Auditing,* page 26-11

Business Assumptions and Other Data

Were the facts recited in the case related to an SEC-reporting company, the solution would be clear, and no reason would exist to present the case. Such a company would simply follow the reporting and disclosure requirements of the Securities and Exchange Commission. The case should interest the students because no authoritative standard covers the accounting private companies should follow when faced with the facts recited.

The case states that the note is "legally enforceable" against Mr. Four by the corporation or its creditors. In that respect, it probably is substantively different from a stock subscription, because in most states, perhaps all, no deficiency judgment can be sought for failure of a subscriber to pay the unpaid balance of a subscription receivable. Also, the stock in this case is "legally issued," which differentiates it from most stock subscriptions wherein stock is not issued until satisfaction of the purchase price.

The case seems to infer, but does not state, that the auditor may evaluate the note as collectible at its face amount. Nor does the case give any indication as to how Mr. Four,

Case 6: Shareholder Accounting 35

who is "cash poor," will be able to raise $950,000 at the end of two years. For the discussion, one can assume that Mr. Four has offered a viable plan for raising the cash and that the auditor is satisfied as to both the plan and the collectibility of the note according to its terms.

The case does not ask whether the $152,000 of interest to be earned over the two years of the note should be recorded as interest income or as additional paid-in capital. However, the issue is very real in cases such as this, and amounts involved can be material in relation to annual earnings of a company.

Discussion

Indirectly, this case raises the "Big GAAP/Little GAAP" question — should they be different for large companies and small companies? Or for publicly traded companies and closely held companies? The FASB, with few exceptions, has maintained that generally accepted accounting principles are applicable in all situations. Nevertheless, there is significant sentiment among smaller and closely held companies to the effect that many GAAP requirements are onerous and meaningless.

The discussion of the merits of one accounting rule for all regardless of size or ownership might well lead the students to discuss an even more annoying situation, at least for privately held companies. Those companies get awfully tired, and with some justification, of being told by their auditors what the SEC would require and that they should go and do likewise, even though not required to do so. The conflict has existed for many years and has intensified in recent years. Whether this trend toward application of SEC rules to non-SEC companies should continue is certainly debatable.

In this case, one good reason why auditors contend that SEC accounting rules should be followed is their concern that to do otherwise could make the financial statements misleading since the receivable may not be collected. One and Two are not going to be misled by classifying the receivable as an asset rather than deducting it from equity. Would creditors who contemplate loans to Fresh Wind be misled by such a classification? It seems that appropriate identification of the receivable and the related equity would suffice to alert creditors, especially given the legal opinion that the note would be legally enforceable by the corporation or its creditors.

Authoritative professional literature is sparse with respect to the fact situation of this case. In paragraph 83 of the AICPA's Interpretation of Accounting Principles Board Opinion No. 15, there is a question regarding stock subscriptions:

Q - How are stock subscriptions included in earnings per share computations?

A - Fully paid stock subscriptions are considered outstanding stock whether or not the shares have actually been issued. Partially paid stock subscriptions are considered the equivalent of warrants and are therefore always common stock equivalents. The unpaid balance is assumed to be proceeds used to purchase stock under the treasury stock method.

Under the facts of this case there is no stock subscription, but rather an actual issue of stock which is partially paid. Yet the purchase of stock on credit is akin to a stock subscription, and some guidance can be obtained by focusing on the accounting followed for stock subscriptions.

Welsch, Zlatkovich and White in their *Intermediate Accounting* text discuss the treatment of stock subscriptions (pages 644-645). They give an example of 1,000 shares of stock subscribed at $102 per share. The journal entry is:

Stock subscriptions receivable	$102,000	
Common stock subscribed		$100,000
Contributed capital in excess of par		2,000

They go on to state:

> Subscriptions receivable are classified as a current asset if the corporation expects current collection. If there are not plans for collection, subscriptions receivable cannot be considered a realizable asset and therefore should be offset against capital stock subscribed in the owners' equity section of the balance sheet.

Thus the collectibility of the receivable is considered by them a valid criterion in the classification decision.

A number of other accounting textbooks conclude that stockholder subscriptions should be treated as assets unless there is some reason to believe that they will not be collectible. And, in fact, it may have been acceptable practice for non-SEC companies to treat those subscriptions as receivables. However, the SEC has always said that stock subscriptions are to be treated as deductions from stockholders' equity. It took that position to avoid the watering of balance sheets. In addition, there probably was some concern that the founding stockholders should not be allowed to simply "subscribe" without cash risk, when the public was going to be invited to participate in the company on a cash basis. But perhaps the SEC has relaxed its long-standing position a bit; in Staff Accounting Bulletin No. 40 it states:

> The staff will not suggest that a receivable from an officer or director be deducted from stockholders' equity if the receivable was paid in cash prior to the publication of the financial statements and the payment date is stated in a note to the financial statements. However, the staff would consider the subsequent return of such cash payment to the officer or director to be part of a scheme or plan to evade the registration or reporting requirements of the securities laws.

That position seems to reinforce the more general proposition of the authors cited above, who advocate classification as an asset based on the receivable's collectibility.

General practice now, however, suggests that stock subscriptions be treated as a reduction in stockholders' equity. The Ninth Edition of *Montgomery's Accounting* offers a different view from the above-cited textbooks and says, "Formerly it was customary to classify them (stock subscriptions) as receivables, but now that treatment is not acceptable." In fact, the Eighth Edition had said treatment as a receivable was acceptable. *Montgomery's* Ninth Edition also says that stock subscriptions should not be treated as capital (and as an asset) because the funds are not fully available for use in the company. That is a good theoretical argument, and probably enough of a basis for the decision in this case. However, it is also likely that the SEC requirement has influenced prevailing practice, and the suspicions which prompted its position are an equally good basis for the answer. The *Handbook of Accounting and Auditing*, edited by Burton, Palmer, and Kay, takes a position in line with the SEC's position and states that private companies should now be adhering to the practice as stated above in Staff Accounting Bulletin No. 40.

Given the SEC's influence, most auditing firms now urge accounting as a deduction from stockholders' equity.

Fundamentally, it comes down to a question of substance, despite all the legalism that attends this transaction; an auditor has every reason to be suspicious of the substance of the transaction. Two divergent points of view are apparent: The first is that until Mr. Four has actually put his cash at risk here, he has really only lent his name to the company; the other is that Mr. Four is a fully responsible individual whose full faith and credit are behind his obligation to the company and the company has an asset there just as good as any other asset on the balance sheet. Which is right? Nobody knows; clearly the first view is more conservative, but that does not make it right.

What is raised by this case is a most interesting reverse twist of a sort to the form-versus-substance issue. If in substance the receivable is as "good as gold," then in substance it is an asset. The Securities and Exchange Commission would say, in effect, it is only as "good as gold" if collected before the financial statements are published. We know that is not necessarily true. The collection simply confirmed the fact that the receivable was collectible; it did not change its collectibility characteristics. So, even though a receivable is substantive, convention says ignore that fact and remove the asset until cash is received. If all receivables were so accounted for, we could forget accrual accounting and revert straight to cash basis accounting. In this part of the discussion, the students may want to explore the substantive differences between a subscription receivable and a "good as gold" note receivable and, particularly, whether the accounting is identical for both.

Lately, a variation of the stock-purchase-on-credit issue, or the related stock-subscription issue has been seen. We don't yet know whether it represents a trend toward substituting form for substance. The variation involves the purchase of stock for cash, followed after some time interval by a substantially equal loan from the corporation to that stockholder. Where the stock purchase and the subsequent loan to the stockholder occur within days of each other, the answer may be clearer than when they are separated by a number of months. Yet, the state of the art seems to permit the loan to be carried as an asset though in substance it is no more than an exchange of checks, separated by some time interval. The Securities and Exchange Commission has attempted to stop the practice in Staff Accounting Bulletin No. 40, noted above, wherein it would consider the subsequent return of the cash to the stockholder to be part of a scheme or plan to evade the securities law. Yet the practice continues, particularly in bank/stockholder relationships.

Authoritative literature does not cover the issue of whether interest received on notes receivable for sale of stock is a credit to earnings as interest income or to capital as additional paid-in capital; and views of corporate management and of practicing accountants can be found on either side. Where amounts are material and an SEC-reporting company is involved, the interest earned probably would be shown as additional paid-in capital. Private companies (and, incidentally, some public companies) carry the interest as an item of income. In time, the pendulum is likely to swing to additional capital.

The sale of the stock to Mr. Four also could be viewed as a related party transaction, and as such would be subject to the accounting considerations (paragraphs 6-8) of Statement on Auditing Standards No. 6. Its considerations are quite general, and include: "Although financial accounting is concerned with both the legal and economic effects of transactions and other events and many of its conventions are based on legal rules, the economic substance of transactions and other events are usually emphasized when economic substance differs from legal form." Which gets back to the starting point — what is the substance of Mr. Four's stock purchase?

The Solution

The receivable from the stockholder should be carried as a deduction from stockholders' equity, and the reasons are (1) the weight of practice and (2) today's environment. Had the company insisted on carrying the receivable as an asset, that position could not be said to be wrong if the receivable were collectible. If such were the client's position, the auditor probably would have modified the audit report either as to possible uncertainty of collection or as to departure from generally accepted accounting principles, dependent on how the auditor perceived the issue.

Employee-Stockholder Transactions

As a partner in the Indianapolis office, you have responsibility for a wide variety of clients. Today you are scheduled to visit the two extremes — Gigantic Corp., a world-wide conglomerate headquartered in Indianapolis, and later in the day, Local Stores, Inc., a family-owned retailer that is a long-time tax and audit client. Gigantic's treasurer has asked you to review a new stock option plan they are considering for top management. The Local family asked you to stop by and meet a new man they have just hired as a store manager. They want this new man eventually to become a key part of the business.

At Gigantic, the treasurer explains that the condition of the stock market has negated the value of their traditional stock option plan which had met most objectives: employees were pleased with their compensation, and the company avoided any charge to income. But now, the employees have asked for a direct participation in the company's growth, apart from the vicissitudes of the stock market.

The treasurer has designed a new plan: The company would create a pseudo stock which would receive dividends but would not vote. Each employee would be given an opportunity to buy a certain number of shares of the pseudo stock at a price equal to the company's net book value per common share at the date of grant, such price being considerably less than market price (based on history to date). It is understood that the pseudo shares would not be tradeable and would have to be sold back to the company when the employee retires or otherwise leaves the firm. The repurchase price would be based on the company's net book value per common share at the time the employee turns in the pseudo shares.

The treasurer argues that this is a normal stock transaction because the employees have actually put their own money at risk. Therefore, he is satisfied that there is no compensation expense connected with the program. After some further discussion, you disagree. You tell him that the program is in essence a profit-sharing plan and, in your judgment, that portion of the company's earnings which increases the book value of the pseudo shares must be considered to be compensation and charged against earnings. After some further argument, you convince the treasurer of your position and he decides to abandon the idea.

Moving on, you stop to visit the folks at Local Stores, Inc. You meet the new store manager and greet the members of the family.

They explain that to get the new manager, they had to give him a piece of the action. The company sold him a newly issued block of shares so that he has about a 25 percent interest in the company. The shares have been restricted, however — the certificates are stamped with the legend, "These shares may only be sold directly to the company." There is no market for the stock and so it was agreed that the new manager would buy in at current book value. It has also been agreed that the company would buy the shares back at book value if for any reason he decided to leave. You congratulate them all and wish them well. As you get ready to leave, the bookkeeper stops you to say that she has never encountered a stock sale, but that she simply debited cash and credited common stock. "That was the right entry, wasn't it?" You agree; that is the right entry, at least for the moment.

SHOULD LOCAL STORES, INC., RECOGNIZE COMPENSATION EXPENSE IF THE BOOK VALUE OF THE NEW MANAGER'S SHARES GOES UP?

Case 7: Employee-Stockholder Transactions 41

DISCUSSION LEADER'S GUIDE

Employee-Stockholder Transactions

Objectives of the Case

What is compensation to employees has never really been defined in authoritative literature and, in a narrower vein, compensation paid through stock also remains undefined, though a number of authoritative pronouncements cope with various types of arrangements. The students should explore the nature of compensation, in general terms if they want, but surely in connection with stock transactions or involvement. Such a discussion could lead to a consideration that discounts on sale of stock and other stock sale arrangements can readily result in an income charge, whereas income credits will almost never result from premiums on sale of stock or other stock sale arrangements.

A specific issue for discussion centers around the appropriateness of using significantly different methods of accounting for what may be fundamentally identical fact situations. Are the two arrangements substantially the same? The case illustrates the difficulty in knowing how to differentiate between apparently substantially identical stock transactions and the fact that often accounting decisions are influenced by circumstantial evidence. The case may suggest that auditors are not always evenhanded in their dealings with large, SEC-reporting clients and smaller, privately held clients. The case should also direct attention (1) to the potentially wide variety of employee stock plans that do not fit the guidelines of Accounting Principles Board Opinion No. 25 or Financial Accounting Standards Board Interpretation No. 28 and (2) to the possibility that, because of this, their solutions will lack uniformity in spite of basically uniform conditions. The students may also want to discuss the merit or the logic of having a stock's change in book value or in market price serve as a measure of the economic benefit of services rendered.

Applicable Professional Pronouncements

No authoritative literature directly addresses the accounting for either Gigantic or Local, much less the anomalous answers given by the auditor to his client. Accounting Principles Board Opinion No. 25, "Accounting for Stock Issued to Employees," may be considered applicable; yet, fitting either the Gigantic or Local situations into its guidelines is difficult.

The Opinion does refer, however, to phantom stock or shadow stock plans. Financial Accounting Standards Board Interpretation No. 28, "Accounting for Stock Appreciation Rights and Other Variable Stock Option or Award Plans," says it does not cover "book value stock option, purchase, or award plans."

Business Assumptions and Other Data

Several years ago the Book Value Stock Option Plan, such as proposed by Gigantic, was invented by one of the major investment bankers. It was adopted by one of the larger SEC-reporting companies and its proxy seemed to indicate that the plan was noncompensatory. A check with the auditors of the company brought out the position that the plan was exactly the same as a qualified stock plan which thousands of companies have adopted, and accordingly was noncompensatory. Structurally, a Book Value Stock Option Plan and a Restricted Stock Plan can be the same and the question then is whether, by analogy, the same accounting impact should follow.

Restricted stock, such as issued by Local, is commonplace, especially in smaller, privately held companies. The accounting followed always is that suggested by the bookkeeper of Local. The solution to the case might be clearer if the restriction were that of granting the company a right of first refusal instead of an unconditional requirement to repurchase; this modified restriction also is commonplace.

Had Gigantic gone ahead with its plan, the auditors would have required that monies paid in by the employees be treated as deposits and any allocations based on net book value would have been added to the deposit account.

The Accounting Standards Executive Committee was asked to consider the matter as a possible emerging practice problem. They'll probably refuse, on the basis that it is a fairly narrow subject.

Since the case was first introduced, Book Value Stock Option Plans have lost some of their popularity, though new ones are still born from time to time. On the other hand, restrictions of one kind or another on the sale or transfer of stock continue as commonplace in smaller, privately held companies.

The case does not tell whether Local Stores' stock owned by the manager can be passed on to his beneficiary upon his death. Assume that upon death the stock must be sold to the company.

Discussion

The rationale for recording an expense, such as compensation, upon sale of stock to employees at a discount is generally understood, though certain managements may disagree with the concept. Management's position is understandable. Compensation is an elusive concept, as witness the fact that no one knows quite how to categorize so-called "perks." Some seem to be compensation; others seem not; and still others are just uncertain. So, while straight discounts on stock sales to employees may smack of compensation, the picture becomes hazy as subtle and sophisticated deviations are devised that would generally produce benefits to employees akin to what would be produced through a straight discount.

Some students may be quick to point out that straight discounts are not always recorded as compensation, or other costs. A good example is the discount sale of so-called promotional stock to promoters, underwriters, insiders, and the like. The state of the art for recording the cost of services or other benefits received from such people has lagged behind accounting developments for cost of services or other benefits received from "plain employees." Yet, one would have difficulty in saying how discount A, to an insider, differs in substance from discount B to a "plain employee."

Case 7: Employee-Stockholder Transactions

But, on to the more subtle arrangements in lieu of discounts! There are many anomalies that should be discussed to highlight the more than ample grounds for differing views as to what is compensation when tied to a stock deal. For example, a company could have a so-called "phantom stock" plan and probably be called on to recognize income, whereas it could sell restricted stock at market price on nonrecourse credit, either by way of bank guarantee or direct financing, and, with a guaranteed buy-back at market, achieve for employees essentially the same result as under the "phantom stock" plan and probably not be called on to recognize income. Some would say the nonrecourse stock sale is in substance a "phantom stock" plan and compensation should be recorded. Some would say such sale is in substance an option to buy at market on the grant date and compensation should not be recorded. Or, the company could remove the restriction, permitting the stock to be sold in the open market and almost assure itself that no compensation need be recorded, as what we then have, clearly, is in substance a stock option. The economics to the corporation of the restricted and unrestricted sales are identical, provided any restricted stock reacquired by the company at current market is resold at current market.

Thus, the presence or absence of compensation in the stock sale plans may turn on the intention of management. Here the students might give some attention to the validity of resolving accounting issues based on management's intention and, as will be seen later, this very point will be of some significance.

In the case at hand, Gigantic steered away from stock plans using market price as an index, for which some authoritative guidance exists, and went to a book value index, which has been explicitly excluded from such authoritative literature as does exist. A conclusion could be drawn that book-value-type plans escape compensation accounting because authoritative literature refused to deal with them. But, that too would likely be unwarranted, because accountants and auditors will continue to search for the substance of such plans. One might also conclude that privately held companies, with no public market for their stock, can use plans indexed on book value without fear of having to account for compensation. At present, that conclusion generally would be a good one, unless the intent clearly was to compensate employees.

Stock option or stock purchase plans in many cases may be intended not primarily as a special form of compensation but rather as an important means of raising capital, or as an inducement to obtain greater or more widespread ownership of the corporation's stock among its officers and other employees. In general, the terms under which options or purchase plans are granted, including any conditions as to exercise of the options or disposal, are the most significant evidence ordinarily available as to their nature and purpose. In practice, it is often apparent that a particular option or plan involves elements of two or more of the above purposes. Where the sale price is not lower than would reasonably be required to interest employees generally or to secure the contemplated funds, no compensation need be presumed.

The structure of the plans at Gigantic and at Local Stores is fundamentally the same, and in both cases there could and should be a presumption of compensation, which may or may not be overcome. The principal difference is in the intent of the companies. In all likelihood, Gigantic intended the plan to be a compensation plan. However, the Local Stores people probably intended their new employee to become an equity participant. But note that even if the assumptions of intent are correct, making accounting determinations based on the auditor's perception of management's intent can be dangerous.

Some other distinctions that may be drawn between the two plans are:

1. Gigantic's plan was truly a plan, and as such would have resulted from a unilateral agreement. On the other hand, Local Stores' plan seems not a plan at all but rather a negotiated agreement essential to obtaining the employment of the manager.

2. As a 25 percent owner, the employee is a principal stockholder with equivalent voting strength that could be decisive in the event of disagreement among the other stockholders of Local Stores. In the case of Gigantic, no stock was ever intended to be issued.

3. Future book value increments at Local Stores have some characteristics of equity earnings. They also have some characteristics of employee earnings. But how to draw a dividing line between owner's equity or return and owner-employee's salary remains unanswered. The real anomaly in the case is that the accounting for the manager's stock is as a stockholder equivalent to the other owners. He is not an ordinary employee; nor is he an owner equivalent to the other owners. Only two accounting choices seem available; yet some accounting recognition of both the owner role and the employee role seems appropriate. In the case of Gigantic, any concept of owner's equity participation becomes more obscure. The plan there simply seemed to be a device or formula by which to calculate additional compensation.

4. Some possibility exists that the manager's stock will never revert to Local Stores. For example, his work could become so vital to the business that the other owners would want him to have full stockholder rights, or he may be able to secure such rights through subsequent negotiation. Similarly, he may be able to buy out and retire the present owners and remove his own restriction. The possibilities are endless. No such prospects would be in store for the management group at Gigantic.

5. Another difference between the two plans is that the Gigantic people probably would not let their employees lose money on their "stock option plan." Should the book value fall, it is reasonable to assume that Gigantic would calculate additional compensation, if warranted, for their employees in some other way. (Experience with the more traditional stock option plans bears that assumption out.) It is also reasonable to assume that the employees would expect, as a minimum, to get their money back and, in all probability, they would. On the other hand, the investment of the manager at Local Stores is at risk. If the company should fail, the family will not be in a position to bail him out. That difference in risk, as well as the difference in intent, probably is enough to justify the different accounting.

The above discussion has been concerned mostly with distinctions that may be drawn between the two plans and possible bases for concluding that the Local Stores stock sale was noncompensatory when the book value of the shares increased. In addition to those considerations, the issue of substance versus form merits more than passing comment. Recording the sale of Local Stores' stock as a stock sale, notwithstanding the "buy-back" arrangement, is largely based on the present-day accounting for sales of stock in closely held companies. In the not too distant past, other types of sales were recorded as sales, even when subject to "buy-back" arrangements. Again, the state of the art was controlling. Abuses based on use of such accounting became apparent in certain specialized industries, notably franchising and real estate. These industries are now required to look to the substance of a transaction, rather than its legal form, and what may have been recorded as sales of franchises or real estate in years past, no longer qualify as sales when the seller is obligated to buy back what was sold. No similar trend toward accounting for substance rather than legal form has been observed regarding common stock sales in privately owned companies. A move in that direction seems warranted, however, and in SEC-reporting companies is already operative. Those companies can no longer carry preferred stock subject to a buy-back arrangement (redeemable preferred stock) as a part of stockholders' equity.

The Solution

No . . . . Any increment in value which accrues to the stock owned by the manager would not be treated as compensation to him.

Troubled Debt Restructuring

Your client, Unsuccessful Inc., a calendar year company, was not generating sufficient cash to meet its loan commitments. After a considerable amount of acrimony, creditors and the principal stockholder agreed that pressing for payment would only cause the company to flounder and seek protection under Chapter XI of the bankruptcy law. All of Unsuccessful's $20 million long-term debt is at a ten percent annual interest rate due in equal installments over the next five years. The long-term creditors and the principal stockholder reasoned that a restructuring of that debt, of which $4 million is the principal stockholder's, would increase their probability of recovery. Further, the principal stockholder believed that this would help to protect his and other stockholders' equity in the company.

In September, the company completed a refinancing that involved a partial conversion of debt into equity. The debt of the principal stockholder was converted into nonvoting common stock B, all of which participates in dividends and liquidating rights to the same extent as the initial issue of common stock. It has a current fair value of $2 million, and is all owned by the principal stockholder.

The other long-term creditors each agreed to the following restructuring of the remaining $16 million of debt:

- Forty percent was converted into preferred stock with a fair value of $5 million and an annual dividend rate of ten percent.
- Ten percent of debt was paid on September 30.
- Fifty percent of the debt remained intact and was collateralized with long-term receivables (net of allowance for uncollectibles) having a fair value of $7 million. The debt was extended from five years to eight years to parallel the long-term receivables. The annual interest rate was reduced from ten percent to five percent.

The current market interest rate is 11 percent. Although contingent interest was not specified, debt repayment will be accelerated if specified future earnings levels are achieved.

WHAT ACCOUNTING RECOGNITION IS REQUIRED FOR THE CURRENT YEAR?

Case 8-1

Case 8: Troubled Debt Restructuring

DISCUSSION LEADER'S GUIDE

Troubled Debt Restructuring

Objectives of the Case

The general objective is to explore accounting questions raised by the FASB's Statement 15 on troubled debt restructuring. In its broadest sense the case suggests the inadvisability of assuming that the FASB has thought of all possibilities and details, and, even with a clear and mechanical statement such as Statement 15, one still has to be alert. Restructurings are seldom alike and, within a single company, subtle differences or nuances in the terms of restructuring may affect the accounting consequences. Or, as stated, the FASB simply may not have covered a situation involved in a restructuring so that the accounting determinations become strictly matters of judgment. The case should also suggest to the students that mechanical application of the statement may produce results that simply do not make sense, in which case alternative solutions should be considered and, in appropriate circumstances, followed — irrespective of their compliance with mechanical standards.

As to the specific concerns, the students may be expected to focus on:

1. Whether the transactions described should be considered a single restructuring of debt or two or more restructurings.
2. The possibility that some or all of the restructurings may be considered a combination of grant of equity in full settlement and a modification of terms.
3. The impact, if any, of the relationships of the principal stockholder with his company on the accounting consequences of the exchange of Class B stock for the stockholder's note.
4. The nature of interest expense.
5. The recognition of income upon issuance of stock.

Applicable Professional Pronouncements

Statement of Financial Accounting Standards No. 15, "Accounting by Debtors and Creditors for Troubled Debt Restructurings"

Statement on Auditing Standards No. 6, "Related Party Transactions"

Code of Professional Ethics - Rule 203, "Accounting Principles"

Business Assumptions and Other Data

The case does not disclose whether the preferred stock has a fixed redemption date or dates. If it does (for example, over the same eight-year period as the 50 percent of debt that remained intact), a position might be sustained that the preferred was in substance still debt, and the accounting for restructuring modified to that basis. Statement 15 does not discuss preferred stock that is essentially the equivalent of debt, but preferred stock with debt characteristics is a matter of concern to the Securities and Exchange Commission and FASB. For this case, assume that the preferred stock has no fixed maturity.

DLG 8-1

The text does not disclose the presence or absence of accrued interest, which is an integral part of an accounting for restructurings in certain cases. In this instance, assume that all accrued interest has been paid to the date of restructuring, though that would seem unlikely in practice.

Fair values were furnished in the case at hand. In practice, fair values for preferred and common stocks are typically difficult to determine, especially in companies having troubled debt restructurings. SFAS No. 15 gives some guidance at paragraph 13 as to how fair values may be determined where no active market exists, as would clearly be true initially in the case of the common B stock and could be true in the case of the preferred stock. The support for the $2 million fair value assigned to the common B stock would need to be very persuasive because of the related party nature of the exchange. Though given in this case, fair value is a key concept that warrants discussion.

In practice, consideration would need to be given to the tax consequences of certain aspects of the restructuring.

Any gains on restructuring, ultimately determined, would be aggregated and, if material, classified as an extraordinary item, net of any related income tax effect. Further, the disclosures required by SFAS No. 15 perhaps will be discussed by the students, even though not a part of the answer called for in the case. These disclosures relate generally to (a) description of the features of the settlement, (b) the amount of gain on restructuring and related income tax effect, (c) the net gain or loss when assets are transferred (not applicable here), and (d) per share amounts of after-tax gain on restructuring. Certain disclosures regarding contingent payments are also required.

Discussion

This case touches on the nature of interest expense, of course, but its principal focus should be on the nature of transactions with stockholders. There is a long-standing prohibition, applicable in most cases, against recognizing income on transactions in a company's own stock. However, recognition of income upon issuance of stock is now actually required by SFAS 15. The discussion on this case should focus on the traditional requirement and how it might be applied and should consider numerous matters.

Some of the alternatives discussed below are tabulated here (in thousands of dollars) and will be referred to from time to time:

	A	B	C
Total debt	$20,000	$16,000	$ 9,600
Deduct applicable settlements:			
Cash	(1,600)	(1,600)	(1,600)
Common stock	(5,000)	(5,000)	
Preferred stock	(2,000)		
Remaining carrying amount of debt	$11,400	$ 9,400	$ 8,000
Compared to:			
Total future cash payments on the debt ($8,000 + $3,200 interest)	11,200	11,200	11,200
Future interest expense	$ -	$ 1,800	$ 3,200
Gain on restructuring	$ 200	$ -	$ -

DLG 8-2

Case 8: Troubled Debt Restructuring

a) Initially a determination should be made as to the appropriateness of applying the restructuring to the entire $20 million debt as though in substance it were a single payable. In considering the propriety of grouping all creditors as one, as in Column A, one should bear in mind a comment in the Introduction of SFAS No. 15:

> ... typically, each receivable or payable is negotiated separately, but sometimes two or more receivables or payables are negotiated together. For example, a debtor may negotiate with a group of creditors but sign separate debt instruments with each creditor. For purposes of this statement, restructuring of each receivable or payable, including those negotiated and restructured jointly, shall be accounted for individually. The substance rather than the form of the receivable or payable shall govern. For example, to a debtor, a bond constitutes one payable even though there are many bondholders.

Though there may be differing views in the discussion on this point, the related party nature of the common B stock settlement suggests considering it separately. Thus, Column A shows only that had a single grouping been appropriate, $200,000 of gain would have been recognized immediately and no interest expense would have been required or recorded applicable to the $8 million of debt over the next eight years.

b) The case stipulates that all of the unrelated party creditors participated pro rata in the settlement for cash, preferred stock, and modification of terms. Some discussion by the students of possible effects on the solution under varying circumstances would improve their insight as to the intricacies of the SFAS. In practice, such a tidy arrangement may not prevail, as different creditors may settle differently from other creditors. The students should appreciate that the solution could vary dramatically depending on the mix between creditors. For example, if one creditor settled for all the preferred stock and no cash or modified terms, the gain called for by SFAS No. 15 would be $1.4 million ($6.4 million, or 40 percent of $16 million minus $5 million, the fair value of the preferred stock); and the company would have $3.2 million in future interest to be recognized over eight years. Other mixes could produce different results, though the above example seems to set the outer limits on income recognition and interest expense related to restructuring the $16 million of unrelated party debt.

c) So far, comments have dealt essentially with the debt to the unrelated parties. A discussion and a decision are needed, however, regarding the gain, if any, resulting from the related party transaction involving issuance of the common B stock for the note payable to the principal stockholder.

The SFAS contains no guidance as to whether the accounting should be different because of the close relationship. Some indication that different accounting might prevail where control relationships exist is found in paragraph 42 dealing with substitution or addition of creditors, and there the accounting does differ based on presence or absence of a controlling interest. In the absence of specific direction, Statement on Auditing Standards No. 6 provides general direction to the effect that if the substance is not materially different from the form of related party transactions, the accounting followed should not be affected by the relationship.

Following that point of view, a decision is needed on the substance-versus-form issue. If the decision is that the form is also the substance of the transaction, then a gain of $2 million would be recorded (being $4 million principal of the note less the $2 million stipulated fair value of the common B stock). If the decision is that the substance of the transaction was a contribution to capital by the principal stockholder, then no gain would be recorded and the $2 million would be credited to additional paid-in capital. To record a gain on a transaction with a controlling interest may be suspect, particularly in this case where the controlling stockholder had the freedom initially to call his $4 million investment either capital or a loan. Whether the $2 million difference is carried as income or as additional capital does not affect the amount of interest expense to be recognized over the next eight years, which would be $1.8 million, shown in Column B.

Some students may hold to the view that the form-versus-substance issue makes for learned conversation, but, nevertheless, income simply cannot be recognized in a stock transaction with a principal stockholder. They would say that if the company traded its stock in any other way with its principal stockholder, it would be precluded from recognizing income on that transaction. Thus, it would seem unreasonable for the company to recognize income in a restructuring in this way.

Still others may choose simply to reclassify the full $4 million of principal-stockholder debt to common B stock on the basis that no meaningful segregation can be made for that amount as between capital and additional capital, reinforced in part by the very real fact that any dollar value assigned as fair value of common B stock is highly subjective.

Regardless of the alternatives followed — unless the method results in recording $2 million of earnings — a highly technical, but very practical, decision will be required:

- First, a company and its auditor could conclude that because of the controlling relationship, because of the uncertainty of the substance of the transaction with the controlling stockholder (which creates earnings from application of an accounting convention), and because of the impracticality of a meaningful determination of the fair value of the closely held common B stock, the exchange of the note payable for common B stock is a contribution to capital (whether shown in total as capital stock or divided between capital stock and additional capital) and that should dictate the accounting to follow. In such case, the auditor's opinion should contain no qualification regarding departure from generally accepted accounting principles.

- Second, a company and its auditor could conclude that generally accepted accounting principles required showing a gain of $2 million but that, due to unusual circumstances, the financial statements would then be misleading. In such case, the auditor's report should be modified, according to Rule 203, to give the reasons why compliance with the principle would result in misleading statements.

- Third, the company could hold to the position that the substance is a contribution to capital, and thus nonrecognition of the $2 million gain conforms with GAAP, while its auditor holds to the position that GAAP requires reporting $2 million of gain but, because of unusual circumstances, to so report would produce misleading financial statements. In this unlikely event, some careful wording, both in the auditor's report and in the footnotes to the financial statements, is necessary to convey each party's position.

- Fourth, and likely, the company could say that not recording income conforms to GAAP while its auditor says, "Not so — income must be recorded." The usual auditor's qualification regarding departure from generally accepted accounting principles may serve adequately in such case, or some further words in the report or footnotes may seem appropriate to state the differing view of the company.

Case 8: Troubled Debt Restructuring

d) Given the above positions as to the common B stock, is it appropriate to consider the "sale" of preferred stock in the same manner? To simply transfer the $6.4 million from debt to preferred stock equity (or, alternatively, to transfer $5 million to preferred stock and the remaining $1.4 million to either earnings or additional capital) leaves the company $3.2 million in interest expense (Column C), which in fact is the stated interest on the remaining amount of the debt.

The position essentially is that stock in exchange for debt can do only one thing — reclassify dollars of former debt to dollars of stockholders' equity, whether classified as stock alone or stock combined with either additional earnings or additional capital. The transfer should in no way suggest that an economic increase had occurred in stockholders' equity, only a "bookkeeping" increase that conforms to GAAP. The "true net worth" of the company may be overstated as a result of the transfer.

Recognizing this, the students may support their position by analogy to a quasi-reorganization, saying in substance that a quasi has occurred, rather than a restructuring. Had the company evaluated its assets and made appropriate downward adjustments, as required in quasi-reorganizations, that position might have been supportable.

All of which leads to a major concern, perhaps outside the narrow confines of our subject, that students may want to discuss. In companies with troubled debt, there is a strong indication (not necessarily a fact) of inadequate return on the assets employed. In that case, there should be a presumption that the assets are overvalued and some downward adjustment of the carrying amount might be appropriate. In every restructuring situation the possibility that assets are overstated should be addressed and a conclusion reached. It is fair to say, however, that FASB has not addressed the issue, though it has discussed the possibility of write-down of productive facilities with low yields; at present, some companies are indeed writing down the carrying amount of low yielding assets while others, the majority perhaps, are not.

e) Some other thoughts that may be expressed in the discussion are as follows:

- Why is it that we account for the stocks at their fair market value, but do not so account for the remaining debt? Under SFAS 15, the remaining debt could be carried at as much as the aggregate of the cash flow requirement, even though its market value will be significantly less. A cynical mind might conclude that the FASB took the "cash flow" approach for the debtor because it was pressured to take the "cash flow" approach for the creditor.

- This case illustrates the possibility of an even more fundamental conceptual problem. When the accounting adjustments in a restructuring result in a credit balance, it has to go somewhere. Because of the profession's emphasis on "clean surplus" the credit has to be run through income even though it is not clearly an income item. The FASB helped a little bit when it said that the "gains" from restructurings could be treated as extraordinary items. Even at that, the discussion of this case ought to touch on the need for a halfway house that could accommodate these transactions which are not clearly income, but may not be completely capital either. The anomaly in SFAS No. 15 may be there simply because the profession has refused to recognize any kind of transaction other than an income transaction or a capital transaction.

DLG 8-5

The Solution

Because of the controlling relationship of the principal stockholder and other considerations discussed above, the exchange of debt for common B stock was treated separately as a capital transaction and no gain or income was recognized. As to the debt to the unrelated parties, the restructuring was treated as a "combination of types" and no gain recorded, with $1.8 million to be charged to interest expense in future years, just as called for by the SFAS (Column B above). Not all practitioners would concur with the unrelated party debt accounting, favoring instead separate handling of the preferred stock, resulting in $3.2 million to be charged to interest expense in future years, the amount that would actually be paid assuming no acceleration of principal payments (Column C).

The answer given would not be affected by the acceleration clause unless the acceleration of principal payments reduced the total future payments below $9.4 million.

Purchase Accounting — Reporting Results

Diddle Stores, a national chain of discount stores, began negotiations to purchase D. Press & Sons, a smaller retail chain, in January, 1978. At January 31, 1978, D. Press's net worth, based on fair value, was $5 million and, by terms of an agreement dated February 3, 1978, Diddle agreed to pay $6 million cash for all of D. Press's outstanding stock. On November 1, 1978, the acquisition was finally consummated. Diddle paid the $6 million even though D. Press's net worth had dropped to $4 million by then. Consistent with its past pattern, D. Press lost $1 million during the nine months between February 1 and October 31, 1978; as in the past, it was profitable in the last two months of the year, earning $1.5 million. Both the seller and the buyer were aware of the seasonal earnings pattern of the past and both presumably expected a similar pattern to be repeated in 1978.

The February, 1978 agreement of purchase provided that control of D. Press would pass to Diddle upon payment of the $6 million purchase price and transfer of the stock purchased. It did not, however, specify an "acquisition date" as that term is used in accounting for business combinations. For many reasons — some major, some minor — delay followed delay, and it was not until November 1, 1978, that the cash and the D. Press stock changed hands. Nonetheless, there were signs, suggestions, and hints that Diddle had some control, though surely less than full control, soon after the February agreement was signed.

At November 1, 1978, D. Press & Sons had cash, receivables, and inventory of $4 million; the fair values of property, plant, and equipment approximately equaled the liabilities. Therefore, when Diddle recorded the purchase, it recorded $2 million of goodwill to balance the purchase price with the net assets received.

Diddle naturally included D. Press's $1.5 milion earnings from November and December in the consolidated results for the year ended December 31, 1978. Of course, the Diddle footnotes describe the acquisition and report pro forma results as if the transaction had taken place at the beginning of the year.

CRITIQUE DIDDLE'S ACCOUNTING AND REPORTING
REGARDING THE ACQUISITION OF D. PRESS & SONS.

DISCUSSION LEADER'S GUIDE

Purchase Accounting — Reporting Results

Objectives of the Case

The case study highlights the possibility that mechanical application of Accounting Principles Board Opinion No. 16 may produce seemingly improper accounting results, and it should promote careful analysis of the situation and the substance of the transaction. The case should elicit the problems in purchase accounting requirements, where we must attempt to allocate total purchase price for an aggregate business over individual assets valued separately. The case brings into sharp focus the importance of the acquisition date in purchase accounting, illustrating both the variety of answers that can result and the importance of understanding the business considerations that surround whatever date is selected.

Though the case seems to center around the uncertainty of the "acquisition date," the students should recognize that the same problems of economic substance could exist even though the date was specified in the contract and, further, the students should discuss criteria pertinent in the determination of an "acquisition date" for accounting purposes. Because "effective control" will undoubtedly be one of the criteria, some discussion should follow as to its meaning and how its presence can be identified.

Applicable Professional Pronouncements

Accounting Principles Board Opinion No. 16, "Business Combinations" paragraphs 93 and 94

Business Assumptions and Other Data

The case states the valuations applicable to inventories, receivables, operating facilities, and liabilities. Though given here, the students should recognize that determination of valuations in a business combination can be the most difficult and elusive aspect in the application of purchase accounting.

In practice, long delays often occur in closing transactions for business combinations. In the case at hand, though the total delay seemed especially long, some justification seemed to exist for each bit of the delay. That is to say, no improper intent was ever proved for the delays; but, the students should pursue the question of delay here just as it is pursued in practice.

The business considerations are numerous and seem to overshadow the technical accounting considerations. One of the more troublesome business considerations suggested by the case, though not stated, is that Diddle agreed, perhaps for a second time, to still pay $6 million even after learning that Press had lost $1 million. It is appropriate to assume that the February contract gave both parties the option of rescinding the transaction under certain circumstances, but the loss (or profit) to date of consummation was not one

Case 9: Purchase Accounting — Reporting Results

of the events that activated the option. Thus, in the case at hand, Diddle agreed only one time, in February, 1978, to pay $6 million.

Tax ramifications to both seller and buyer could be numerous and varied in their impact. The tax consequences are not the focal point of the case. Some students may want to explore, however, the potential tax impacts deriving from some of the alternatives.

Discussion

The mechanical application of Accounting Principles Board Opinion No. 16 results in the solution as proposed by the company; that is, $2 million of goodwill (to be amortized over not more than 40 years) recorded as an asset and the November and December earnings of $1.5 million recorded as 1978 income. But does this make sense? The students will recognize that if D. Press holds to the same operating cycle pattern in 1979 any comparison of the consolidated, two years' operating results will be highly distortive.

The recited terms of the agreement between Diddle and D. Press are not all that easy to understand and could cause students to wonder, "Can something like this really happen in the business world?" It can and does. And that should lead the students to explore the likelihood of the existence of a better solution than the one derived from the rule book; that is, $2 million goodwill and $1.5 million 1978 earnings. Were the acquisition date specified as February 3, 1978 (effectively January 31, 1978), the accounting should result in $1 million of goodwill and $.5 million 1978 earnings. But no such early date was specified in the agreement. Were the acquisition date specified as December 31, 1978, the accounting should result in $.5 million goodwill and $0 1978 earnings. But no such late date was specified, and, worse yet, Accounting Principles Board Opinion No. 16 has absolutely no provision for specifying an acquisition date subsequent to the date the cash and stock certificate changed hands. And, any acquisition date other than the three dates above should still produce a result. The discussions that follow deal with some of the considerations implicit in the accounting choice. The students should be aware that the solution to the case (there may be no one correct solution) is less important than understanding the possibilities that need to be explored before reaching that solution.

Some of the business considerations:

The business aspects appear more challenging than the technical accounting requirements.

The delay of almost nine months should raise questions: was it justified or contrived? If the delay was planned, as it may have been, the students should recognize that the planned economic substance of the transaction could be significantly different from its casual appearance. For example, the stock price of Diddle could be sagging in the marketplace and $1.5 million of earnings not burdened by anticipated off-season losses of $1 million could be just what the company needed to regain investor confidence.

Closely related is the absence of a designated acquisition date in the contract of sale. This absence could suggest lack of due care in preparation of the sale/purchase agreement, unless omission was deliberate on the part of one or both parties. If deliberate, one should focus very carefully on the issue of substance versus form. If inadvertent, the intent of the parties possibly could be determined by verbal or written contract with each party. However, the parties' recollected perception of their intent at the time of agreement is not always a reliable indicator of fact. For example, the parties may express different recollected perceptions; or events subsequent to the date of agreement may make it most advantageous to recollect one intention in preference to another intention, which could be true in this case, though it does not have to be. And, from an auditor's view, it may be impossible to determine conclusively whether the omission was deliberate or inadvertent if the parties were bent on deception — such are the risks of auditing. Nor would the specification of an acquisition date in a contract be conclusive as to the substance of the transaction were the seller willing to accommodate the buyer in achieving the apparent earnings growth of $1.5 million.

The fact that the price remained the same, $6 million, though the fair value declined $1 million opens avenues for interesting conjecture by the students. Why would either party enter into such a loose arrangement regarding future losses (or earnings)? That simply does not make good business sense no matter what one says; yet, it is done. And the next question should be, "Whose loss is it?" That is an accounting issue as well, to be discussed further below. But, on the business side, no one would logically pay for a $1 million loss needlessly. A company may be able to point to the $1 million of heretofore unidentified assets, such as favorable leases, that caused a reassessment that $6 million was still a fair price in spite of the $1 million loss. More commonly, as in this case, no new assets will be located. So the trick seems to lie in finding a quid pro quo — if any.

While taxes generally are to be ignored in this discussion, they could indeed be the quid pro quo sought. For example, from the seller's view, assuming for convenience that the fair values are the same as the tax basis at each of the significant dates above and assuming further that the corporation's taxable income flows through to its owners (Subchapter S corporation), the tax on the $1 million gain if the transaction closed on February 3, 1978, could be material, whereas the tax on the $2 million gain if closed on November 1, 1978, would likely be zero. Further, though taxes are not a part of the case, the students should realize that often, when business terms seem to make little economic sense, the apparent concessions or advantages in a contract may be no more than unmarked tax consequences to either or both parties.

If Diddle and D. Press in substance had a transaction that could have been closed with proper effort on February 3, 1978, or soon after, one has to question why D. Press was willing to forego interest or other earnings on its $6 million cash sale price for a period up to nine months. Again, it does not make sense. One wonders if there is a quid pro quo hidden in the agreement, or, worse yet, spelled out in an undisclosed side agreement.

The students should understand that not all contracts offer such a wide range of uncertainty as to who is getting what for what; though in practice, some offer even more. They should understand that intent and/or substance may be vital to the accounting solution.

Some of the accounting considerations:

In this case the price paid is fixed ($6 million) but the fair value of the assets purchased is variable. In other cases, usually involving purchases by issuance of capital stock, the fair value of the assets purchased is fixed but the fair value of the consideration given is variable. And, further, in some cases, the price paid and the fair value of the assets purchased are both variable. It seems fair to say that in the presence of variables in the purchase arrangements, variables are likely to result in the proposed accounting solution. The student should be mindful of these variables and be willing to conceptualize beyond the dictates of accounting literature.

Paragraph 94 of Accounting Principles Board Opinion No. 16 states: "The cost of an acquired company and the values assigned to assets acquired and liabilities assumed

Case 9: Purchase Accounting — Reporting Results

should be determined as of the date of acquisition. The statement of income of an acquiring corporation for the period in which a business combination occurs should include income of the acquired company after the date of acquisition by including the revenue and expenses of the acquired operations based on the cost of the acquiring corporation." Diddle contends that the date of acquisition is November 1, 1978, the date of closing, and, if correct, then the accounting proposed by Diddle would be proper.

Accounting Principles Board Opinion No. 16 says the following regarding Acquisition Date:

> The Board believes that the acquisition of a company should ordinarily be the date assets are received and other assets are given or securities are issued. However, the parties may for convenience designate as the effective date the end of an accounting period between the dates a business combination is initiated and consummated. The designated date should ordinarily be the date of acquisition for accounting purposes if a written agreement provides that effective control of the acquired company is transferred to the acquiring corporation on that date without restrictions except those required to protect the stockholders or other owners of the acquired company — for example, restrictions on significant changes in the operations, permission to pay dividends equal to those regularly paid before the effective date, and the like.

Thus, the Opinion clearly offers a choice of two different dates as the acquisition date. And one of those dates, the earlier alternative date, would seem inapplicable to the Diddle/Press transaction because no such alternative was designated in the contract. (As noted above, however, such an omission may have been planned or contrived.) The Opinion makes no provision for a third choice, that is, a date subsequent to the date of consummation, which, if permitted, would result in all or part of the $1.5 million earnings subsequent to comsummation being carried as a reduction of goodwill otherwise determined.

The above-cited material regarding what is an "earlier acquisition date" referred to the date upon which effective control was transferred. That is the only criterion given for earlier acquisition dates. The students might discuss what additional criteria should be used in establishing an earlier acquisition date. And they should discuss what is meant by "effective control." The Opinion cited above enumerates as an example a number of restrictions on the buyer that do not destroy effective control. These are negative criteria; the students might wonder, assuming those criteria are no problem, what positive signs may warrant a judgment that effective control was passed. When new management is virtually running a purchased company, does that constitute effective control irrespective of how a contract is worded regarding transfer of control? The case suggests that Diddle had its people running around and controlling some things, "though surely less than full control." Where on a scale below full control is the stratum called "effective control"? And, were it concluded that Diddle had effective control long before the closing date, can that be ignored simply because the agreement did not specify an earlier acquisition date? The students should visualize the vast uncertainties that surround all definitions of control no matter how modified (except full or absolute control), and how a little slippage one way or the other in the time of passage of effective control can materially alter accounting consequences.

Turning back to an earlier business-oriented question, "Whose $1 million loss is it?", the answer probably is, "There is no way of knowing," either from an economic view or an accounting view. For a fact, D. Press recorded the loss; and, for a fact, Diddle paid the

DLG 9-4

same purchase price in spite of the loss. From there on, the water gets murky. The possibilities of who did what to whom are endless. For example, one possibility is that the transaction was planned from the start to pay $6 million for a $4 million company. That seems highly unlikely but, strangely, gives the same answer as a literal application of the Opinion; that is, $2 million goodwill and $1.5 million 1978 earnings. At the other end of the possibilities is the suggestion that there is indeed no loss at all, but rather there is another asset available to Diddle at November 1, in the form of capitalized overhead. One could reason that the stores would not have been available to earn the profits of the last two months of the year if the company had not been in a position to absorb the losses during the first ten months. If a company in manufacturing can capitalize plant downtime in its inventory overhead, for example, capitalization of seasonal losses then may be said to be reasonable for a retail business. This accounting tends to produce the same results as selecting the earlier acquisition date, that is, earnings of $.5 million for the year and goodwill of $1 million. Accounting Principles Board Opinion No. 28, "Interim Financial Reporting," is not clear as to whether it would prohibit or support such accounting, but the possibility for support seems remote.

It's possible that from the start the plan was that the $1.5 million earnings of November and December, 1978, should be offset against the "goodwill" determined as of November 1, 1978. The thought could go along the line that this had to be what the parties anticipated because it was unreasonable to try to put a value on a seasonal business at any other point; instead a valuation should be made as of the end of its business cycle. The theory sounds good, but we know from experience that purchases of cyclical businesses are made on the basis of valuations other than at the end of the succeeding business cycle. This suggested approach produces the same result as would be obtained if the acquisition date were said to be December 31, 1978, two months after consummation; that is, $.5 million goodwill and $0 1978 earnings. Neither the business cycle concept nor the post-consummation concept are supported by authoritative pronouncements. Nor is an auditor typically in a position to maintain "what the parties had anticipated." That information typically should be evident in an agreement or should be provided by the contracting parties.

Because of the importance of the acquisition date in the assignment of values, one should also explore the analogy where the securities are given as consideration for a purchase, and where the values assigned to those securities are the average values over a period of time. Paragraph 74 of Accounting Principles Board Opinion No. 16 specifically recognizes that measuring consideration at a specific date may be distortive. By analogy, could one reason that it would be distortive to measure the fair values of assets received as of a specific date and thus some kind of averaging should be used?

The Solution

The company agreed with the auditor that the $1.5 million earned in November and December should be offset against the "goodwill" on the grounds that this was what the parties anticipated. Concurrence as to what the parties anticipated may not be obtainable in other situations, leaving the auditor to decide what must be done if the auditor's preferred solution is unacceptable. In this case, the company did not offer an explanation as to why they had been trying to record the $1.5 million earnings in 1978 when both parties had anticipated an adjustment of goodwill. Maybe it was just another case of "testing the

Case 9: Purchase Accounting — Reporting Results   59

water" to see how much they could get past the auditor, which is very understandable when the authoritative literature seems to support the position initially taken.

The answer produced the most conservative results of the alternatives discussed above, and for this reason had some considerable appeal. To follow the company's suggested solution could enable companies to time a closing to produce the most favorable earnings results. Here, also, one had to weigh the advantages and disadvantages of immediate recognition of $1.5 million earnings against the advantages and disadvantages of relieving future earnings of a $1.5 million charge over a period of 40 years through amortization of goodwill.

The answer is not perfect, and it may not comply with GAAP. The auditor would have to evaluate that, and if he concluded that GAAP was not followed but that the results reached were necessary to keep the financial statements from being misleading, he might need to disclose the facts in his opinion as provided by Rule 203 of the Code of Ethics of the American Institute of Certified Public Accountants. In this case, the conclusion was that the accounting fit the substance of the transaction, and thus what was an apparent departure from Opinion No. 16 accorded with the broader principle of recording economic substance.

Purchase Accounting — A Bargain Purchase

Matrix Mfg. Co. has purchased, in a stock for stock transaction, 100 percent of West Taxicab Company, which owns operating permits issued by three major cities for fleets of taxicabs. Matrix exchanged nonvoting, cumulative preferred stock for all of the West common. The market price of Matrix shares issued in the purchase is $5 million. Vital statistics for West, formerly a subsidiary of a large corporation, and the accounting Matrix proposes for the purchase are as follows:

($000s omitted)

Balance Sheet Accounts	West's Net Book Value	Fair Value of West's Identifiable Assets	Allocation of Excess	Matrix's New "Cost" For West
Taxicabs	$ 3,000	$ 1,500	$ (600)	$ 900
Garages and Equipment	1,000	2,500	(1,000)	1,500
Permits	—	6,000	(2,400)	3,600
Goodwill	1,000	—	—	—
Liabilities	(1,000)	(1,000)	—	(1,000)
Total	$ 4,000			$ 5,000
Fair Value of "Purchased Assets"		9,000		
Cost of Purchase		5,000		
Excess of Fair Value Over Cost		$ 4,000	$(4,000)	

Proposed Accounting Application

The valuation of the permits is based on bona fide offers made by three other taxicab operators within the last two months. The permits probably can be said to have an indefinite life, but they will be amortized over 40 years. The fair values of the other assets are based on sound appraisals. The average useful remaining life of the taxicabs is three years and of the garages and equipment, 15 years.

West's operations have suffered recently due to fuel difficulties and related economic dislocations. As a result current profits are depressed.

CRITIQUE THE ACCOUNTING WHICH MATRIX HAS PROPOSED FOR THIS PURCHASE.

Case 10-1

DISCUSSION LEADER'S GUIDE

Purchase Accounting — A Bargain Purchase

Objectives of the Case

The case should promote the students' thinking and discussion of the economics of the transaction. And the discussion should relate closely to the accounting requirement to apportion an aggregate purchase price for a going business over the fair value of individual assets when a reasonable presumption is that the individual assets cannot have those fair values. In much the same vein, the students should focus on possible abuses that can be encountered when significant intangible assets are included among noncurrent assets. The case also addresses the procedures to be followed in allocating to individual noncurrent assets the excess of aggregate fair value over aggregate purchase price, and in the process permits the students' discussion of some of the tax consequences that vary with the structure of the transaction.

Applicable Professional Pronouncements

Accounting Principles Board Opinion No. 16, "Accounting for Business Combinations," paragraphs 22, 66, 69, 74, 75, 76, 87, 88, and 89

Accounting Principles Board Opinion No. 17, "Accounting for Intangible Assets," paragraphs 27 to 31

Business Assumptions and Other Data

The statement of the case furnishes the market value of $5 million for the shares of stock issued by Matrix to acquire West. Often, the most difficult determination required in the accounting for an acquisition is the fair value of the transaction, but here it is given.

The students may properly raise the question whether there are leases that should be included among West's assets as the garages appear to be on leased land. They would be correct in that there are land leases but none were evaluated as being "favorable leases."

The students should also bring into the discussion the uncertainty that attaches to perpetual permits and whether accounting recognition can, or should, be accorded such uncertainty, or perhaps disclosure, or perhaps complete silence. We have all seen perpetual permits rendered worthless by action of the issuing authority. Examples would include taxicab permits, liquor licenses, and notary public licenses that were rendered essentially worthless because the issuing authority lifted the restriction on the number of permits or licenses it would issue, making them generally available to all applicants. A recent nationwide example concerns interstate operating rights of trucking companies that the FASB mandated could no longer be carried as assets in recognition of the provisions of the Motor Carrier Act of 1980.

An interesting point, not bearing directly on the case, that may be reflected upon by the students is the fact that Matrix's depreciation rate on taxicabs does not reduce the carrying cost sufficiently to keep pace with the reduction in their economic value. True, accounting-style depreciation is not intended to measure "fall in value," yet it should be of some concern both that it does not and (as here) that it can greatly deviate from fair values.

The students will recognize that the acquisition of West does not meet the criteria for pooling-of-interests accounting because (1) it was a subsidiary of another company and (2) nonvoting preferred stock was exchanged for common stock, which also disqualifies the transaction as a tax-free exchange.

Had the transaction been a tax-free exchange, the accounting proposed by Matrix would have been different. In such case, the market or appraisal values specified in the case study for assets would differ from the income tax bases of those items. Estimated future tax effects of differences between the tax bases and amounts otherwise appropriate to assign to an asset or a liability are one of the variables in estimating fair value. Amounts assigned to identifiable assets and liabilities should, for example, recognize that the fair value of an asset to an acquirer is less than its market or appraisal value if all or a portion of the market or appraisal value is not deductible for income taxes. The impact of tax effects on amounts assigned to individual assets and liabilities depends on numerous factors, including imminence or delay of realization of the asset value and the possible timing of tax consequences. Assuming a 50 percent tax rate, and assuming the book values of West's tangible assets are also their tax bases, a solution Matrix could propose, to give effect to the loss of tax benefits, would have been:

	Initial Fair Value in Excess of Tax Basis	($000 omitted) Loss/ (Gain) in Tax Benefit	Adjusted Fair Value	Allocation of Excess	Matrix New Cost
Taxicabs	$(1,500)	$ (750)	$ 2,250	$ (321)	$ 1,929
Garages and Equipment	1,500	750	1,750	(250)	1,500
Permits	6,000	3,000	3,000	(429)	2,571
Goodwill	—	—	—		—
Liabilities			(1,000)		(1,000)
Total	$ 6,000	$ 3,000	$ 6,000		$ 5,000
Cost of Purchase			5,000		
Excess of Fair Value over Cost			$ 1,000	$(1,000)	

This solution illustrates the potentially significant differences that can result to the buyer dependent upon tax status, even though the initial tax impact would apply to the seller rather than to the buyer. The illustration also highlights the fact that a mechanical application of the rules can result in a computed new cost basis in excess of fair value. The fair value of the taxicabs is stated in the case at $1,500,000. But, if one grinds out the numbers "by the book," one arrives at a meaningless valuation for accounting purposes of $1,929,000 or over $400,000 in excess of fair value. Is $1,929,000 the number to use?

DLG 10-2

Or, should the $400,000 plus be reallocated on a proportional basis to the remaining properties and permits? Authoritative literature does not address the specific question. A second allocation that reduces the taxicabs to an amount no greater than $1,500,000 would seem warranted.

This illustration also should introduce the students to discussion of the questions of whether the loss (gain) in tax benefit should be discounted (accreted) in arriving at "Adjusted Fair Value" and whether the gain in future tax benefit should be recognized unless its realization is assured beyond a reasonable doubt. Some accountants take the position that loss of tax benefits should be discounted (they would not accrete gains), all of which poses a further interesting question, if followed. What is the discount period for the loss of tax benefit on the perpetual permits? These accountants would view loss of tax benefit as not in the nature of deferred taxes, which are not discountable, nor can they be carried through in an acquisition accounted as a purchase. They also base their position on Accounting Principles Board Opinion No. 16 which, as noted above, says that the impact of tax depends on a number of factors including the possible timing of tax consequences.

Some accountants would also say that the gain in tax benefit should not be recognized until its realization is assured beyond a reasonable doubt. But, to take that position puts the gain in the nature of a tax. It is strange that the credit adjustments to initial fair values (that is, loss of tax benefits) are not in the nature of taxes, whereas the debit adjustments (that is, gain in tax benefits) are in the nature of taxes. Still other accountants would take the position that the whole thing is nothing but meaningless allocation and reallocation of purchase price (which should be constant), and nuances such as discounting, accreting, and realization beyond reasonable doubt add nothing to the economic reality of the purchase transaction. No matter which school of thought is on the side of right, the illustration has ignored such nuances, or refinements, in the interest of simplicity. Nevertheless, it seems appropriate that the students understand the impact of a tax-free exchange for tax purposes in a purchase transaction and the related unsettled issues attendant thereto. In the actual situation on which this case is based, the transaction qualified as a tax-free exchange. In order to simplify the case, the circumstances were changed slightly to make the transaction taxable, and it is assumed that the fair value of West's assets will be established, through liquidation of West, as tax bases for the future.

Discussion

The Economics of the Transaction — Matrix Mfg. Co. has purchased a company that has a net book value of $4 million by issuing stock having a market value of $5 million. The estimated value of the net assets of West Taxicab Company is $9 million, including $6 million for permits, an intangible that had no recorded book value. The economics of the transaction seem to make no sense. Why would a conglomerate sell everything for $5 million when it could sell the permits only and retire its liabilities for an equivalent $5 million and still have left over, in the latter instance, operating properties with a fair value of $4 million? Why would a company walk away, as it were, from assets having $4 million of estimated fair values, fully recognizing that the operating properties may not bring $4 million in an open market sale but could conceivably bring in something approximating that amount? The business side of the transaction should prompt the students' discussion of the strong likelihood that one or more of the fair values being bandied about is obviously unrealistic. It cannot be reasonable that the individual assets have those fair values if the aggregate purchase price is also fair value. There may be rare cases of so-called "bargain purchases," but Accounting Principles Board Opinion No. 16 recognizes they should be few in number — and presumably the number should be zero where the cost of the acquired business was paid for with a company's stock. Accounting Principles Board Opinion No. 29, "Accounting for Nonmonetary Transactions," specifically states that it takes no position on acquisition of nonmonetary assets on issuance of capital stock of an enterprise; of course, that sidestepping is overcome by the same Opinion saying that it takes no position on business combinations, which brings the case back to the jurisdiction of Accounting Principles Board Opinion No. 16. However, until general rules are formulated by the Financial Accounting Standards Board as to accounting for stock issued in exchange for assets, highly specialized rules, as found in Accounting Principles Board Opinion No. 16, could continue to produce under certain circumstances the unrealistic results observed above.

There generally are no "bargain purchases" available in a market with reasonable market transparency and the fair value of the consideration given for the purchase would seem to produce clearer evidence for the total "cost" than the individual valuations of the property acquired; such theoretical considerations make the solution appear questionable, since a strict adherence to the Opinion results in an erosion of "hard" assets by ballooning the intangible asset, "permits." Thus, from a practical standpoint, it seems to make more sense to isolate the intangible asset and assign as small a value to it as possible in view of the uncertainty surrounding the various estimates of fair value. This line of reasoning is supported by the fact that the purchase determines the value of the permits as $2 million (purchase price less fair value of net tangible assets) through an arm's-length transaction. Though theoretical deliberations are in congruence with practical considerations, present accounting rules may not permit valuing the operating rights at only $2 million.

By interpretation, one may believe the $2 million result can be reached under GAAP. Paragraph 22 of Accounting Principles Board Opinion No. 16 says that applying the purchase method to business combinations effected primarily by issuing stock may entail difficulties in measuring the cost of an acquired company if neither the fair value of the consideration given nor the fair value of the property acquired is clearly evident. There follows an extensive discussion of the difficulties and dangers inherent in using the purchase method of accounting when stock, rather than cash or a monetary obligation, is used. Paragraph 16 brings up the necessary restraints on measurement, again, when stock is used. And paragraph 75 has this to say: "If the quoted market price is not the fair value of stock, either preferred or common, the consideration received should be estimated even though measuring directly the fair values of assets received is difficult. Both the consideration received, including goodwill, and the extent of the adjustment of the quoted market price of the stock issued should be weighed to determine the amount to be recorded. All aspects of the acquisition, including the negotiations, should be studied, and independent appraisals may be used as an aid in determining the fair value of securities issued. Consideration other than stock distributed to effect an acquisition may provide evidence of the total fair value received."

In interpreting the above, some accountants have concluded that, indeed, some flexibility in applying the strict mechanics of Accounting Principles Board Opinion No. 16 is available — that good judgment (or estimates) can be used in lieu of relying on the formula "cost may be determined either by the fair value of the consideration given or by the

Case 10: Purchase Accounting — A Bargain Purchase   65

fair value of the property acquired, whichever is more clearly evident," when apparently neither of the fair values is "more clearly evident." The interpretation seems to accommodate the preferred valuation of the permits at $2 million.

The case does not reveal why Matrix chose to use the market value of the stock issued as cost of the acquisition. Surely, it is more conservative, but is that a criterion? The students should discuss the judgments involved in selecting "either the fair value of the consideration given or the fair value of the property acquired, whichever is more clearly evident." Though in no way conclusive, Accounting Principles Board Opinion No. 16 seems to lean toward acceptance of market price as cost of a transaction by stating, in effect, that the fair value of securities traded in the market is normally more clearly evident than the fair value of an acquired company. Thus, the quoted market price of an equity security issued to effect a business combination usually may be used to approximate the fair value of an acquired company after recognizing possible effects of price fluctuations, quantities traded, issue costs, and the like. The market price for a reasonable period before and after the date the terms of the acquisition are agreed to and announced should be considered in determining the fair value of securities issued.

The Allocation of Negative Goodwill — Accounting Principles Board Opinion No. 16, paragraph 91, requires allocation of the excess of fair value over cost to reduce proportionally the value assigned to noncurrent assets (except marketable securities). The mechanics of this requirement result in eroding "hard" assets (and reducing immediate-term depreciation) to enhance "soft" assets (and increasing long-term amortization), with the resultant financial effect:

- $600,000 of the fair values of taxicabs have been effectively shifted to permits. The effect on income will be an annual amortization charge of $15,000 (assuming the permits are written off over 40 years) instead of a depreciation charge annually of approximately $200,000 on the taxicabs.

- $1 million of the fair values of garages and equipment have been effectively shifted to permits. Here the income effect will be annual amortization of $25,000 instead of a depreciation charge of $66,000.

- While the permits are stated substantially below this "fair value," they still constitute a significant asset, and the valuation of that asset is increased through reduction of the "hard" assets. In essence, this accounting treatment resulted in increasing the valuation of a "soft" asset with a 40-year life out of "hard" assets with much shorter lives.

Valuation of Permits — Another issue of this case deals with the perpetual permits. Industry practice indicates a considerable value for these rights in bona fide sales. Evidence in the case is provided by the recent purchase offers. However, the purchase offer for the permits is out of line with the total purchase price for West Taxicab Company, which makes the offer questionable. Unfortunately, Accounting Principles Board Opinion No. 16 does not deal with the valuation of assets when neither the value of the consideration given nor the assets received are "clearly evident." Certainly, the proposed purchaser who made offers to purchase the permits applies future earnings potential in determining the fair value of the exclusive right, and considers such factors as fuel cost and other economic problems. However, if the fair value assigned to the permits is incorrect on the high side, even on a "going concern" basis, then present purchase accounting rules have resulted in excessive deferrals of asset diminution, which in turn could produce misleading income and balance sheet statements.

On the other hand, if the fair value of the permits is correct, then a true "bargain purchase" has occurred, unless the valuation of the stock is wrong. However, Accounting Principles Board Opinion No. 16 does not permit recognition of negative goodwill so long as tangible property and intangibles remain. Yet the economic reality of a typical bargain purchase is that the reduced price recognizes the future excess costs that will be required to stem the operating drains and turn the business into a profitable or more profitable operation. On that theory, any deferred credits, often called "negative goodwill" (though a misnomer), typically would be amortized over the so-called turnaround period, which ordinarily would be quite a bit less than 40 years.

Amortization of Permits — Permits must be amortized over no more than 40 years (APB Opinion No. 17). The amortization of a "perpetual life" right is difficult to understand and impossible to properly apply. It may be that in 40 years the permits are worth ten times as much, but there is also the chance that in 40 years' time taxicabs, as now known, will no longer be operating, or the permits may have been rendered worthless. A 40-year write-off limit seems an appropriate end to "amortization," though it is clearly arbitrary and cannot be sustained by a useful life measure.

The Solution

The solution — which could go in more than one direction — should not be considered a key part of the case. The treatment proposed by Matrix accords with generally accepted accounting principles, as stated in Accounting Principles Board Opinion No. 16, and was considered appropriate. However, the results seem to offend one's business judgments and to substitute a mechanical solution for one that could better display the economic substance of the transaction. Presently, about the only course of action available is a strong challenge of the fair values assigned. A natural inclination, that would seem to better accord with economic substance, is to assign the excess ($2 million) of the purchase price ($5 million) over the fair value of net tangible assets ($3 million) to the permits. Should the company and the auditor be able to support that such accounting accords with economic substance, it could be used, presumably. A decision that accords with GAAP would be needed however, or else, as a departure from promulgated standards, etc., would require disclosure in the auditor's report under Rule 203 of the Code of Ethics.

Pooling of Interests Accounting — Intent

Your client, Conglom, Inc., a New York Stock Exchange favorite, has acquired over a period of years several businesses that have worked out quite well. It has profitable subsidiaries in lines such as home computers, seismographic operations, agricultural chemicals, and solar energy. Its earnings have shown steady growth, and the stock market shows its appreciation and expectation by way of a high price-earnings ratio.

A month or so ago you and Conglom's treasurer discussed the proposed acquisition of Byum, Inc., a nationwide real estate brokerage operation with a number of subsidiaries, some of which own and operate apartment houses in various cities. What with the depressed real estate market, high interest costs, inflation, and flat earnings, the stock of the real estate company was trading at less than book value. The acquisition was to be made by a simple, straight-forward exchange of common stock for common stock using market prices. After reviewing the criteria for business combinations, the treasurer and you readily agreed that, if the deal went through, the accounting would follow the pooling-of-interests method.

But now the treasurer is on the line — with other ideas. He says, "It looks like the deal for Byum will go through. As I see it, if we intend to sell off some of those apartment house subsidiaries, or any of our other assets, we have to use the purchase method of accounting; and, no matter how I figure it, we'll have a minimum of $20,000,000 negative goodwill to take into income over the next three years. We can discuss whether three is the right number of years later, but I just wanted to check and be sure that purchase accounting is OK before we close the deal." With considerable lack of enthusiasm, you say, "Yeah, that's what the 'book' says, provided it's a significant part of the assets and not a disposal in the ordinary course of business." He quickly responds, "That's great; you can tell us later what is significant and that's the amount we intend to sell. And, thanks."

Your lack of enthusiasm centers around the thought that here is a company that may be able to "manipulate" $20,000,000 or more into its future earnings stream by expressing an intention to sell off some properties. Your uneasiness is fortified by your recollection of a situation that confronted you some six months earlier. Another client had acquired a ladies' apparel manufacturing complex in a pooling-of-interests transaction with no intention (represented in writing) of selling off any assets. But, notwithstanding such intention, it had in fact sold off a significant, unprofitable girdle and corset manufacturing subsidiary 16 months after acquisition. So much for intentions then and now.

DID YOU GIVE THE RIGHT ANSWER TO CONGLOM?

WHAT WILL YOU TELL THE TREASURER IS A "SIGNIFICANT PART OF THE ASSETS"?

IF THE PURCHASE METHOD OF ACCOUNTING IS FOLLOWED, WHAT WILL YOU DO IF CONGLOM DOES NOT SELL OFF A SIGNIFICANT AMOUNT OF ASSETS?

Case 11-1

DISCUSSION LEADER'S GUIDE

Pooling of Interests Accounting — Intent

Objectives of the Case

A broad objective is to have the students debate the validity of the pooling-of-interests method of accounting. Many accountants and others have long questioned the concept, except perhaps in limited situations such as a business combination of affiliates or companies under common control. Related considerations include (a) the appropriateness of an accounting policy that produces significant accounting swings based on intention alone, (b) the accounting consequences of a subsequent deliberate violation of that intention or an existing intention to violate conditions negotiated at the time of acquisition. Further, the students should focus on the form-versus-substance issue — that is, whether one can identify the economic substance of a pooling as contrasted to the economic substance of a purchase. Part and parcel of the form-versus-substance issue is the need to focus on the practice of "structuring" transactions to achieve different accounting results without necessarily changing the economic effects of the transactions.

In a narrower sense the objective is to have the students deliberate on the meaning of "significant part of the assets" and "in the ordinary course of business."

Applicable Professional Pronouncements

Accounting Principles Board Opinion No. 16, Accounting for Business Combinations

Business Assumptions and Other Data

By way of background the students should be aware that a time-honored practice has been to try to structure business combinations as purchases (rather than pooling of interests) where the purchase price results in substantial "negative goodwill" (a "deferred credit" according to APB Opinion No. 16). The attraction of purchase accounting can be even stronger if material, noncurrent assets do not exist that have to be reduced to zero before determination of negative goodwill. While not all companies have pressed to qualify for purchase method accounting when acquired net assets exceed cost, the temptation sways many companies because of the boost in future earnings resulting from amortization of negative goodwill.

The stock-for-stock exchange ratio was based on market prices, as stated. Though not necessary for the solution, that fact, with others, tends to make the acquisition generate substantial negative goodwill. Some of the other factors are:

- Market price of the brokerage company stock is already below book value.
- Apartments had been held for a number of years, and depreciated cost is less than net realizable value, which has been influenced by inflation.

- If apartments are to be sold they are required to be valued at net realizable value (which is not reduced to zero by by an excess of acquired net assets over cost).
- Because it is a service organization, the brokerage company has relatively little in noncurrent assets which also would need to be reduced to zero.

Though not necessary to the solution as stated, the students should be aware of the circumstances which attracted the treasurer to do a flip-flop in roughly a month's time. (Some students may be quick to suggest that the auditor should have pointed out this attractive possibility a month or so ago and not waited for the treasurer to come up with it. Others may disagree.)

Though not stated in the case, Byum has never sold a subsidiary. Further, the apartment house subsidiaries, which have been in existence for varying periods from three to nine years, have never sold any of their owned properties. They are jealously trying to guard a tax position that they believe will allow a more favorable tax rate if and when any properties are sold. (The parent, Byum, buys and sells properties from time to time for its own account, but never carries an inventory held for sale, as such.) As to Conglom, it has on occasion sold unprofitable subsidiaries and operations and is expected to continue to do so.

Discussion

The students may recall that a number of years ago, perhaps in 1968 or 1969, when the world was sick and tired of "pooling abuses," the Accounting Principles Board circulated a draft opinion that would have effectively dispatched the pooling-of-interests method — it would no longer have been acceptable. But the draft failed to gain sufficient support and APB Opinion No. 16 followed in 1970. The "Background" section in that Opinion does a good job in summarizing the pros and cons of pooling-of-interests accounting. Those arguments are not repeated here, but the students may want to discuss some that are of interest to them.

Roughly three years later, in 1973, the Accounting Principles Board issued its Opinion No. 29 on Accounting for Nonmonetary Transactions, wherein it stated, "The Board concludes that, in general, accounting for nonmonetary transactions should be based on the fair values of the assets (or services) involved which is the same basis as used in monetary transactions." But, that principle is stated not to apply to business combinations accounted for as a pooling of interests. Also, the students may want to discuss, as part of the conceptual support for poolings, the anomaly that is provided in APB Opinion No. 20 (1971) whereby a business combination reported by the pooling-of-interests method results in a different reporting entity but remains the same entity if the purchase method is followed. We all know the entity is the same in either case. Saying it is different does not make it different.

One of the principal positions stated in opposition to the purchase method (thus supporting the concept of pooling) was the inability to determine fair value in many cases. If inability to determine is a valid argument, the students may want to discuss why it loses its validity when the uncertainty of such things as intent and contemplation (keystones of the pooling concept) are understood. Some students may want to discuss the soundness of an accounting principle that requires one to wait two or more years before knowing if, when all facts are known, the right accounting decision was made. Estimates of future events are made all the time; they are a part of accounting. But, when estimates are later discovered to be in error, the result is typically a change in dollar amount, not a change in accounting principle or a belated recognition that the wrong accounting principle was used.

The intention of management plays a part in accounting in situations other than pooling-of-interests accounting. (It is fair to say auditors like to hold intention-based accounting to a minimum.) In many cases, the intention bears solely on classification of assets or liabilities, for example, intention to hold marketable securities as an investment. In perhaps fewer cases intention bears directly on net earnings, for example, intention not to repatriate foreign earnings or intention of a savings and loan association not to pay dividends from tax-restricted reserves. In still other cases, intention alone is insufficient, for example, not only must management have an intention of refinancing short-term debt as long-term debt after the balance sheet date, it must also have an irrevocable contract so that the intent can become reality.

Authoritative literature offers little guidance toward concepts that would establish when intention alone is enough to affect the accounting. The students may perceive the unwritten guidelines to be that when management has the ability to unilaterally carry out its intention then the accounting can follow that intention. But, when action of an outside interest is necessary to carry out management's intention, the accounting must await the outside action. The theory is sound; unfortunately many of the situations are not clear-cut as to management's ability to perform in what appear to be unilateral actions. For example, management may not recognize a loss from market declines in a bond portfolio on the basis it intends to hold the bonds to maturity; yet adverse future developments could make it imperative that the bonds be sold before maturity to provide needed working capital. Such is the situation here; Byum intends to sell apartments, or failing that, some other assets not in the ordinary course of business, within two years to "break" the requirement for pooing-of-interests accounting. While management's intention may be good, market conditions or other factors may operate in such a way that the intention cannot be carried out.

Professional literature gives some guidance here and there as to what to do if accounting recognition is given an intention and that intention fails. For example, in the foreign earnings and savings and loan reserve cases, literature says accrue the taxes previously not accrued. In the case of an intention not to sell assets (the opposite of this case) in order to qualify for pooling treatment, it says disclose the failed intention and show any gain or loss on the sale as extraordinary. But nothing is said about a failed intention in the fact situation applicable to this case.

In discussing failed intentions, the students may see a need to differentiate between deliberate violation of an intention (such as Conglom now likes all its assets too much to sell any of them off) and a preconceived plan at the time of combination not to carry out the stated intention that threw the accounting from one method to the other. Professional literature offers no specific guidance as to the sort between the two types of failure. Were the latter situation known at the time of initial accounting, the intention would be disregarded in the selection of an accounting method. (And, some serious question would result as to whether to continue a professional relationship with a client who attempted to deceive.) Were the latter situation to come to light after the initial accounting, some students would opt to reverse the purchase accounting retroactively and restate under pooling concepts. The students should understand that proving, in an audit sense, an earlier

DLG 11-3

Case 11: Pooling of Interests Accounting — Intent

design to deceive would be most difficult. Even an admission of deceit would be viewed with skepticism — it may be a false, self-serving admission simply to switch to what now is a greener pasture. (Again, continued client relationship would become a question.)

In most situations involving the form versus substance issue, the answer speaks for itself; for example, a sale of property for a note receivable bearing one percent interest. Such a clear distinction is missing in the case of purchase/pooling as to legal form and economic substance. Instead the distinction between the two is devoid of any form/substance comparison but rather rests on a number of man-made criteria, which as noted can be subject to rather easy manipulation — particularly going in the direction of "making" a pooling a purchase; it is considerably more difficult in the opposite direction. What the students might discuss is whether a so-called pooling has economic substance, as such, or whether it is an accounting form only (surely not a legal form). If such be the thinking then what follows logically would seem to be that poolings are devoid of economic substance but rather are manufactured by following prescribed form. Stated differently, companies combining by stock-for-stock exchange possess the same economic substance regardless of whether called purchase, pooling, merger, amalgamation, consolidation, acquisition, or some other name - only the accounting differs. So, rather than the accounting following substance, it may be following form.

The students should discuss the pros and cons of "structuring deals." It would be a poor businessman who did not "structure" a deal to the extent possible to obtain the best economic advantage. But, when transactions are structured solely to give a different accounting answer, they tend to be more suspect. In the case of Conglom the students should recognize that the $20,000,000 additional income it is proposing to structure into the deal is not hard, quality earnings such as can be used to liquidate debt, pay out in dividends, invest in inventories, and the like. Though the income is illusory, some companies continue to strive to create it.

Opinion No. 16 does not define what is meant by a "significant part of the assets." The natural inclination of the students may lean toward ten percent of total combined assets because some of the other criteria in the Opinion use ten percent as a break point. Others may consider a higher percentage — say 15 or 20 percent — because the test is applied to total assets of both companies rather than the assets of the company being "acquired."

"Ordinary course of business" seems not to be defined explicitly in professional literature. Everyone seems to know what it means. But in Conglom's situation, slight interpretation one way or the other triggers a monumental swing in future income. Presumably Conglom, as a service company, would be limited in the type of assets it would have for sale. Byum has plenty of assets it can sell but the question is whether any can be sold other than in the ordinary course of business of the formerly separate company. Conglom has sold subsidiaries before — presumably in the ordinary course — and is unlikely to be able to sustain further sales of subsidiaries as not in the ordinary course of business. Sale of a subsidiary by Byum may be said to be "in substance" a sale by Conglom. Byum has not sold subsidiaries but Byum has sold apartment houses and a sale of apartment subsidiaries may be in substance the sale of apartment buildings. As stated earlier, Byum has sold apartment buildings before but never any that it had designated as held for operations. Yet it seems probable that in the world of real estate, even apartments held for operations will be sold from time to time. The character of the property, alone, in the hands of a real estate company may be enough to say that any sales qualify as "in the ordinary course." Arguments can be made both ways; the answer is not clear as to what sales, if any, will meet the test.

The Solution

The auditors had a feeling that the declared intention may have been a manipulation to produce a preconceived accounting result, but for lack of substantiation that the declaration of intention was false and misleading, or, if bona fide, could not be carried out by the company — accepted the answer given by the audit partner.

Ten percent was given as the amount of assets to be disposed of in other than the ordinary course of business.

If the dispositions are made in the future other than in the ordinary course, the third question is moot. If the future produces no such qualifying sales, a whole host of questions will need to be resolved. If the failure seems to be a deliberate violation for cause, full disclosure of the facts should suffice. If a lack of good faith can be shown in declaring the intent (most difficult) or if the deliberate violation has no cause but to manipulate earnings, retroactive accounting should be considered. In such case, some other auditors may have to deal with the issue as the present auditors will likely have terminated their relationship.

Some students may want to know what happened in the other situation of concern six months earlier that involved future sales when the client had represented none would be made. The auditors' investigation produced no evidence of lack of good faith in the declaration of intention so the pooling-of-interests accounting was allowed to stand and the required disclosures were made, with gains on sales being shown as extraordinary income.

Case 12: Interim Accounting — Deferral of Costs

Interim Accounting — Deferral of Costs

The Kool-Komfort Ice Cream Company is a publicly held manufacturer and retailer of ice cream products. Their products are sold by vendors from mobile units which cover residential areas during the summer months. The product line includes the standard ice cream bars and Popsicles and also features several novelty ice cream treats as promotional items. These novelty items have usually been big sellers. The 1978 summer novelty hit was the Jaws Breaker, a grape Popsicle shaped like a shark.

The company's fiscal year ends October 31, which historically has been the end of the summer season. The selling season begins again in April. Between October 31 and April 1, the company expends a great deal of its effort to develop novelty treats for sale during the next selling season. The company does not start product research and development prior to October 31 because the theme is usually topical, as evidenced by their 1978 hit, the Jaws Breaker. The product research and development effort includes the following stages:

1. Identification of products for sale,
2. Market research as to consumer acceptance and enthusiasm,
3. Product design,
4. Production planning, and
5. Advertising.

The company's controller has asked how he should account for product development costs in the statements for the first quarter ending January 31, 1979. The company has settled on its main novelty product for the 1979 selling season, the Star Licker, a double Fudgsicle with the figure of a space ship on top. They have completed the first three steps described above and have incurred some costs for steps 4 and 5. By January 31, they have incurred a significant amount of development cost, but they are satisfied that the product will be a hot item. The controller believes that all the costs of developing the Star Licker should be deferred to the selling season and then amortized to cost of sales by October 31. But, he knows he must have them written off by October 31 because Financial Accounting Standards Board Statement No. 2 prohibits the deferral of research and development costs at year-end. He is not sure how the theory of Statement of Financial Accounting Standards No. 2 should be applied in interim reports, however, and he would like your advice.

HOW SHOULD KOOL-KOMFORT ACCOUNT FOR ITS DEVELOPMENT COSTS IN ITS INTERIM FINANCIAL STATEMENTS?

DISCUSSION LEADER'S GUIDE

Interim Accounting — Deferral of Costs

Objectives of the Case

The objective of this case study is the development of an understanding of the two conflicting pronouncements on interim financial reporting (Accounting Principles Board Opinion No. 28 and Statement of Financial Accounting Standards No. 2), and of the practical difficulties in applying these pronouncements. Kool-Komfort illustrates the difficulties in the determination as to certain items — whether they should be accounted for as belonging to a separate and discrete interim accounting period or as an integral part of an annual period.

Applicable Professional Pronouncements

Accounting Principles Board Opinion No. 28, "Interim Financial Reporting"

Statement of Financial Accounting Standards No. 2, "Accounting for Research and Development Costs"

Business Assumptions and Other Data

In practice, companies which derive a significant portion of their revenues on a seasonal basis, such as in the last quarter, have adopted different policies in accounting for certain costs on an interim basis. The costs in the known situations would not be identical necessarily to those in this case study; yet some similar characteristics are present and some characteristics of research and development are present.

A position may be taken that a company's business cycle should be used for the application of the provision of Statement of Financial Accounting Standards No. 2. If one concurs that the provisions may be applied to a company's business cycle and since Kool-Komfort's business cycle is April 1 through October 31, the research and development expenses should be deferred on an interim basis and expensed over the business cycle. However, assuming that position is supportable so as to accommodate deferral and amortization of research and development costs within a company's business cycle, it would seem allowable only if a company's business cycle were 12 months or less. For companies having business cycles extending beyond one year, as may be true in the automobile and aircraft industries, for example, deferral of research and development costs beyond a fiscal year-end would seem contrary to the spirit of Statement of Financial Accounting Standards No. 2.

Of the activities whose costs are under consideration at Kool-Komfort, not all would seem to qualify as a research and development cost. Market research and advertising plan-

DLG 12-1

Case 12: Interim Accounting — Deferral of Costs 75

ning would seem clearly outside the scope of Statement of Financial Accounting Standards No. 2 and the same would seem true of production planning.

Discussion

A first reading of this case study probably suggests deferral of the development costs in the earlier interim financials so that they may be properly matched with the associated revenues produced in the later interim periods. Yet, on the other hand, Statement of Financial Accounting Standards No. 2 states that all research and development costs should be expensed as incurred. The case is truly an anomaly.

The primary conceptual issue is whether

1. An interim period is a discrete accounting period in itself, or
2. An interim period is an integral part of the annual period.

Under the view that an interim period is a discrete accounting period, deferrals, accruals, and estimations at the end of each period are determined by following essentially the same principles and judgments that apply to annual periods.

Under the view that an interim period is an integral part of the annual period, deferrals, accruals, and estimations at the end of each interim period are affected by judgments made at the interim date as to results of operations for the balance of the annual period. Thus, an expense item that might be considered as falling wholly within an annual accounting period (no fiscal year-end accrual or deferral) could be allocated among interim periods based on estimated time, sales volume, productive activity, or some other basis.

Accounting Principles Board Opinion No. 28 adopted the position that "each interim period should be viewed primarily as an integral part of an annual period." Proponents of the "discrete" view cricized the Opinion by stating that it encourages normalizing and smoothing income and, therefore, conceals the actual level of activity. Furthermore, the Opinion is criticized by those who favor the "discrete" view because it ignores the fundamental concept of consistency by condoning the use of interim principles and practices inconsistent with accounting policies used in the preparation of annual financial statements.

The Accounting Principles Board adopted the position that the interim period is an integral part of the annual period and that the usefulness of interim financial statements rests on their relationship to the annual results of operations. The Board recognized that the shorter a reporting period, the less useful it is as a predictive tool. Thus, to the extent interim financial statements can more closely reflect the anticipated results of operations for the annual period, the more their usefulness will be enhanced.

However, the Financial Accounting Standards Board, in Statement No. 2, adopted the position that all research and development costs should be "charged to expense when incurred." Basically, the Board adopted the view that research and development cost should be expensed because:

1. It was objective.

2. The idea that there was a direct relationship between research and development costs and specific future revenue was rejected. (The Board cited "three empirical research studies, which focus on companies in industries intensively involved in research and devel-

opment activities that generally failed to find a significant correlation between research and development expenditures and increased future benefits as measured by subsequent sales,[1] earnings,[2] or share of industry sales."[3]

The Financial Accounting Standards Board also believed that financial statements of all entities would be more comparable if such costs were expensed as incurred.

Considering the previous discussions, one can understand the difficulty in applying current accounting principles to resolve how Kool-Komfort should account for its development costs in its interim financial statements. It could be argued that the Kool-Komfort development costs are associated directly with the products to be sold in the later periods as evidenced by past history. Accordingly, under Accounting Principles Board Opinion No. 28, such costs should be charged against income in those interim periods in which the related revenue is recognized. On the other hand, one can view such costs as being research and development costs as defined by Statement of Financial Accounting Standards No. 2. Accordingly, they should be expensed as incurred.

Statement of Financial Accounting Standards No. 2 does not deal specifically with interim financial accounting, perhaps because its authors considered the words "when incurred" to cover both interim and full fiscal periods.

The *Handbook of Accounting and Auditing*, Burton, Palmer, and Kay, contains a comprehensive chapter (No. 5) devoted to interim financial statements. Regarding seasonal revenues, costs, or expenses it has this to say:

> There is no authoritative guidance for seasonal businesses to follow in deciding whether to defer slack-period costs and expenses. Each set of circumstances must be viewed on its own merits, and industry practices often will govern. Seasonal businesses that do defer such costs and expenses should disclose their accounting policies and the nature of their activities in their interim financial statements. An example of such a disclosure might be:
>
>> The interim results of ABC Baseball Team, Inc. are not necessarily indicative of the annual results of operations. Substantially all of the company's revenue is earned during the regular baseball season, which except for post-season games, extends from the middle of April to the beginning of October. Expenses such as players' and coaches' salaries, stadium and game expenses, and broadcasting expenses, which are directly related to the playing of baseball, are deferred and will be amortized to expense on the basis of the number of games played. Expenses such as general and administrative expenses, public relations, scouting, player development, and spring training have been expensed as incurred.

The *Handbook* (page 5-3) cites one author, Michael Schiff, who sees the integral/discrete issue somewhat differently. He is quoted as follows:

> Interim income numbers are the important ones and the annual income number provides merely a confirmation of the previously reported numbers . . . . The central thrust for the de-

---

[1] Maurice S. Newman, "Equating Return from R&D Expenditures," *Financial Executive*, April 1968, pp. 26-33.

[2] Orace Johnson, "A Consequential Approach to Accounting for R&D," *Journal of Accounting Research*, Autumn 1967, pp. 164-72.

[3] Alex J. Milburn, "An Empirical Study of the Relationship of Research and Development Expenditures to Subsequent Benefits" (Unpublished Research Study, Department of Accountancy of the University of Illinois, 1971).

Case 12: Interim Accounting — Deferral of Costs

velopment of accounting reporting standards should be directed to interim reporting, and modifications in annual reporting standards should be made to accommodate the interim period. The interim period is a fraction of the annual period, much as the annual period is a fraction of the entity's life. The problem of integral vs. discrete is therefore viewed as a nonproblem. . . .

Though some may consider interim reporting a "nonproblem," in practice interim reporting issues continue unabated and are likely to do so for some time to come. In practice, most, if not all, interim financial statements contain some elements of both the integral and the discrete concepts. For example, companies who fancy themselves as pure "discreters" could end up with some pretty wild and meaningless financial statements if they ignored the implication of annual amounts for such things as LIFO adjustments; investment-type tax credits; certain income tax provisions, such as loss carrybacks; and other singularly annual accounting determinations.

The differences in present day practice may narrow when the Financial Accounting Standards Board finally takes a position on standards for interim financial statements. In 1978 it took a step in that direction when it issued its Discussion Memorandum on an Analysis of Issues Related to Interim Financial Accounting and Reporting. But the FASB has deferred further consideration, perhaps pending resolution of a conceptual framework for accounting, both annual and interim. And, the record to date does not furnish a strong sense of direction for guidance in the interval pending its authoritative pronouncement.

As discussed above, Statement of Financial Accounting Standards No. 2 on research and development costs would seem to suggest the discrete concept. Statement No. 3, Reporting Accounting Changes in Interim Financial Statements, seems to suggest the integral concept when dealing with the cumulative effect type accounting change (paragraph 10):

> If a cumulative effect type accounting change is made in *other than the first* interim period of an enterprise's fiscal year, no cumulative effect of the change shall be included in net income of the period of change. Instead, financial information for the pre-change interim periods of the fiscal year in which the change is made shall be restated by applying the newly adopted accounting principle to those pre-change interim periods. The cumulative effect of the change on retained earnings at the *beginning of that fiscal year* shall be included in restated net income of the first interim period of the fiscal year in which the change is made (and in any year-to-date or last-twelve-months-to-date financial reports that include the first interim period). Whenever financial information that includes those pre-change interim periods is presented, it shall be presented on the restated basis.

FASB takes a similar position in Interpretation No. 33 regarding capitalization of interest in the full-costing portion of the oil and gas industry, and ducks the issue completely in Statement No. 43, Accounting for Compensated Absences: "This statement does not address the allocation of costs of compensated absences to interim periods."

At the present time, even with the "integral view" in place in Accounting Principles Board Opinion No. 28, the answer to this case is clouded. The students should refer to paragraph 16 of Opinion No. 28 where the Board talks about spreading costs over the year, when the costs benefit the operations of the year. Before one could agree to spread this company's interim development costs, one would have to be satisfied that those costs benefited the operations of the later quarters. And given the logic of Statement of Financial Accounting Standards No. 2, it will be difficult to argue that there is a direct correlation between those development expenditures, and sales in later quarters. If the product is successful, one would have some proof of a relationship — but that later success will do little good in the earlier interim periods. The students might discuss the nature of these development expenditures and ask whether they come under the logic of Statement of Financial Accounting Standards No. 2.

Somewhere in the discussion, someone ought to ask whether the decision they are being asked to make is really all that important. Surely the reader of an interim statement recognizes that the company has seasonal variations. And the reader must understand that there is development effort required even when no revenues are being generated. In fact, a logical argument could be made that the larger the write-off of these early costs, the happier the investor will be because it will indicate a more extensive research program and opportunities for greater seasonal sales. In fact, the right theoretical answer to this case probably is that the company should use a rolling 12-month statement at interim dates, and should de-emphasize the importance of any single quarter's reported results.

The right practical answer to this case is "it depends." The students really cannot answer the case with the facts they are given, because they do not know how different the current activities might be from successful research activities of the past. The answer to the question, as asked, will depend on the facts gathered by the auditor and on the auditor's judgment. The students might want to think about how much judgment was removed from year-end reporting upon issuance of Statement of Financial Accounting Standards No. 2.

The Solution

There are obviously several answers to the case and different answers, as noted, have been given in practice to cover essentially the same factual situations.

The decision was that Kool-Komfort's development costs should be expensed as incurred on its interim financial statements. Although the costs incurred in the prior year to develop their novelty hit resulted in substantial revenues, such costs were not considered to have a direct relationship with the revenues produced and there was no assurance that the cost incurred in the current year would be similarly productive. Each year there is a high degree of uncertainty about the future benefits to be derived from such development costs. Furthermore, had the decision been to defer expenditures in the interim period, it would have been difficult to determine which expenses should be deferred.

In summary, the conclusion was that an asset should be recorded only if its future benefits can be identified and objectively measured. In the Kool-Komfort case, neither of these criteria was met and, accordingly, such costs were expensed in the interim period.

However, as noted, some companies do defer such expenses to be amortized in the period of revenue production, so long as the deferral and amortization occur within the same fiscal period. If such accounting is supportable, and support is the key issue, a better matching of revenues and expenses, indeed, will occur. Kool-Komfort is certainly a borderline case and the answer would not necessarily be the same from all accountants reviewing the same factual situation. Perhaps the strongest case to avoid expensing as incurred could be made by supporting that such costs are related to seasonal or other periodic design changes to existing products, such costs being excluded from the accounting re-

Case 12: Interim Accounting — Deferral of Costs

quirements of Statement of Financial Accounting Standards No. 2. The determination that Kool-Komfort's costs qualify for exclusion would be a matter of judgment.

Further, as noted above, not all of the activities identified in the case study seem to meet the test of a research and development expenditure. To the extent those activities are outside the purview of Statement of Financial Accounting Standards No. 2, they should be considered separately from the other activities, and deferral and amortization could be appropriate for those costs under the interim accounting concepts of Accounting Principles Board Opinion No. 28.

Uncertainties — Accounting and/or Reporting

You are partner in charge of the audit of Shangri-La, Inc. The company is a real estate developer, specializing in luxury vacation areas. The company's operations have been profitable, although not spectacular. Most of the development property is pledged as collateral for bank loans; there is a reasonable stockholders' equity of about $10 million.

Shangri-La has a substantial investment in a large parcel of land in Key Biscayne, Florida. The company originally paid $25 million for the property two years ago and has since capitalized an additional $5 million in taxes and other carrying costs.

The property is zoned for single-family homes, but Shangri-La has been working diligently to have it rezoned for condominiums. As a site for condominiums, the property would be very valuable and the company has an appraisal to that effect. However, if sold as single-family home sites, it probably would be worth no more than $15 million.

Shangri-La management concedes that their efforts at rezoning have met stiff local resistance, but they refuse to admit defeat. They are planning subtle social pressures on local political groups. Your audit inquiries confirm that the company has carried its rezoning campaign through the necessary legal steps and has been turned down each time. It will clearly be difficult to obtain rezoning for multifamily use but it is not clear that the job is impossible.

Your staff people on the engagement report real frustration on this matter. They have concluded that the client cannot be successful in its rezoning efforts, and, therefore, they have suggested that the land be written down to $15 million. The client has obviously objected, arguing that any such adjustment prejudges their ability to do their job.

The treasurer takes the position that the uncertainty regarding the carrying amount of the Key Biscayne land is just that — an uncertainty — and for your people to insist, or really even suggest, that a write-down in value is necessary is merely showing your strong bias. He then launches into a voluble exhortation of why your people are off base, and he quotes generously from the so-called Trueblood Objectives Report (page 58), on which he has obviously been priming himself. In essence, the applicable portion of that report cautions against bias which benefits one group at the expense of another and further cautions that conservatism for its own sake may actually introduce bias.

While the treasurer graciously acknowledges the existence of an uncertainty, he goes on to say: "It seems to me that any big write-down on that land would reflect a bias, benefiting only you. Your benefit would be the reader's loss. I believe that a frank disclosure of the uncertainty results in a fairer presentation."

WILL DISCLOSURE RESULT IN A FAIR PRESENTATION OR MUST YOU INSIST ON A WRITE-DOWN?

DISCUSSION LEADER'S GUIDE

Uncertainties — Accounting and/or Reporting

Objectives of the Case

The objective of the case is to explore the difficulties encountered in making a judgmental determination as to whether, with regard to an uncertainty, disclosure alone may be adequate to make the financial statements not misleading. If not, of course, an amount must be recorded in the financial statements. The specific case focuses on an uncertainty concerning the market value of the land in relation to its intended best use and in relation to a possible alternative use.

Applicable Professional Pronouncements

Statement of Financial Accounting Standards No. 5, "Uncertainties"

American Institute of Certified Public Accountants, "Objectives of Financial Statements," Report of the Study Group on the Objectives of Financial Statements (called Trueblood Report), page 28 (nonauthoritative)

Accounting Principles Board Statement No. 4, Chapter 6, "Conservatism" (AC 1026.35), "Measuring Unfavorable Events" (AC 1027.09/M-5A), and "Loss Recognition" (AC 1027.09S-5A) (nonauthoritative)

Accounting Research Bulletin No. 43, "Current Assets and Liabilities" (AC 4311.75)

Business Assumptions and Other Data

Accounting for real estate activities is often troublesome and to a large extent is dependent upon management's intention and representation. In the real estate industry, valuation of real estate held for development or sale is often the most troublesome of the accounting issues. The case study states that if the property were sold as single-family home sites, it probably would be worth no more than $15 million, and that amount, given so easily in the study, is the key number, whether disclosure or a write-down is required.

How that number is arrived at is outside the objective of this case study. Yet some recognition, and some discussion, of the difficulties in arriving at the amount is appropriate. Often such amounts derive from appraisal reports on a property. And the appraiser often is an officer or employee of the client company, but sometimes is an "independent" appraiser and may have even been selected by the auditors.

One might assume that the "house" appraiser will be less objective than would the so-called independent appraiser. While this may be true in many cases, it is possible for the "house" appraiser to arrive at equally or even more realistic valuations just as it is possible for all appraisers to arrive at unrealistic values. The use of two, three or four appraisers for a single property does not necessarily result in a more precise or realistic valuation. The fact that appraisals do not establish value needs to be understood; all too often, people view them as pronouncements of certifiable value.

Methods other than appraisals may be used. For example, where available, comparable recent sales may be most useful in arriving at a probable selling price. In considering the method used to determine a valuation and the reasonableness of such valuation, the previous experience with a client company should furnish some guidance and comfort to the auditor. For example, where management has been forthright and objective in its efforts to arrive at a fair valuation, the auditor can be expected to show less concern than in situations where management has attempted consistently to obtain higher valuations by whatever means in order to "puff" earnings or to fulfill some other objective.

For this case study, one should assume that the $15 million determination was made in a forthright manner, is free of suspicion of management manipulation, and does not appear unreasonable to the auditors.

The case gives no information as to the prospective land valuation if zoned for condominiums except "very valuable." Why would an astute businessman in Shangri-La pay $10 million more for property than it is worth as presently zoned, unless re-zoning was assured? Ten million dollars is quite a gamble for any company on something as fickle as a zoning board's behavior. Nor is it likely that the economics of the area have deteriorated to the extent of $10 million in two short years. For the case study, one should assume that the purchaser was overexuberant and the seller did a fine job of convincing the buyer that permits for condominium construction were easily obtainable. Even so, the business economics of the relationship of the purchase price to the fair value based on present single-family zoning are difficult to understand, and the students should have their doubts, too.

Discussion

Statement of Financial Accounting Standards No. 5, "Uncertainties," is the governing, authoritative guide in this case and it perhaps gives better guidance as to when disclosure alone is appropriate than does the referenced nonauthoritative material above; however, as this material was the principal source of guidance available to clients and practitioners for a number of years, it still offers room for theoretical considerations that would challenge the write-down as being arbitrary, or biased, considering the unquantified certainty of the loss. The Trueblood Report attempts to make the reader aware of the fact that not all assets are alike in respect to liquidity and degree of certainty as to realization. The Committee's recommendation actually proposes more than a footnote disclosure in this area; they would rather provide the reader with a new set of financial statements, disclosing the degree of uncertainty for all items, so that the reader is in a position to make an informed judgment based on unbiased facts. The Financial Accounting Standards Board's conceptual framework project seems to parallel somewhat the recommendations of the Trueblood Committee. The Financial Accounting Standards Board, however, has not implemented that part of the Trueblood Committee's recommendation.

Therefore, the company and the auditor have to follow current applicable rules, which are found in SFAS 5. A charge to income would be required if both the following conditions are met:

(a) Information available prior to issuance of the financial statements indicates that it is "probable" that an asset has been impaired . . . at the date of the financial statements. (It is implicit in this condition that it must be probable that one or more future events will occur confirming the fact of the loss.)

(b) The amount of the loss can be "reasonably estimated."

Case 13: Uncertainties — Accounting and/or Reporting

The students may be interested in discussing some of the background of SFAS 5, as it may bear on their solution. The Statement ws conceived, in part, with the help of the Securities and Exchange Commission, to correct perceived abuses in the insurance industry through use of catastrophe and other general reserves to "smooth" earnings. From such a humble purpose, which it serves quite well, it was expanded to cover many other items — including real estate held for sale or development and, in fact, just about everything on the balance sheet and off the balance sheet. In its sweeping coverage it has undoubtedly improved significantly the accounting practices related to uncertainties. But, because it is dealing with the universe, essentially, some generalizations are used which are subject to diverse interpretations. Words such as "probable," "reasonably possible," "remote," and "reasonably estimated" will always mean different things to different people no matter how extensive the attempts to tighten up their meaning.

The treasurer is aware of the ambiguity in the key words above, and like any right-thinking treasurer he expects to interpret those ambiguous words to suit Shangri-La's purpose. Simply stated, his position is that the situation does not meet the criterion that it is "probable" an asset has been impaired. He does not question that the amount of the loss can be "reasonably estimated" if, indeed, one exists.

The students may be quick to point out that generally accepted accounting principles are not consistent as to treatment of the various types of estimates and uncertainties in financial accounting and reporting. For example, the FASB has decided it is inappropriate to allow financial statement preparers to estimate the recoverability of general research and development which, by an interpretation, would seem to fall within the sweeping reach of Statement of Financial Accounting Standards No. 5 to be marked as an "uncertainty." Since any such estimates of recoverability are considered too subjective, all such costs must be expensed. However, estimates as to the future utility of other assets, including those that appear to be very similar to research and development expenditures (e.g., pre-operating expenses and start-up costs), may still be deferred based on estimates of future utility. The incongruity seen here is prevalent elsewhere in authoritative literature.

With such incongruities in accounting, the audit judgments required usually become quite difficult. To delineate between conditions requiring accounting for a loss from those requiring disclosure only is often difficult; yet those judgments must be made in all borderline cases. Presumably to resolve the issue in favor of disclosure only, the evidence should be especially convincing. The students should discuss what evidence would be convincing to them.

The essence of the case, then, is that the auditor will have to decide what is acceptable to him as an auditor, notwithstanding the arguments of the client company. He will need to conclude whether he can issue a "clean" opinion based on full disclosure in a footnote (assuming the company intends to make no write-down); whether he will issue a "subject to" opinion regarding the uncertainty; or whether he will issue an "adverse" opinion, stating that the financial statements are not fairly presented because the write-down has not been taken. There are a number of ramifications to that basic question, however. The discussion should consider:

1) Evidence

Before an auditor can express his opinion saying that the financial statements are *not* fairly presented, he has to have as much evidence in his file as if he were to express an opinion that the statements *are* fairly presented. The text of the case study does not present enough information to enable the student to determine whether he could form an opinion as to the fairness of the $15 million written-down value. But the discussion ought to ask about the kind of evidence an auditor would need before he could be in a position to express that opinion.

2) Expertise

D. R. Carmichael, in Auditing Research Monograph No. 1, argues that the decision as to the type of opinion should consider the expertise the auditor can bring to the matter, and the degree to which the different kinds of opinions communicate the facts. The relevant sections of the monograph (pages 85 through 88) are interesting, but they reach no conclusion. Nonetheless, the students could be referred to that monograph, and they should understand the efforts the profession has made to think through the problem.

3) Effort

There is another more practical aspect of Carmichael's "expertise" argument. An auditor may not hide behind a "subject to" opinion or an "except for" or an "adverse" opinion, if in fact the scope of the audit has been restricted. When the audit report begins by saying that an examination has been performed in accordance with generally accepted auditing standards, the auditor should have applied every reasonable procedure possible in an attempt to resolve the problem. And, this observation may highlight the major auditing uncertainty in this case — what more might the auditor have done to have a basis for concluding whether the write-down was or was not necessary.

4) Limits

There is a corollary to this "expertise" argument. If the auditor has made an honest and a reasonable effort to search out the facts, but still cannot resolve the uncertainty persuasively, he ought not to play God. He ought not put himself in a position where he claims to know the company's business better than company management. He is responsible to bring objectivity to the reporting process, but he is not responsible for the accounting decisions and should be precluded from putting himself in management's position.

5) Risk

The Carmichael monograph and the Trueblood Objectives Study both ask whether the reader is more properly informed as a result of a strongly worded qualified opinion, or a substantial recorded loss. The question is interesting theoretically, but in these days of frightening litigation, it may not be much help; further, Statement of Financial Accounting Standards No. 5 may have eliminated some of the old options. The Carmichael study further suggests that the readers of the financial statements should be educated to understand the nuances of the accountant's reporting procedures, but acknowledges that to do so is a long-term proposition. Practically speaking, it seems clear that an auditor extends his risk when he agrees to a "subject to" opinion in the face of an impending write-down.

6) Policies

An interesting side question here is the continued capitalization of costs in the face of such significant uncertainties. Irrespective of the ultimate decision as to the appropriate

DLG 13-4

Case 13: Uncertainties — Accounting and/or Reporting

accounting and reporting, a case could probably be made for changing the capitalization policies with respect to the troubled properties.

7) Ambiguity

With rules so clear, and yet so ambiguous, vis-a-vis Statement of Financial Accounting Standards No. 5, the students should appreciate the need for not one, but two, interpretations of key words in the Statement and the likelihood of two different interpretations, all made in good faith. As in this case, what may seem "probable" to one party, be it client or auditor, can seem a "reasonable possibility" to another party, with each party sincere in its interpretation of the facts in relation to the rules.

The students may observe that were the assets in question "operating assets" not held for sale, Statement of Financial Accounting Standards No. 5 would be inapplicable (paragraph 31). Though operating assets and real estate held for sale or development are both tangible property having similar characteristics, the exclusion described in paragraph 31 should not be considered pertinent to this case study.

The Solution

The client was not persuaded that a write-down to $15 million was the better course of action. The auditor was not persuaded that the properties should be carried at $30 million with a footnote explaining the zoning problem and the related uncertainty. The audit firm considered that it had carried out all steps appropriate in the circumstances and that further auditing would produce no further reliable information; accordingly, the firm expressed a strongly worded "subject to" opinion on the financial statements. The firm was fired as a result; but, it is interesting to note that in the succeeding year the company agreed to write the property down and to accept a clean opinion. Those actual facts point out how important age is to an uncertainty. The more mature an uncertainty is, the easier it is, usually, to take a categorical position.

The students should recognize a number of things about the solution here:

1. The qualification in the accountants' report was a so-called "subject to" opinion. It expressed uncertainty as to realization of the carrying amount of the Florida property. But, why should the qualification have not been a so-called "except for" opinion? If the loss were "probable" and could be "reasonably estimated," the accounting to follow is clear — a write-down in carrying amount is required. Since the reduction in carrying amount was not made, generally accepted accounting principles were breached, and "subject to" -type qualifications are inappropriate for opinions covering generally accepted accounting principles violations. Or, if the amounts were material, and they would seem to be in this case ($15 million possible loss compared to some $10 million stockholders' equity), why was an "adverse" opinion not given in the face of a generally accepted accounting principles violation? Seldom are satisfactory answers available for questions such as these. The answers most often are judgment calls. The line of demarcation between what goes as "subject to" and what goes as "except for" (or "adverse") is often quite thin, and often as not beyond the understanding of the typical reader. Yet, the auditor cannot treat the demarcation as casually as it is treated by typical readers. If the wrong choice is made and can be linked with resultant damages, litigation against the auditor can follow, and has followed.

2. The desired rezoning could have been obtained subsequent to the firing of the auditors. The fact that the rezoning was obtained would tend to support, as they say, with benefit of hindsight, the company's contention that they were going to obtain it and that, accordingly, it was not "probable" that their Florida property had been impaired. Had damages been suffered and a causative relationship established between the damages and the nature of the auditor's opinion, litigation could follow. In practice, litigation in such situations is not common.

3. The qualified opinion given could have caused the lenders to Shangri-La to draw in their credit lines (they did not in this case) and, as a consequence, force the company to petition for bankruptcy or suffer some other damages. The cause-and-effect relationship between type of opinion and availability of credit is fairly commonplace and, on occasion, results in damage claims against the auditors.

4. The auditor could have been satisfied, in good conscience, with the client's position and given a "clean" opinion. Had a write-down of the property been required in later years, as it was in this case, the appearance of a $15 million downward adjustment, presumably untimely recognized, would serve as a basis for litigation, and often has.

5. Where material dollar amounts are involved in an uncertainty and judgment calls must be made by the auditor as to the type of opinion to express because of the uncertainty, irrespective of the judgment call made, the door opens wide for possible litigation, and in more situations than one cares to reflect on, litigation walks right in.

Liquidity Problems

You are in the final stages of completion of the December, 1981, audit of Revolutionary, Inc., which has been your client since it was formed in 1978. The company was organized to develop a new method of residential construction. The original impetus (and the original capital) came from American Home Builders Co., a very large construction company audited by another CPA firm. American originally put up $2,500,000 but Revolutionary went through that in no time at all. American put in another $2,500,000 and, simultaneously, Revolutionary had a public offering of stock, raising an additional $5,000,000. Revolutionary's experimentation looks promising and, in fact, several of the pilot projects have been very successful. However, the company has been eating up cash at a startling rate. Cash drain has been $1,500,000 a month. Up until now, American has been willing to loan funds to Revolutionary for operating purposes. The loans were always five-year notes and so are due in 1984 and 1985.

Most of Revolutionary's expenditures have been for salaries and supplies, and expensed as incurred. However, the company has also invested substantially in an assembly line plant and has capitalized a significant amount of legal and similar expenses related to patent rights.

This has been a difficult year for home construction, and American is having troubles of its own. In fact, one morning you read in the *Wall Street Journal* that American has announced its intention to sell its 50 percent interest in Revolutionary. When you stop by the office of the treasurer to discuss this development, you find that he has already anticipated your question. He has been in contact with American's chief financial officer, and Revolutionary has been assured that American will continue to provide operating finances as might be required. American apparently feels a moral obligation to the stockholders who came in on the public offering. You wonder out loud whether American would be willing to put that commitment in writing. The Revolutionary treasurer suggests that they probably would not, simply because they could not afford to encumber their own financial picture with a legal obligation. You point out that unless American will give some form of written commitment — or unless Revolutionary can line up some firm source of financing — you will have to reflect this new uncertainty in your audit report on Revolutionary's financials. The treasurer observes dryly, "How can it be any worse; your opinion is already subject to all of our assets. Do you mean you're now going to be subject to our liabilities as well?"

HOW WILL THIS NEW DEVELOPMENT AFFECT YOUR OPINION ON REVOLUTIONARY'S FINANCIAL STATEMENTS?

స
DISCUSSION LEADER'S GUIDE

Liquidity Problems

Objectives of the Case

The objectives of the case are to explore the reporting alternatives confronting auditors with clients in financial difficulty and to consider the impact of one decision over another. The student should develop an appreciation of the difficulties faced by auditors in forming their opinion in going concern situations where so little professional guidance exists.

Applicable Professional Pronouncements

Statement on Auditing Standards No. 34, "The Auditor's Considerations When a Question Arises About an Entity's Continued Existence" (AU 340)

Statement on Auditing Standards No. 2, "Reports on Audited Financial Statements" (AU 509)

Securities and Exchange Commission Accounting Series Release No. 115

Statement of Financial Accounting Standards No. 5, "Accounting for Contingencies"

Statement of Financial Accounting Standards No. 7, "Accounting for Development Stage Enterprises"

Accountants' SEC Practice Manual, Poloway, Waxman, Willis, "Qualifications Relating to Necessary Additional Financing," paragraph 5155 (nonauthoritative)

Handbook of Accounting and Auditing, Burton, Palmer, Kay, Chapter 16-8, "The Auditor's Report" (nonauthoritative)

Montgomery's Auditing, Ninth Edition, Chapter 19, "The Auditor's Report" (nonauthoritative)

Business Assumptions and Other Data

American Home Builders Co. (American), the former parent company and present 50 percent owner, is the dominant figure in this case in terms of economic substance. American put Revolutionary together, and, in a most atypical arrangement brought in public shareholders pari passu, resulting in no dilution in relation to the simultaneous purchase of shares by the promoter, American. And, American continued to finance the cash needs of the company, presumably on related-party loans. Further, in the final analysis, American has "assured" Revolutionary that it will continue to provide operating finances even after it sells its ownership interests. No "godfather" could be be expected to comport himself in a more selfless manner. The students may want to explore just what might be at the root of American's openhandedness.

DLG 14-1

Case 14: Liquidity Problems

The case suggests, though it does not so state, that the $10,000,000 received for sale of capital stock is exhausted. The students would be correct in that assumption and may be interested in the fact that the related party advances totalled some $6,000,000, all on an interest-free basis.

Of interest to the students should be the question of the probability that American can find a willing buyer for an unproved company chewing up cash at the rate of $18,000,000 a year and dealing in an industry suffering a certain amount of economic pain. Were American's continued financing to cease and were the company unable to find other financial support, the new buyer could be purchasing a bankrupt, literally from inception. Not too many buyers are keen to move into such a situation unless, possibly, it can be done at a throwaway price.

The case does not tell how Revolutionary was "assured" of American's support in the past, though it does say that American does not want to make a legal commitment to continue to advance funds in the future. The documentation of the past arrangement was somewhat loose — a letter from American stating that it intended to provide funds, interest free, as needed and to the extent supported by invoices, payrolls, and the like. Such unilateral expression of intent could undoubtedly have been changed at any time at the desire of American, and as such may not have been enforceable. The auditors in the past may have preferred a more formal, legally binding agreement, but as a practical matter the stated intent and the actual performance to date by American seemed to afford sufficient comfort so that the auditors' opinion had not then been qualified regarding the liquidity of the company.

As noted, previous opinions did not deal with liquidity problems; what the report did say was that realization of certain plant, machinery, and inventory in the development stage was subject to the success of the company in producing and profitably marketing the new residential units. The opinion expressed was qualified "subject to" the effects of such adjustments, if any, as might have been required had the outcome of the uncertainty regarding realization been known. It is fair to point out that opinions given on development stage companies, such as Revolutionary, seem to follow no set pattern; some are unqualified; some are qualified; some are denials, though the latter are few in number; and, more to the point, authoritative literature gives little guidance in how to pick and choose between the available variations. It is usually a matter of an individual auditor's judgment.

In dealing with going concern situations, accountants have typically focused on whether there was an immediate threat to continuation as a going business. Some accountants hold to the view that "immediate" covers a period of one year from the date of the accountants' report. Others hold that "immediate" covers a period of one year from the date of the financial statements. Still others hold to the view that "immediate" covers the period of an operating cycle when such cycle is longer than one year but would not look to the operating cycle when shorter than one year. In this case, if Revolutionary ever gets going, its operating cycle should exceed one year. The students may want to think in terms of a period longer than one year in their solution, should they consider "immediate threat" as an integral part of that solution.

Statement on Auditing Standards No. 34 (March, 1981) does not pick up on "immediate threat" (which derives from Accounting Series Release No. 115) though it does suggest that emphasis is ordinarily on plans that might affect solvency within one year of the "date of the financial statements on which the auditor is currently reporting." The Statement on Auditing Standards also suggests, but does not state, that some recognition may need to be given to lengthy operating cycles.

In this vein, company projections or forecasts would be expected and the students may want to know what they show. Revolutionary's most recent projections show that the company will become marginally profitable ten months from the date of the discussion with the treasurer. It is fair for the students to understand, in addition, that the preceding projection had the company entering a profitable stage some 15 months earlier than the present projection.

Discussion

Before March, 1981, when Statement on Auditing Standards No. 34 was issued, auditors had little authoritative guidance in dealing with going concern issues. About the best information around could be found in Accounting Series Release No. 115, for SEC reporting companies. That release said the SEC would consider defective a registration statement in which auditors qualified their opinions because of doubt as to whether a company will continue as a going concern. The Release went on to say:

> . . . The Commission does not intend to preclude companies with pressing financial problems from raising funds by public offerings of securities. It does, however, believe it clear that an accountant's report cannot meet the certification requirements of the 1933 Act unless the registrant can arrange its financial affairs so that the immediate threat to continuation as a going business is removed. The independent accountant must be satisfied that it is appropriate to use conventional principles and practices for stating the accounts on a going concern basis before a registration statement under the 1933 Act can be declared effective.

This pronouncement was applied administratively to permit 1933 Act filings if the qualification ran to a specific event, such as sale of the securities contemplated by that 1933 Act filing. But, it would not permit general qualifications such as " . . . subject to the company's ability to attain profitable operations and/or to successfully obtain additional capital, the accompanying financial statements . . . ." Such general qualifications are still found in non-SEC practice, but in SEC practice, auditors were forced to conclude whether the funds to be raised by the 1933 Act offering, or some other specific event, would be enough to remove the "immediate threat" to the company's continued existence.

In the case of Revolutionary, their auditors could run their qualification subject to the continued support by American — a specific event — and possibly meet the Securities and Exchange Commission's test under Accounting Series Release No. 115. Yet, the specific event described may seem all too general to other auditors and the SEC, who could say that unless American contracted through an enforceable agreement to provide $18,000,000 during the next year, the auditors cannot be satisfied that the immediate threat of continuation as a going business has been removed; and, thus a disclaimer of opinion was necessary. (Few, if any auditors, had been advocating unqualified opinions for clients whose continued existence is threatened, though such advocacy may be expected to increase, as Statement on Auditing Standards No. 34 now offers the so-called clean opinion as a viable option.)

The profession has argued against the position of those advocating a disclaimer of opinion, suggesting that the auditor's ability to predict "imminence" or "immediate threat" was in itself an uncertainty. It was argued that it was very difficult to make a dis-

Case 14: Liquidity Problems

tinction between a general going concern and one where the company was in more immediate danger. As a result of that line of thinking, Statement on Auditing Standads No. 2 specifically says that a "subject to" qualification is appropriate for any uncertainty, including going concern problems. The Statement acknowledges that some auditors may wish to express a disclaimer of opinion when faced with a significant uncertainty. That footnote was a concession to those firms which, in going concern situations, follow the Accounting Series Release No. 115 approach.

The argument still continues within the profession and within certain firms whose policies advocate the use of a disclaimer rather than a "subject to" opinion in egregious situations. There are those who argue that such firms extend their liability unnecessarily by assuming an obligation which the profession is not willing to impose. And it is true that firms have backed away from some situations where their policy would seem to require a disclaimer, because they could not support their position with a professional pronouncement. That argument is the essence of this case.

Unfortunately, Statement on Auditing Standards No. 34, when issued in 1981, did little to dampen the above argument or put it to rest. Some auditors had hoped it would resolve the issue. What it says is this: After the auditor has considered a number of matters, " . . . the auditor may conclude that the question raised about the entity's ability to continue in existence should not result in a modification of his report. On the other hand, the auditor may conclude that a substantial doubt remains about the entity's ability to continue in existence. In such a case, he should consider the recoverability and classification of recorded asset amounts, and the amounts and classification of liabilities, in light of that doubt. Identifying the point at which uncertainties about recoverability, classifications, and amounts require the auditor to modify his report is a complex professional judgment. No single factor or combination of factors is controlling." The Statement on Auditing Standards goes on to say what was said before; that is, the modification can be a qualification of the opinion or a disclaimer of opinion.

The students should understand the dilemma auditors are facing on the going concern opinion. Professionally they can get by with a "subject to" opinion where doubt remains about an entity's ability to continue in existence, and no one-year time limits or any other time limits are set. For Securities and Exchange Commission reporting under the 1933 Act, a harder line is taken; a disclaimer is required unless the client can arrange its financial affairs so that the immediate threat to continuation as a going business is removed, and, administratively, the SEC is saying that means one year. The students should also understand that some auditors try to apply the more onerous SEC requirements on SEC and non-SEC clients alike.

The *Accountants' SEC Practice Manual*, paragraph 5155, comments, in part, as follows, with regard to auditors' opinions filed with the Securities and Exchange Commission:

> In ASR 115 relating to the Securities Act the SEC discussed a difficult situation that concerns a company and its auditors where the company is in dire need of additional funds in order to maintain itself as a going concern. The SEC will accept a certificate that is qualified as subject to the obtaining of financing only if sufficient financing to remove any existing 'immediate threat' to continuation as a 'going concern' is covered by firm commitments. A firm commitment under a proposed offering, or an 'all-or-none' best efforts offering, under a Securities Act registration, if adequate funds are contemplated thereby, would ordinarily be accep-

table. Firm commitments for funds from other sources, such as loans, may also be acceptable, provided they do indeed permit the company to continue as a going concern.

An 'open-end' qualification such as 'subject to the obtaining of adequate financing' is not acceptable to the SEC. An acceptable opinion paragraph would state that the financial statements are fairly presented, but the opinion may be qualified 'subject to' completion of the offering contemplated by this prospectus and, if applicable, consummation of the commitment to obtain additional financing. This form of opinion would appear in the preliminary prospectus or offering circular. However, if prior to the effective date of the registration statement, it is determinable that the offering will be successful, in which case the contingency giving rise to the qualification is thus removed, then a revised opinion may be substituted by amendment. Alternatively, if it is determined that the offering will not be successful in which case the contingency becomes real, then the opinion, along with the registration statement, should be withdrawn.

The certifying accountant is, therefore, placed in the position of having to make an evaluation of the company's financing needs and resources to determine if there is an 'immediate threat' to continuation as a 'going concern.' Some accountants have interpreted 'immediate' as covering a period of one year from the date of the accountants' report contained in the registration. The staff of the SEC has informally supported this interpretation.

In deciding on the adequacy of financing, it is necessary to consider the disclosures under 'Use of Proceeds' and review the client's forecasts. If acceptable financing is not available, if the forecasts are not reasonably credible, or if the client has no basis on which to build a forecast, it is not possible to conclude that the 'immediate threat' to continuation of operations has been removed; a disclaimer of opinion would be necessary. The SEC will not accept a 'going concern' disclaimer of opinion as satisfying certification requirements for any filing under the Securities Act. The SEC will accept such a report for a filing under the Exchange Act.

If either a qualified 'subject to' opinion or a disclaimer of opinion is appropriate, the certifying accountants must state the reason. When a continuation as a 'going concern' is in question, a middle paragraph is included in the certificate explaining the uncertainty and usually referring to a footnote explaining financial commitment arrangements.

The SEC's discussion in ASR 115 should serve as a reminder that if a company is in a position where it cannot continue to operate without additional funds, and the necessary funds are not available through commitments or a combination thereof with reasonably certain future operations, the company is no longer a 'going concern' and anything but a disclaimer of opinion cannot be justified.

Montgomery's Auditing, page 777, would seem pretty much in line with the above quoted material wherein it states:

In many situations, a 'going concern' qualification is unnecessary because the problems are diagnosed early enough for corrective action or the enterprise is able to show that it can otherwise overcome its difficulties. When doubts about the ability of a company to continue as a going concern cannot be satisfactorily resolved, they sometimes, but not always, constitute a pervasive uncertainty. SAS No. 2, paragraphs 21 through 26, 35, 39, and 45 (and the various footnotes thereto) describe several circumstances in which a qualified opinion or disclaimer of opinion may be appropriate, but provide an auditor only broad suggestive guidance about analysis of the going concern problem and wording of any opinion he might wish to express in the circumstances. The authors believe that the same guidelines as are described in the section on 'Qualified Opinions Versus Adverse Opinions or Disclaimers' can be applied. If, as frequently is the case, the problem causing the going concern question can be

Case 14: Liquidity Problems

adequately measured and described, then a 'subject to' qualified opinion is appropriate. Otherwise, the middle paragraph should describe the problem and the pervasiveness of its effect, and a disclaimer of opinion should follow.

The guidelines for choosing between qualified opinions and disclaimers (referred to above) are:

The usefulness of financial statements containing problems.

The auditor's assessment of users' ability — and his own, for that matter — to understand the problems.

The auditor's ability to measure the potential impact of the problems.

The auditor's ability to describe his reservations about the financial statements with clarity.

The extent of the auditor's disagreement with his client's handling of the matter.

The *Handbook of Accounting and Auditing*, in speaking of uncertainties, generally has this to say: "Although the auditor is not precluded from issuing a disclaimer of opinion in cases involving uncertainties, this is no longer frequently done. Prior to 1975 it was common to observe disclaimers when the uncertainties were pervasive, and there will always be those few very serious situations when an uncertainty disclaimer is best" (pages 16-18). And, as to an entity's continued existence, this:

The auditor uses the enterprise's earnings and financing history as predictors, with other evidence, to gauge the potential success of future operations and financings. Other evidence includes the liquidity of assets, the prior reliability of budgets and forecasts, and whether the enterprise's current situation will affect its access to credit or equity markets. How long a company might be able to hold out in the face of adversity is also crucial.

The auditor may conclude that a disclaimer of opinion should be issued when the going concern assumption is in question, failure may be imminent, and the effect of failure on the financial statements would be pervasive. Technically, the auditor need not disclaim an opinion in this situation, but he may do so, depending on the risk that the financial statements and his relationship thereto may be misunderstood if he issues a less onerous report.

The imminence of the uncertainty, as the auditor sees it, is one of the important factors in determining the type of opinion to issue. For example, when it is evident that the entity cannot operate indefinitely if the losses of the last several years continue, but it can withstand another year of such losses without going out of business, the auditor may determine that a going concern qualification is not necessary (pages 29-25).

The students should appreciate that no right or wrong answer to the case exists. As between firms, different opinions would be reached on the same fact situation, and the same is true as between individual members of the same firm. Some auditors believe that a disclaimer of opinion regarding uncertainties tells the readers nothing and ordinarily should not be used (the AICPA position). Other auditors believe the Securities and Exchange Commission is on the right track in Accounting Series Release No. 115. And, others think the "clean" opinion is appropriate as long as footnotes adequately describe the going concern uncertainty (the so-called Cohen Commission position).

The students should give attention to the timing of the events in the case. For example, does the expression of intention by American in a newspaper trigger an opinion change, or would it take an actual sale of the 50 percent interest? What assurance, one way or the other, does the auditor have that American can ever find a buyer? Perhaps even if American were successful in finding a buyer, it would continue to advance monies with an eye toward protecting the $6,000,000 of advances already on the book. Also, for example, if the audit report had been issued just a month before *The Wall Street Journal* article and the next one was not due until approximately eleven months later, would the auditors have the same concern? Would they even consider withdrawing and revising their opinion now outstanding?

The students should also discuss whether the opinion of the preceding year should be changed if their opinion for this year is other than "clean" on the going concern issue — that is, either a disclosure or a qualification on the year under audit. Again, positions will vary. Statement on Auditing Standards No. 34 says the auditor "ordinarily should modify his report on only the current period's financial statements because of an uncertainty due to a substantial doubt that arose in the current period about the entity's ability to continue in existence." Even so, in practice, auditors often are observed modifying their opinion on the prior year as well. Accounting Series Release No. 115 offers no guidance on the matter.

The case seems to suggest, but does not state, that if American were to agree in writing to continue to provide operating finances after its sale of the 50 percent interest, the auditors might well take a different view regarding the type of opinion they could issue. The students should discuss their views as to how a written commitment versus an oral commitment should affect their opinion. Their discussion probably should include the fact that American may be having financial difficulties of its own, which could make its commitment less viable and the fact that if it proceeds to honor its "moral obligation," whether that commitment is in writing or not, it will have "encumbered its own financial picture." This sounds like an attempt by American to mislead its auditors — if it's in writing, it's "legal" and will show in a footnote; but if it keeps advancing to satisfy a moral obligation, no mention is made. So to improve its report, American refuses to confirm in writing what it intends to do, and the refusal could result in a worsening of Revolutionary's report. American's auditors have a dilemma too, but they may not know it.

The students may also want to discuss the probable effect on Revolutionary if the opinion is qualified or is disclaimed. The students ought to try their hand at drafting a report that will be necessary given Revolutionary's current status. They should be encouraged to draft the middle paragraph of the report first, before they try their hands at an opinion. That middle paragraph should cover:

- The fact that the assets are stated at cost where it presumes continuation of the company as a going concern.
- The company is still in the developmental stage, and has accumulated substantial losses.
- It seems likely that there will be other threats to the going-concern status of the company, including a negative net worth and negative working capital.

The group favoring a qualified opinion might focus on the words in footnote 8 of Statement on Auditing Standards No. 2 regarding uncertainties, which states "The quali-

Case 14: Liquidity Problems

fication of the auditor's opinion contemplated by this section should serve adequately to inform the users of financial statements." Those students who have concluded that a disclaimer is appropriate should be asked how they would deal with the client who threw those words at them and argued that the profession disagrees with their opinion. Students should be confronted by a dilemma — they should be forced to choose between their own logical conclusions and a professional pronouncement.

The Solution

Because American would not enter into an agreement to advance funds necessary for the ensuing year, and because the company had arranged no other firm commitments to assure its continued existence for the coming year, the opinion was issued as a disclaimer. The opinion of the prior year was changed to a disclaimer also.

Accounting for Hindsight

Chicago Properties is a publicly held company dealing in all kinds of commercial real estate, but specializing in apartments and condominiums. Since you have been assigned to the engagement, the mainstay of the company's business has been the development and construction of apartment complexes which they ultimately sell to individual investors or tax shelter partnerships.

One of the company's best customers is a local entrepreneur, Mr. T. M. Wacker. Mr. Wacker bought one of the company's apartment projects in 1975; he bought two more in 1976; and he bought a large complex in 1977. There were no sales to Mr. Wacker in 1978; however, during the 1978 audit, your staff tells you that the 1977 transaction has been rescinded and the $800,000 profit which had been recorded last year has been reversed this year. The profit on that transaction was very material to 1977's earnings, and the reversal is a material part of the 1978 loss.

You look back at your 1977 work papers and see that the transaction was structured as follows:

Downpayment in cash	$ 200,000
Downpayment by bank letter of credit	800,000
Note receivable	4,000,000
Total Sales Price	$5,000,000
Cost	4,200,000
Gross Profit	$ 800,000

The work papers show that the note receivable was examined and confirmed. Last year's audit team obtained a Dun & Bradstreet report on Mr. Wacker, and it showed that he was a man of some means but perhaps "cash poor." His credit was not seriously challenged, however, because all the notes he issued in previous transactions had been paid off in advance.

Your people also had gotten a confirmation from Mr. Wacker's bank confirming that they issued a letter of credit in favor of Chicago Properties drawn against Mr. Wacker. In effect, the bank confirmed that they would pay $800,000 to Chicago Properties on demand; Mr. Wacker was apparently committed to either pay the bank or take out an $800,000 bank loan in satisfaction of the bank's payment to Chicago Properties. The letter of credit was good for 180 days, issued at the date of the sale October 1, 1977, and expiring March 31, 1978, three months after Chicago Properties' December 31 year-end.

Case 15-1

Case 15: Accounting for Hindsight

As it was originally structured, this 1977 transaction met the criteria specified in the American Institute of Certified Public Accountants Audit Guide, "Profit Recognition on Sales of Real Estate." For completed apartment houses, the guide requires a 20 percent downpayment, and Mr. Wacker's combination cash/letter of credit totalling $1,000,000 exactly qualified.

You ask what happened to the Wacker transaction and the client's controller explains that Mr. Wacker asked for a 90-day extension of the letter of credit in March and then again in June of 1978. Finally, in September he acknowledged that he did not have enough cash or borrowing power to meet his commitment and he asked to be excused. The controller explained that, although the apartment complex was not fully rented, it was a showplace and Chicago Properties was happy to take it back. Besides, management felt they could "not lean too heavily" on Mr. Wacker because of their long-time business association.

You inquire into that long-time association in more detail. You find that Mr. Wacker prepaid all of his earlier commitments to Chicago Properties because he was able to resell the apartment houses quickly — as soon as he got them rented up. In fact, earlier transactions appear to follow a pattern — new sales to Mr. Wacker closely followed his payments on earlier purchases, and these payments themselves followed resales by Mr. Wacker of the apartment houses.

Rhetorically, you ask the controller whether Mr. Wacker really intended to go through with the 1977 transaction unless he was able to sell the apartment complex before the letter of credit expired. The controller assures you that Mr. Wacker will be happy to confirm his honest intentions and that the management of Chicago Properties will give you a letter of representations attesting to the bona fides of that transaction. When you ask why the company let Mr. Wacker extend the letter of credit twice and then let him out from under the deal, the controller explains condescendingly, "You don't kick a good customer when he's down."

WHAT WILL YOU DO ABOUT THE $800,000 PROFIT RECISION IN THE 1978 FINANCIAL STATEMENTS?

DISCUSSION LEADER'S GUIDE

Accounting for Hindsight

Objectives of the Case

The real issue here seems to be not so much what the accounting should be, but what is the nature and substance of the sale, and later recision of the sale, to Mr. Wacker. Conclusion as to the substance of the transactions might well affect the accounting and this issue should be covered as well. Also, dependent on the conclusion as to substance, the students will most likely find they need to focus on the sales to Mr. Wacker in 1975 and 1976, exploring whether the substance of the first sale to him may be different from what was perceived when the sales were initially recorded. Of interest, too, is whether all these Wacker sales might have been related party transactions and if so, what the attendant consequences were. Further, the case should focus attention on the business and legal aspects of what has happened and how they should be handled.

Applicable Professional Pronouncements

American Institute of Certified Public Accountants Audit Guide, "Accounting for Profit Recognition of Sales of Real Estate"

Statement of Financial Accounting Standards No. 16, "Prior Period Adjustments"

Accounting Principles Board Opinion No. 20, "Accounting Changes"

Statement on Auditing Standards No. 6, "Related Party Transactions"

Statement on Auditing Standards No. 15, "Reports on Comparative Financial Statements"

Burton, Palmer, Kay, *Handbook of Accounting and Auditing*, Chapter 28-12, "Related Party Transactions" (nonauthoritative)

Business Assumptions and Other Data

The case does not specify the source of the $200,000 downpayment by Mr. Wacker. The students can assume that the auditors were satisfied in the previous year that the downpayment did not come from Chicago and nothing learned during the recision discussion provided information to the contrary. The students should be aware, however, that reaffirming the source of cash in the 1978 audit would be necessary to an understanding of the substance of the sale and recision.

Nor does the case state, though one may say it infers, that Chicago gave Mr. Wacker his $200,000 back. In the business world such a generous gesture would not be expected to occur often. The more conventional business attitude in case of nonperformance by a buyer is to foreclose the property, but keeping any cash paid in. As the problem suggests, when it states that $800,000 of profit (not $600,000) was reversed, Mr. Wacker did get his $200,000 downpayment back.

Case 15: Accounting for Hindsight

The students should assume that the 1975 and 1976 sales were all perfected with cash during the year of sale and did not have a holdover letter of credit such as existed here.

The case says nothing about whether Mr. Wacker made interest and principal payments on the $4,000,000 note in the period from October 1, 1977, to September, 1978. The students can assume that no payments were made and that, upon return of the $200,000, Mr. Wacker was made completely whole except for a minor excess of operating expenses over rental income during the rent-up period.

The attitude of the Securities and Exchange Commission regarding inflation of earnings is well known, as is its position regarding real estate transactions generally and questionable ones particularly. Regardless of the accounting decision made, the students should recognize the case portends even greater legal and business problems. In this case legal counsel of the client and of the auditor should be consulted in the process of formulating a decision. And, the students should point out that the Securities and Exchange Commission should be consulted also. In the actual case, the company and the SEC decided to stop trading in the company's stock before news of the loss was released to the public. The students should recognize that the auditor, regardless of the action taken or the accounting decision made, is virtually 100 percent certain of being sued. When prior year's financials are restated, as could be proposed here, litigation is virtually automatic. Litigation may or may not follow reporting the loss in 1978, as is the client's desire, but it should be expected and with a high degree of confidence.

While the students' discussion may concentrate on the accounting issue at hand, they should appreciate the real problems surrounding the re-audit and the legal and business considerations.

Discussion

Foreclosures against buyers who cannot fulfill their obligations for property purchased are daily occurrences — a way of life for sellers of real estate. To rescind a real estate sale is not all that common, however, and it is the recision rather than the foreclosure that makes this into a case. The students should recognize that "beware" is the key word for auditors in virtually all material real estate transactions. The list is long, and regretfully still growing, with names of auditors who found profit recognition acceptable on real estate sales that probably were not sales at all. And that is what this case is about. Did a sale take place in 1977? If it did, all well and good, and the fact that the property bounced back in 1978 simply confirms that some real estate sales do not "stick." But is that the substance of what happened? A word of caution to all auditors, in situations such as Chicago, is given by Securities and Exchange Commission ASR 173 wherein it says "auditors should recognize the attempts by management to structure transactions in a contrived manner to meet the technical criteria of existing accounting literature."

The case gives a good set of circumstances that can contribute to an understanding of the need to be ever vigilant in pursuit of the substance of real estate transactions and not to be taken in by historical performance or other superficial criteria. A close reading of the case will develop the following facts: Mr. Wacker had a good prior history of meeting and, indeed, exceeding commitments with Chicago. The case states he paid off his notes in advance; the Dun & Bradstreet indicates he had significant property holdings but was "cash" short; the letter of credit had less significance than it would appear as it was based on a commitment by Mr. Wacker (who was cash short) of either reimbursing the bank or being able to separately obtain a loan for this same amount. The note was confirmed, and the letter of credit was confirmed by the bank issuing the letter. All good audit procedures — all pointing toward recognition of income.

Good as the audit was, it now raises a question, "Was it good enough?" Perhaps the auditors could have done a better job in assessing the import of annual sales of property to a customer who was reselling the property and buying more. There is nothing wrong with doing that, but it may suggest the possibility of an accommodation between the parties. On accommodations, the *Handbook of Accounting and Auditing* has this to say:

> One party may participate in a transaction as an accommodation for another, sometimes receiving a fee or commission for the service. Such direct compensation is not always apparent, but in practice it is advisable to assume the existence of a quid pro quo. Accommodations can look very real on paper, but their usual substance is commonly summed up in such descriptors as *swap, sham, parking, laundering,* and *strawman*. The party being accommodated usually conceals the transaction. The need to record fee income makes concealment by the accommodator less likely.

If an accommodation or sham can be identified, the accounting to follow is usually apparent. And, if the transactions were accommodations that have been deliberately concealed, we may be faced with the equivalent of management fraud.

In the absence of subpoena powers, proof of concealed accommodations is highly unlikely. The case says both Mr. Wacker and the company will be happy to confirm the bona fides of the unknown. It could come out that both parties never intended to perfect the sale until the time of resale. Testimony of the banker could well reveal an understanding that the letter of credit would not be exercised at all, or at least not until a new, qualified buyer was nailed down. The banker's testimony on the basis of his granting a letter of credit should be revealing also. What banker performing with due care would grant an $800,000 irrevocable letter of credit to a "cash poor" customer without collateral, guarantees, understandings, or the like?

Further, what is the quid pro quo for giving Mr. Wacker back his $200,000 and letting the bank off the hook for an $800,000 letter of credit, all of which denies the stockholders $800,000 profit? It has to be more than "you don't kick a good customer when he's down."

One could go on and on as to what auditors can learn from subpoenas that may be outside their reach through use of conventional audit techniques. Thus, the audit aspects of the possibility of related-party transactions, accommodations, and concealment, and the business and legal considerations should be the focus of the students' discussions. And those discussions should develop the students' further pursuit as to what should be done, if anything, about the earlier years' sales to Mr. Wacker. And is a search warranted as to whether other customers are fulfilling a similar buy-sell role, as apparently displayed in Mr. Wacker's dealings?

The case raised an accounting question which the students should discuss. But, they should have in mind that, in spite of what has been said before about auditing, they still have no proof that the transactions were accommodations, parkings, shams, or anything else other than what Mr. Wacker and management represented them to be. Thus, the students will find themselves relying on their judgment to find the accounting solution.

For the initial recording of income, the Audit Guide on real estate transactions would govern. The key points at issue would be whether continuing involvement of the seller

Case 15: Accounting for Hindsight

existed after the sale and whether the buyer was financially able to perform his end of the transaction. As to the first point, the case gives no indication of known continuing seller involvement at the time of sale. What happened since can surely raise a question as to whether the usual risks of ownership had been passed from seller to buyer.

As to the second point, based on the facts given in the case, at the time the transaction took place, "his credit was not seriously challenged, however, because all of the notes he issued in previous transactions were paid off in advance . . . . " The case also states that the letter of credit was contingent on Mr. Wacker being "either able to pay the bank or take out an $800,000 bank loan in satisfaction of the bank's proposed payment to Chicago Properties." When pressed, Mr. Wacker admitted he did not have the financial resources to meet such a commitment and asked to be excused.

The American Institute of Certified Public Accountants Industry Audit Guide, "Accounting for Profit Recognition on Sales of Real Estate," in paragraph 9 states specifically:

> Uncertainty about collectibility of the sales price may require another method of accounting in which the effective date of a sale is deferred until the uncertainty is satisfactorily resolved. No revenue or profit is recognized before the date the sale is considered to be effective, and all cash received before then is accounted for as a deposit on the sales price.

Since Mr. Wacker's financial condition alone could not meet this criterion, the original accounting for this matter may seem incorrect and the sale should have been considered either a lease or a financing arrangement. However, in 1977, Chicago had a bank's irrevocable letter of credit and did not need to rely on Mr. Wacker's credit. What was not known then, and perhaps could not have been known without use of subpoena power, was that Chicago would voluntarily relinquish its right to demand payment by the bank in order to protect its "good customer" who lacked the financial ability to qualify the transaction for income recognition.

With these inconclusive facts, the students might conclude either way as to whether profit should have been recognized in 1977. Those who conclude that it should not have been recognized, probably because it appears now Mr. Wacker may not have been the real purchaser but merely a "parking lot," would then be governed in the accounting to follow by Statement of Financial Accounting Standards No. 16, "Prior Period Adjustments." They should recognize that the criteria for prior period adjustment would be met by way of correction of an error and that such error would be deemed an oversight or missue of facts that existed at the time the financial statements for 1977 were prepared.

If this is their position, they should further be aware of:

(1) The consequences and audit risks inherent in taking a position, unsupported in an audit sense, that is contrary to the position of management and the buyer, both of whom contend (not under oath, however) the 1977 sale was bona fide.

(2) The strong probability that such a position leaves the auditor in the posture of not trusting management or its representations. In such a posture, the auditor has little choice but to disclaim an opinion or resign or require resignation of management.

On the other hand, students may say that nothing has been proved one way or the other as to whether the sale was in fact an accommodation and, in the absence of such proof, 1977 should remain as is and 1978 should carry an explanatory footnote of what happened.

Perhaps the students will suggest that neither approach above is correct. Instead they might say the auditor should describe to the Board of Directors what has happened — the recision, the meeting with the Securities and Exchange Commission, the stop-trading order, the inconclusiveness of the auditor's inquiry into what happened and why — and then request that the Board investigate the matter, using legal counsel and such other investigators as needed, to conclude, one way or the other, just what happened.

Irrespective of the course of action followed, the auditor has further accounting issues to consider which the students should recognize: (1) The valuation (or carrying amount) for the property returned in the recision — appraisals may be needed, the strength of market would need to be assessed, and so on to confirm that $4,200,000 was not in excess of current market, and (2) the 1975 and 1976 sales and other major sales would need to be reviewed to attempt to ascertain whether they have characteristics suggesting that they too might be sales to "parking lots."

If the decision is to restate 1977, the students should recognize that Statement on Auditing Standards No. 15, "Reports on Comparative Financial Statements," is the guide to how their report should be modified to cover the restatement.

The Solution

The auditors took the position that they must submit the matter to the Board of Directors and request that the directors conduct an investigation. The Board authorized such investigation. The president of the company admitted that he, Mr. Wacker, and the banker all had an understanding that the whole deal was contingent upon resale which, at the time, he saw as assured within a few weeks based on negotiations then underway with a tax shelter which was to be the ultimate owner. Thus, he recorded the sale earlier as made to Mr. Wacker, simply to get the income in the year where it belonged.

The 1975 and 1976 sales were not similarly tainted nor were any other major sales according to the president, and the auditors saw no similar suspicious characteristics.

Thus, the 1977 financials were restated to eliminate the $800,000 profit, with appropriate revision in the auditors' report. The president was moved to the sales department and ultimately resigned. The lawsuits against the auditors showed up on schedule.

Contingencies

The controller of Big Deal Stores calls to complain that your auditors are creating chaos in his Executive Office. Specifically, he complains that your senior has been arguing accounting with the company's insurance manager. The senior suggested that the company treat all of their premiums as deposits and that casualty expense be accured based on actual loss experience. The controller goes on, "He tried to tell me that Statement No. 5 from the Financial Accounting Standards Board prohibits income smoothing and permits accrual of a loss only when a loss can be measured. I told him that SFAS No. 5 prohibits income smoothing by insurance *companies*, but it says nothing about insurance *policies*." You ask your senior to come by the office that afternoon.

Your senior reports his side of the story: "I didn't say that all their insurance premiums should be treated as deposits. But, I really don't think their public liability policy should be considered insurance." He explains that Big Deal carries a large public liability policy with Lloyds of London. Premiums for the policy are based on the company's loss experience during the last five years. He argues that the company should have no expense in any years when they have no claims. But if they have a bad year with a number of claims filed, that year should bear *all* of the cost of those claims. He says, "The spirit of SFAS No. 5 is to prohibit income smooting and, specifically, it says that insurance premiums must be treated as deposits unless the insurance company has in reality accepted the risk."

Together, you review the provisions of SFAS No. 5. The controller is correct in his understanding. The original purpose of the Statement was to stop insurance companies from providing general, unspecified catastrophe reserves. But your senior's understanding of the Statement is also correct. The Statement says that a loss should be accrued only when both of the following conditions are met:

a) Information available prior to issuance of the financial statements indicates that it is probable that an asset had been impaired or a liability had been incurred at the date of the financial statements. It is implicit in this condition that it must be probable that one or more future events will occur confirming the fact of the loss.
b) The amount of loss can be reasonably estimated.

The objective of the Financial Accounting Standards Board Statement seems clear — income smoothing is no longer acceptable. Although the Lloyds' policy is primarily a cash flow smoothing device, it effectively smooths income as well. Still, you have got to wonder whether the Financial Accounting Standards Board was thinking about Big Deal's policy with Lloyds when Statement No. 5 was written. After all, every insurance premium is based on the insured's experience, at least to some degree. Your senior has raised an interesting problem.

HOW SHOULD BIG DEAL ACCOUNT FOR ITS PUBLIC LIABILITY INSURANCE?

DISCUSSION LEADER'S GUIDE

Contingencies

Objectives of the Case

This case should focus the students' attention on the general nature of contingencies and contrast them with incurred expenses or costs. The case asks whether payments for insurance are in substance premiums paid which should be charged to expense or are in substance insurance deposits which should be carried as assets. By indirection, the case also should focus the students' attention on the possibility that Big Deal chose that particular type of insurance policy as an income smoothing device.

Distinctions between contingencies to be recorded and contingencies to be disclosed are often obscure, as would seem to be the case at Big Deal. Accordingly, there may be no right or wrong solution to the Big Deal case. Most students probably would agree that "income smoothing" is bad and should not be permitted. However, that is not to say that circumstances at Big Deal automatically brand their accounting for public liability premiums as an income smoothing device. Again, no right or wrong solution may be evident.

In all likelihood, the students will emphasize the issue of materiality in their attempt to arrive at a decision, but that should not be the focus of the case. Yet, it is quite true that in some years, in almost any company, the impact of the difference in accounting could be material, whereas in other years the impact would be inconsequential. Still, focus on the general nature of contingencies.

Applicable Professional Pronouncements

Statement of Financial Accounting Standards No. 5, "Accounting for Contingencies"

Business Assumptions and Other Data

Every insurance policy is experience-based to a certain degree, and the more experience-based it is, the more it is like self-insurance. Statement on Financial Accounting Standards No. 5 discusses why true self-insurance is not really insurance. It is that discussion that framed the question raised in the case study. Some of the common gradations of insurance and self-insurance seen in practice involve: (a) situations where a number of companies deposit monies in a common fund to be available in cases of casualty with risk protection nonexistent as the casualty costs will be paid ultimately by the damaged company; (b) situations where elements of real protection (insurance) and elements of self-protection or "self-insurance" both are present, as is common in many retrospective rating policies such as illustrated in the case study; and (c) situations where all, or substantially all, of the risks of loss are insured by an insurance company. Even with the specific provisions of Statement of Financial Accounting Standards No. 5, it is difficult to know whether a contingency or a business risk as this case shows, should be ignored; whether it should be recorded; whether it should be disclosed in a footnote; or whether it should be the subject of a qualification in auditors' report.

The original project which culminated in Statement of Financial Accounting Standards No. 5 had its origins in the SEC's concern over certain insurance companies which were effectively smoothing income over the years by use of catastrophic or similar reserves. Though Statement of Financial Accounting Standards No. 5 was issued as a general purpose Statement, covering gain and loss contingencies of every nature, it is heavily concerned with insurance reserves, illustrated in numerous examples in Appendix A of the Statement.

Any number of companies have retrospective rating policies of one kind or another, and Big Deal illustrates one such type of policy. In practice, the accounting often follows that at Big Deal. Whether that should be, is not receiving a great deal of attention within the profession at present. Because of its apparent conservatism, it finds tacit acceptance, yet the conservatism is illusory for in any year a company could sustain a catastrophic loss that would be measured in the earnings statement in a future year or years when the retrospectively rated premiums are charged.

The students may be aware that the insurance carrier is fully liable to successful claimants, irrespective of whether it is able to recoup its loss payments from the insured company through future premium increases. For example, following a catastrophic loss, or an ordinary loss for that matter, a company may cease business and cancel its insurance. Or, a company may cancel its insurance following a major loss in order to shift the burden of the loss to the insurance carrier. The latter course of action would seem improbable in an ongoing company as such action can reduce, or completely remove, the possibility that other insurance carriers would find their risk an acceptable insurance risk.

Discussion

Statement of Financial Accounting Standards No. 5 defines a loss contingency as an existing condition, situation, or set of circumstances involving uncertainty as to possible loss to an enterprise that will ultimately be resolved when one or more future events occur or fail to occur. Resolution of the uncertainty may confirm the loss or impairment of an asset or the incurrence of a liability. When a loss contingency exists, the probability that the future event or events will occur can range from very probable to reasonably possible to remote. The Statement provides that

> an estimated loss from a loss contingency shall be accrued by a charge to income if both of the following conditions are met:
>
> a) Information available prior to issuance of financial statements indicates that it is probable that an asset had been impaired or a liability had been incurred at the date of the financial statements. It is implicit in this condition that it must be probable that one or more future events will occur confirming the fact of the loss.
>
> b) The amount of the loss can be reasonably estimated.

One of the primary motivations for Statement 5 was preventing the accrual of arbitrary loss reserves by corporations in general, and so-called "catastrophe reserves" by insurance companies. That's why both conditions are to be met prior to the accrual. Before those conditions were imposed, some companies would accrue reserves in good years or in years with major operating losses (i.e., the "big bath" syndrome). This accrual would benefit income in future periods or, in general, have a smoothing effect on income. The Financial Accounting Standards Board felt that such smoothing was inappropriate and did not reflect economic reality. Managements do not necessarily agree that smoothing is bad, and neither will the students.

Reserves for self-insurance are a type of loss contingency reserve that is generally not allowed by Statement of Financial Accounting Standards No. 5. The Statement argues against self-insurance as follows:

> At the date of an enterprise's financial statements, it may not be insured against risk of future loss or damage to its property by fire, explosion, or other hazards. The absence of insurance against losses from risks of those types constitutes an existing condition involving uncertainty about the amount and timing of any losses that may occur, in which case a contingency exists as defined [above]. Uninsured risks may arise in a number of ways, including (a) noninsurance of certain risks or co-insurance or deductible clauses in an insurance contract or (b) insurance through a subsidiary or investee to the extent not reinsured with an independent insurer. Some risks, for all practical purposes, may be noninsurable, and the self-assumption of those risks is mandatory.
>
> The absence of insurance does not mean that an asset has been impaired or a liability has been incurred at the date of an enterprise's financial statements. Fires, explosions, and other similar events that may cause loss or damage of an enterprise's property are random in their occurrence. With respect to events of that type, the condition for accrual . . . is not satisfied prior to the occurrence of the event because until that time there is no diminution in the value of the property. There is no relationship of those events to the activities of the enterprise prior to their occurrence. Further, unlike an insurance company, which has a contractual obligation under policies in force to reimburse insureds for losses, an enterprise can have no such obligation to itself and, hence, no liability.

Though it is clear that the Board believes that there should not be reserves for self-insurance established, it is less clear when dealing with insurance policies covering possible losses. It seems to feel that if a company purchases insurance against a loss and if the risk of loss is indeed transferred to the insurance company, then the premium may be expensed. However, it goes on to say:

> To the extent that an insurance contract or reinsurance contract does not, despite its form, provide for indemnification of the insured or the ceding company by the insurer or reinsurer against loss or liability, the premium to be retained by the insurer or reinsurer shall be accounted for as a deposit by the insured or the ceding company. Those contracts may be structured in various ways, but if, regardless of form, their substance is that all or part of the premium paid by the insured or the ceding company is a deposit, it shall be accounted for as such.

This last quote seems to be the key consideration in the case. The narrow issue is to decide whether the risk of loss has been transferred from Big Deal Stores to the insurance company, or, in other words, whether the policy provides for indemnification. Pragmatically, it is true that insurance for major companies is determined on their individual loss experience and may be, in effect, self-insurance through payments of premiums. The Financial Accounting Standards Board seems to indicate that such premiums should be treated as deposits, but this may be an overly rigid interpretation of Statement of Finan-

DLG 16-3

Case 16: Contingencies

cial Accounting Standards No. 5. If the insurance policy provides indemnification, the premiums should be expensed.

The broader issue in the case is the distinction, generally, between contingencies that should be recorded and those that should be disclosed or not disclosed. The students should recognize the broader issue in their discussion while at the same time addressing the narrow issue. This case involving a public liability policy was presented because it was compatible with the initial focus of the Securities and Exchange Commission on the use of contingency reserves as a means of either (1) providing a reserve for unknown future losses likely to occur or (2) leveling income over a period of years, or both.

The discussion should help students to see that in dealing with contingencies, of whatever type, the accounting is most often in shades of gray.

The Solution

In the case at hand, the decision was to accept the accounting followed by the client in charging the insurance premiums to expense when paid. As a practical matter, casualty insurance for major companies, irrespective of the type of policy; may be determined to a large extent by their own loss experience; also, as a practical matter, the client in the case at hand could terminate the insurance and close off any future premiums based on retrospective rating. (Such action would not be likely, however, because of the probable effect on attempts to obtain insurance from another insurance carrier.) Experience under Statement 5 will doubtless provide more and more guidelines on which to base insurance decisions in borderline cases.

DLG 16-4

Profit Recognition

Our client, Sunflower Ship Building, began construction of two seagoing drilling rigs designed for service in North Sea oil fields. When they had invested about $30 million in the two rigs they ran short of cash and realized that at least $30 million more was necessary. Coincidently it became apparent that there was a serious shortage of drilling rigs and that their work in process had considerable value. Sunflower was approached by Cash Inc., a personal investment company wholly owned by a wealthy individual. Cash Inc. offered to buy a 50 percent interest in the two drilling rigs under construction, to pay 50 percent of the cost incurred to date and 50 percent of whatever future construction costs might be incurred. In addition, Cash offered to pay Sunflower a $5 million premium for the opportunity to buy in at this time.

The two parties negotiated a deal and formed a partnership. Sunflower donated its work-in-process inventory as its capital contribution and Cash Inc. contributed $30 million in cash. In addition, Cash paid the promised $5 million directly to Sunflower. The partnership then negotiated a line of credit with a group of banks to be sure to have sufficient funds to complete the rigs if construction costs should exceed the estimated $60 million. In their agreement, the partners state their intention to lease the drilling rigs to independent exploration companies — several already have expressed an interest in chartering the rigs. Sunflower is to be responsible for the completion of rigs should the costs exceed the estimated $60 million plus the amount provided by the line of credit. Sunflower will also act as leasing agent, for which it will earn a nominal fee.

As you review Sunflower's year-end financial statements, the controller explains that the cost of the work in process was simply transferred to an account called "Drilling Rigs Partnership." The $5 million premium has been included in this year's income; the controller smiles, "It's an ill wind that blows no good."

DO YOU AGREE WITH THE CONTROLLER'S PROPOSED ACCOUNTING?

Case 17-1

Case 17: Profit Recognition

DISCUSSION LEADER'S GUIDE

Profit Recognition

Objectives of the Case

There are indeed problems surrounding profit recognition as this case illustrates. Accounting practice and accounting literature abound with revenue recognition criteria applicable to specific situations (none of which is exactly on point in this case, however). There is not much in the way of authoritative guidance when it comes to general revenue recognition rules. The nonauthoritative Accounting Principles Board Statement No. 4 gives some guidance. Consequently, the objective of the case should be to promote the students' discussion of the general rules and the varying interpretations that might be applied in this case and that could result in dramatically different answers. At the same time, the students should recognize that changes in the fact situation in the case, though apparently not all that distinguishing and important, could also result in dramatically different answers. And, as is true for so many major transactions, the students should discuss whether the substance of the transaction is materially different from its legal form.

Applicable Professional Pronouncements

Accounting Principles Board Statement No. 4, "Basic Concepts and Accounting Principles," paragraphs 147 through 153

Statement of Position 78-9, "Accounting for Investments in Real Estate Ventures," paragraphs 30 and 36

Industry Accounting Guide, "Accounting for Profit Recognition on Sales of Real Estate"

While the real estate references are not applicable to personal property, for which no similar guidance is given in AICPA literature, they should offer some guidance in determining the appropriate accounting.

Business Assumptions and Other Data

It can be assumed that the present estimated cost of $60 million is a realistic estimate that likely will not be overrun. The degree of reliability in the estimate may or may not affect a student's analysis of the requirement that Sunflower is to be responsible for completion of the rigs. While this responsibility could take any number of forms, each of which may affect the various solutions, it should be assumed that the responsibility is about as suggested. If more monies are needed to complete the rigs they will be advanced by a group of banks and then by Sunflower, and such advances will not affect the respective partner's equity interest or profit-sharing percentage and will be repaid by the partnership to Sunflower in due course.

The case makes no suggestion that Sunflower and Cash, or their respective principals, are related parties, and arm's length should be the assumption. Had the parties been related, the students may perceive a different accounting solution from that applicable to arm's-length trading. The students may discuss the possibility that the parties became related upon execution of the partnership agreement. Though the state of the art is unsettled on this point, the parties were unrelated at the pertinent time in this case.

In arriving at the substance of the transactions, the students should pursue a line of discussion directed toward the fair value of the rigs at the date of the transaction with Cash. Without knowledge of fair value, a realistic conclusion as to what is the substance of any transaction becomes a matter of luck. The students should also recognize that determination of fair value is not easy where the property involved lacks an active trading market, is only partially completed, untested, and void of sale or lease commitments. It should be assumed here that the best estimate of fair value of the two rigs in their present state of completion is $40 million.

Discussion

Joint ventures and partnerships are increasingly common, and for several reasons. The risk inherent in major projects often makes sharing a necessary strategy. Accounting rules permit investments in these ventures to be handled on the equity basis, which usually means the debt of highly leveraged ventures is not reflected in a participant company's financials. Further, the formation of a joint venture may signal the transfer of assets in a taxable event, if structured in an appropriate manner, thus resulting in a stepped-up basis to the venture. Larger depreciation charges may then be deducted against venture income. The above business considerations are not directly related to the solution of the case; yet students may want to discuss them in the context of how such ventures and partnerships are, increasingly, a necessary business method.

Students who have some background in federal income taxation may recognize that Section 721 of the Internal Revenue Code provides that no gain or loss is recognized to the partnership or the partners upon a contribution of property to the partnership in exchange for a partnership interest. Further, the illustrations of partnership accounting presented in some advanced accounting texts conform to the tax treatment. Also, a question arises when cash is received by the partner as a result of, or in a transaction related to, the transfer to the partnership. The tax law would probably look to the form of this transaction; that is, "a premium for the opportunity to buy in," and treat the $5 million as ordinary income. At a minimum, it would be treated as a receipt of boot in a tax-free exchange which becomes taxable to the extent of any boot received less than the gain. Though these tax considerations are inapplicable as accounting principles, they may be pertinent to the students' thought processes in selecting a solution.

The state of the art in 1981 remained unsettled as to the appropriate accounting for the formation of a partnership or joint venture under the circumstances described. Some may view it as a financing transaction, with Cash being the lender of $30 million for an unspecified interest return equal to 50 percent of future profits reduced by the $5 million paid directly to Sunflower. Others may view it as the contribution of property to form a partnership, accompanied by receipt of a fee for allowing another party to participate in future operations. (This seems to be the legal form.) Still others may view the transactions as a sale of a one-half interest in the rigs for $20 million with a concurrent contribution by

Case 17: Profit Recognition

each joint owner of its one-half interest in the rigs plus $15 million cash to a partnership formed for the purpose of completing and operating the rigs. And, others may see the substance of the transaction still differently.

Where the interpretation is that of a sale of a one-half interest, further consideration should be given to what is called the "seller's (Sunflower's) continued involvement." The quoted term derives from the Industry Accounting Guide for real estate transactions. Though not applicable to sales of personal property, the guide should figure in the students' thought processes because the transactions are similar; guidance for personal property is not covered by professional literature. In this case, the students should discuss whether the agreements to be responsible for completion of construction of the rigs and to act as leasing agent affect the accounting solution. The discussion should include whether reasonable estimates can be made of the future costs of development (in excess of $60 million plus the bank line of credit) and also of the cost of leasing activities to be performed for nominal compensation.

The Solution

Though the substance of this transaction, and other similar transactions, is the subject of varied interpretations, it seems to be a sale of 50 percent of two units of personal property for $20 million, such sale being effected legally through the use of a joint venture, and the contribution of $15 million so received to the partnership along with half of the property. As the units "sold" were 50 percent complete at the time of sale, the real estate guide would permit 50 percent of the profit to be recorded after deducting from total profit an amount which would provide compensation at prevailing rates for the leasing activity. Though the property in the case is not real property, the guide should support the above position as to the amount recognized as income, with the remainder to be deferred and recognized as the balance of the work is performed.

Cost of Goods Sold - and Otherwise Disposed of

On April 1, 1980, your client, Radetronics Corporation, an SEC-reporting company, acquired Korphone, Inc., a manufacturer of portable radios. Your acquisition investigation included observing Korphone's March 31, 1980 inventory, which consisted mainly of purchased parts — transistors, speakers, tubes, and such — kept in a controlled storeroom. The inventory was carefully taken and your people on the observation team were well satisfied.

During the year, you reviewed Korphone's system of internal control and came away with some serious concerns about the controls over inventory and cost of goods sold. There appear to be adequate controls over receiving and shipping: the company is reasonably assured that it pays only for what it receives and that it bills all of the finished goods shipped out. But there is no perpetual inventory system to control quantities of purchased parts, nor does the accounting system establish book value control over the inventory every month-end. Cost of goods sold is determined by the traditional formula: beginning inventory plus purchases less the ending inventory equals cost of goods sold.

Because of the control weaknesses — the lack of any perpetual records or book value controls — you insisted that your people observe the physical inventory at December 31 rather than at an interim date. Your manager reported that it went off without a hitch. He also told you that he inspected the storeroom and was satisfied with the physical controls over the purchased parts. Further, he observed the guards at the gates and was impressed that the employees all stopped to have their lunch boxes inspected.

Nonetheless, he is still concerned about Korphone. The gross margin from nine months of radio production is about 40 percent of sales, which is consistent with last year's results. But gross margin percentages month to month vary dramatically, from 52 to 35 percent. The variance is not due to product mix, because the company's cost/price worksheets indicate a standard 50 percent spread between cost build-ups and planned sales prices. Your manager says he has looked everywhere but cannot find an explanation of the variance in monthly gross margin statistics or the variance between the planned gross margin and actual. And, he points out that every percentage point change in gross margin is worth $200,000 annually at the bottom line and of course the variances are even more significant to the earnings.

When you discuss this issue with the client's controller, he acknowledges that your people have raised an interesting question. He even acknowledges that the problem may be due to employee theft of very small, very expensive purchased

Case 18: Cost of Goods Sold — and Otherwise Disposed of

parts. The controller asks that you send a letter detailing your findings and your recommendations, but concludes, "to be honest, I have to tell you that we're not going to do anything drastic at Korphone. Our labor relations are good, but tenuous. We're not about to establish any controls which might upset our people or stir up the water in any way. And besides, the company is very profitable as it is, and is meeting the projections we established when we bought it." As an afterthought he adds, "I'm not at all sure that a more elaborate control system would pay for itself."

When you report the results of this meeting to your audit staff, the manager suggests that the traditional line on the income statement be expanded to read, "Cost of Goods Sold and Stolen." But then he asks seriously, "OK, so we tell management about the weaknesses in the system; should we insist that the stockholders be told too, by mentioning it in a footnote?"

HOW WILL YOU ANSWER YOUR MANAGER?

DISCUSSION LEADER'S GUIDE

Cost of Goods Sold - and Otherwise Disposed of

Objectives of the Case

The question posed by the manager on the engagement may concentrate the student's attention:

(1) on the auditor's responsibility for adequacy of financial statement disclosure of real or suspected irregularities and of weaknesses in internal control;
(2) on the auditor's professional and implied responsibilities for detection of irregularities; and
(3) on the auditor's exercise of judgment in the discharge of those responsibilities.

But, there is more to the case. The student should also focus on:

(1) the difficulties of evaluating whether additional controls would be cost effective;
(2) the uncertainty that thefts in fact have occurred;
(3) the difficulty in categorizing the control weaknesses as material weaknesses;
(4) the possibility that control weaknesses may fit some design or pattern of management operations; and
(5) the possibility that the financial statements omit a contingent asset should thefts in fact have occurred that are recoverable from the company's insurance carrier.

Applicable Professional Pronouncements

AICPA Codification of Statements on Auditing Standards Sections 320.32 and 302.46, "Auditor's Study of Internal Control"; Section 331.09, "Inventories" (SAS-1)

Statement on Auditing Standards No. 16, "The Independent Auditor's Responsibility for the Detection of Errors and Irregularities"

Statement on Auditing Standards No. 20, "Required Communications of Material Weaknesses in Internal Control"

Statement on Auditing Standards No. 30, "Reporting on Internal Accounting Control"

Foreign Corrupt Practices Act - Section 13(b) of Exchange Act of 1934

Business Assumptions and Other Data

The controller said the month-to-month variance in gross margin *may* be due to employee theft — and at this point, there could be a number of explanations. The standard cost/price work sheets could be in error, such that product mix in sales will result in variations in gross margin. Or, some of the internal recordkeeping activities inadvertently could produce the monthly variances. Or, the month-end physical inventories could be inaccurate, as can be envisioned easily for work in process. Or, the monthly pricing could contain errors. It is easy to suspect employee theft, but there *can* be answers other than theft.

The case does not categorize the control weaknesses — material or otherwise. Management tends to think the weaknesses are not material as evidenced by the controller's comment that the company is not going to do anything drastic. Yet, the weaknesses are potentially material. And if they are, then the company may be in violation of the Foreign Corrupt Practices Act, which requires SEC-reporting companies to maintain an adequate system of internal control. Material weaknesses and potentially material weaknesses should be discussed with the client's legal counsel to obtain their opinion as to whether a violation of the act has occurred.

Statements on Auditing Standards Nos. 20 and 30 contain no language suggesting inclusion of comments regarding material weaknesses in a footnote or in an accountant's report. However, in practice, comments about weaknesses in internal control have appeared with some regularity in published reports on SEC-reporting companies, but most of these companies have been facing financial difficulties. In healthy, ongoing companies, such comments are the exception. But the pattern of disclosures could change with more experience under the Act — there is still little to go on. Some students may recall that the case of *Adams vs. Standard Knitting Mills, Inc.* (United States District Court, Eastern District of Tennessee No. 8052) is very much on point. The Court found in *Adams* that the failure of the auditor to disclose or compel management to disclose in the financial statements the fact that the company audited had serious and continuing electronic data processing control problems constituted a material misrepresentation.

As no theft loss has yet been established, the possibility of a contingent receivable from the insurance carrier seems remote. While the potential of insurance recovery sometimes motivates managements to investigate further the possibility of employee theft, Radetronics' management has no intention of stirring up its employees or their union.

The overall operating results presumably are fairly stated, assuming no potential insurance recovery. That being the case, the classification of employee theft, if indeed it did occur (or the absence of some kind of disclosure), may be the only thing incorrectly stated. Employee theft and shoplifting losses are commonplace, reputedly aggregating staggering sums annually that are seldom if ever recovered. In practice, managements most often view such irregularities as another cost of doing business — one that cannot be avoided. The retail industry, for example, has lived with such thefts seemingly forever, and even plans for them. Such theft losses conventionally are included in the caption "cost of merchandise sold" with seldom a second thought, to the end that the manager's suggestion to add "and stolen" appears to be in jest.

But one should not pass over this jestful suggestion in too much of a hurry. The "business as usual" syndrome may be on its deathbed, and the manager's suggestion shows incisive thinking — "Does it have to be that way because it has always been that way?" The SEC says, definitely, "No." For example, their position is that bribes should be disclosed, even though relatively small in relation to the financial statements, and should not be "buried" in operating costs as has always happened in the past. Admittedly, bribes and theft have different characteristics, but the disclosure principles appropriate for each may not be so far apart.

New reporting movements, those that buck the tide of "business as usual," often come obliquely, as is the case with bribes. The profession often has not anticipated but has reacted (and at times slowly) and thus has received unwelcome criticism. In the mid- to-late 1970s substantial concern was expressed over auditors and auditors' reports and internal control. Congress (Senator Metcalf and Representative Moss, initially) voiced some of those concerns; the SEC, others; and the so-called Cohen Commission on Auditors' Responsibilities, still others. Insofar as internal control is concerned, the impact of these and other studies seems to be in the direction of public reporting on the adequacy of internal control by management and auditors, at least for publicly held companies. The SEC apparently is dedicated to having auditors express their opinion on the adequacy of internal control and may even try to tie such opinion into an evaluation of compliance or noncompliance with the accounting requirements of the Foreign Corrupt Practices Act. But substantial resistance remains, and the internal control reporting or disclosure requirements were unsettled at the beginning of 1981.

Discussion

Disclosure

A new accountant probably would assume that the audit firm should do as the manager suggested — that is, use the caption "cost of goods sold and stolen." And the old, experienced accountant — steeped in years of common usage — would probably consider the suggestion unworthy of a response. Yet, the profession needs young auditors who are able to look beyond "the books" and beyond common usage to seek better solutions to apparently mundane issues.

Because theft was not established, use of the suggested caption could be considered presumptive. However, employee thefts most likely had occurred and must be considered. First, if no thefts have been identified but everyone knows they occur in the ordinary course of business, as in the retail industry, should all financial statements disclose this fact to the readers with language that goes like this — "Management is aware that merchandise is stolen on a recurring basis by employees and others. Recovery on the thefts is unlikely and such theft losses, included in Cost of Goods Sold, are considered a normal cost of doing business. The amount of loss through thefts is indeterminable but could be as much as ____% of sales, or ____% of earnings before taxes."?

Whether such disclosure is essential to a reader's understanding of the financial statements has not been addressed by the profession to any extent. As one moves further away from retail-type operations to companies where employee theft is less likely, as with Korphone, the meaning of "essential to an understanding" remains uncertain. The expectation of disclosure may be stronger, however, because such thefts would be further from the ordinary course of business.

On the other hand, if thefts had been identified for a certainty in Korphone, should they be disclosed? The state of the art is unsettled, but leans toward disclosure if the amounts are material. What is material is also a complex subject; still, identified theft losses in excess of three percent of pretax income of SEC-reporting companies are surely of sufficient size to prompt careful consideration.

Although the above reasoning may be logical, the fact remains that the state of the art in 1981 had not prescribed disclosure in any of the various situations above. Statement on

Case 18: Cost of Goods Sold — and Otherwise Disposed of

Auditing Standards No. 16, discussed below, deals with how the auditor should report when the audit indicates possible irregularities, and that dissertation may be helpful.

As to disclosure of weaknesses in internal control, the state of the art is equally unsettled. If the weaknesses are considered material weaknesses, disclosure to management is required; if reporting publicly, so is public disclosure, but in a separate report. An inference exists (in paragraph 43 of Statement on Auditing Standards No. 30) that a material weakness is unlikely to affect an accountant's report. What this says is that auditors can "audit around" material weaknesses. And, this has been considered true for years — witness the small company with a single bookkeeper. Though material weaknesses can still be "audited around," we still have the question of whether they should be disclosed in the financial statements. The student will recognize that not too much comfort should be taken in the inference above. Where a material weakness exists, at least in an SEC-reporting company, disclosure in the financial statements seems highly probable. Auditors probably should consult their own legal counsel if they are contemplating writing a "material weakness" letter to a client's management without also seeing that the weakness is disclosed in the annual financial statements.

Internal Control and Detection of Irregularities

In cases where an auditor has determined that the internal control over inventories may be deficient, further substantive tests are appropriate.

In this case study, the auditor is satisfied with the physical inventory procedures and the client's representations about the quantities and physical condition of the inventories. He is concerned, however, that cost of goods sold may be overstated due to possible theft.

Statement on Auditing Standards No. 16 addresses this issue:

> If the independent auditor's examination causes him to believe that material errors or irregularities may exist, he should consider their implications and discuss the matter and extent of any further investigation with an appropriate level of management that is at least one level above those involved. If after such discussions the auditor continues to believe that material errors or irregularities may exist, he should determine that the board of directors or the audit committee is aware of the circumstances. Also, he should attempt to obtain sufficient evidential matter to determine whether in fact material errors or irregularities exist and, if so, their effect .... When the auditor's examination indicates the presence of errors or possible irregularities, and the auditor remains uncertain about whether these errors or possible irregularities may materially affect the financial statements, he should qualify his opinion on the financial statements and, depending on the circumstances, consider withdrawing from the engagement, indicating his reasons and findings in writing to the board of directors.

> The independent auditor's examination may reveal errors or possible irregularities that he concludes could not be so significant as to materially affect the financial statements he is examining .... The auditor should refer such matters to an appropriate level of management that is at least one level above those involved, with the recommendation that the matter be pursued to a conclusion.

The key to the portion of the case dealing with internal control and detection of irregularities is the evaluation of the auditor's uncertainty about whether the possible thefts may materially affect the financial statements. What is material in the case of fraud or theft? How can materiality be evaluated if absolute amounts are unknown? Can upper limits of an unknown loss be calculated; not likely, but if so would it be fair to use the upper limit, or something less than that and, if less, how much less? Determination of a material effect on financial statements is difficult under most circumstances, but such a determination borders on the unreal when dealing with an unknown amount. Yet, that is what is required professionally and what must be done at Korphone.

Statement on Auditing Standards No. 1 (AU 320.32) recognizes that the cost of internal control should not exceed the benefits expected to be derived. Management has the prerogative of concluding whether the cost of correcting control weaknesses, material or otherwise, is likely to exceed the expected benefit. However, the fact that correction of control weaknesses should be cost effective does not mitigate the auditor's need to consider whether such weaknesses are material.

In general, under Statement on Auditing Standards No. 1, the auditor is to plan his examination to search for irregularities, and an unqualified report conveys a belief that the financial statements taken as a whole are not materially misstated as a result of errors or irregularities. In the case of Korphone the auditor "looked everywhere," which presumably meets the professional requirement for extended auditing procedures when the examination indicates material irregularities may exist. The auditor is satisfied with the numbers — that is, the financial statements taken as a whole are not materially misstated as a result of irregularities. Thus, we are back to the question of disclosure and/or classification.

The Solution

As to internal control:

- The absence of perpetual records and bookkeeping control probably is a material weakness but when considered in conjunction with the mitigating monthly physical inventory, the overall impact is less than material.

- The cost-benefit issue should be reviewed again by management. Perpetual record keeping is unlikely to disturb the management/labor relationships but would increase control.

As to the auditor's responsibility for detection of irregularities, that has been accorded required professional handling.

As to disclosures:

- The management and board of directors should be advised by letter of the concern over accounting controls. The letter should recommend that they use perpetual records, that they have an internal review or audit of (a) the accuracy of the physical inventory and its pricing of the cost/price sheets, and of (b) the internal record keeping in an effort to identify causes for the monthly variances, if any, resulting from the record keeping.

- The financial statements overall were considered not to be misstated. In the absence of known theft, no further consideration was given to changes in financial statement captions or classifications or to disclosure of possible employee theft. In the future, if theft is identified or believed beyond reasonable doubt to have occurred in material amounts, the questions of classification or disclosure should be reconsidered in light of the then-existing state of the art.

DLG 18-5

Accounting for Doubtful Real Estate Loans

New World Development Co. is developing a new community to consist of single-family homes, condominiums, and retail establishments. Because of the economy, progress has been slow, and New World has dramatically scaled down its planned activities. Management is confident that the project will ultimately prove out but, in the near term, intends to let the development hibernate.

Earlier in the current fiscal year, New World sold a piece of the property to a local partnership with the understanding that the partnership would construct a shopping center. The sale was for $1,000,000 — New World got $250,000 in cash, took a $750,000 note, payable in equal annual installments of $75,000 a year over ten years plus interest at ten percent, and recognized a $750,000 profit. New World's "hibernation" policy is obviously going to delay the cash-flow payout from the proposed shopping center. The partnership has not yet committed any funds to the construction of the center and as the fiscal year draws to a close, there is some talk of default on the note.

New World has been scrambling to find alternatives to prevent the partnership from defaulting and several proposals are under consideration. Another development company has offered to buy the shopping center site from the partnership for $600,000 cash. The partners have suggested that they sell the land and settle the note for a $600,000 lump sum payment. As a second possibility, the partners have also agreed to stick with the original deal if New World will give them a three-year moratorium on the note, suspending requirements for principal and interest payments. They offered to pledge additional collateral on their loan in an effort to induce New World to agree to the moratorium. Of course, there is a third alternative — New World can simply let the default happen, repossess the property, hold it for a while, and then sell it again when the project comes out of hibernation.

New World's president is concerned with the accounting implications of these alternatives and calls to ask your advice. He explains that the company's financial position is such that they can afford to wait out the hibernation period. The company has over $2,000,000 in equity and has access to an $8,000,000, eight percent, five-year revolving credit agreement. He explains that this decision on the alternatives might be influenced by the accounting impact. He has concluded that if he accepted the cash deal, he would have to step up to a $150,000 loss today and he is reluctant to take that kind of loss in the current year's earnings. And yet he observes that a bird in the hand is always worth two in the bush. Before he makes any final decision, he wants your advice.

HOW DO YOU ADVISE REGARDING THE REQUIRED ACCOUNTING FOR EACH OF THE THREE ALTERNATIVES?

DISCUSSION LEADER'S GUIDE

Accounting for Doubtful Real Estate Loans

Objectives of the Case

This case is a good illustration of the interrelationship of accounting consequences and business decisions. In the more conventional situations the business decisions have already been made, and all that remain are determinations of accounting consequences. In theory, at least, accounting consequences should not shape business decisions. Such decisions should, instead, rest on a foundation of greatest economic benefit over the long term to the reporting company. Pressures of the marketplace have a way, however, of placing emphasis on near term earnings and earnings per share.

The three alternatives available to management are:

1. Settle the $750,000 note for a $600,000 lump sum payment from the original partners.

2. Grant the partners a three-year moratorium on interest and principal payments.

3. Allow the default to occur and repossess the property.

The students might want to spend some time discussing the economics of the three alternatives without regard to the accounting consequences to gain insight into the evaluation of choices between alternative actions.

Each business choice is likely to produce different accounting results. The students will probably focus on (a) the accounting for restructuring of debt in troubled loan situations and (b) the valuation or carrying amount of receivables or real property. Collateral issues that may come up for discussion could involve (a) the presence or absence of a related-party relationship between New World and the partnership, (b) the possibility that the sale should not have been recorded in the first place, (c) the possibility that, upon receipt, the note should have been discounted to provide a yield greater than the stated interest rate, and (d) the possibility that the interest cost to carry doubtful loans or foreclosed property should be taken into account in the valuation of the asset.

Applicable Professional Pronouncements

Statement of Financial Accounting Standards No. 15, "Accounting by Debtors and Creditors for Troubled Debt Restructurings"

Statement of Financial Accounting Standards No. 5, "Accounting for Contingencies"

Accounting Standards Executive Committee Statement of Position 78-2, "Accounting Practices for Real Estate Trusts"

Accounting Standards Executive Committee Statement of Position 75-2, "Accounting Practices for Real Estate Investment Trusts"

Though not dealing with an investment trust in this case, guidance given in the Statements of Position may be relevant.

Business Assumptions and Other Data

The validity of the original sale transaction is an issue which should be addressed, simply because it is a recurring problem in real estate transactions. Was the original sale a bona fide transaction conducted at arm's length? And is the subsequent event (i.e., the prospective default) in fact a second event to be accounted for separately? Or was the original transaction a "sham" or accommodation transaction conducted between related parties? If the latter, the original sale transaction would be reversed.

The arm's-length nature of the original transaction should be affirmed; avoid allowing the discussion to digress to the philosophical and practical problems inherent in related-party transactions. Define the sale as devoid of related-party involvement and devoid of "sham" or accommodation characteristics. Accordingly, the original sale need not be reversed.

However, factors which students would need to consider to determine the arm's-length character of the original transaction are as follows:

1. Sales price, repayment terms of the note, and the interest rate in comparison to sales of similar properties.
2. Previous dealings or relationships between the two entities.
3. Any stockholder, directorship, or family relationship between the two entities.

The timing of the sale in relation to the date New World first became aware of the purchaser's need for relief suggests a question as to whether the sale should be reversed. Both events occurred in the same fiscal year, and are assumed to be separated by some eight to 11 months. Though the timing of both events within the same fiscal year may suggest reversal of the sale, reversal would be inappropriate in the state of the art as practiced in 1981.

Whether the interest rate of ten percent on the note represents fair and adequate compensation to the seller for the use of funds is not stated. That it does may be inferred from the stated fact that the seller can borrow money at eight percent. Accordingly, the issue of discounting the note at the time of sale to provide a fair return need not be discussed exhaustively. It is fair to state that the provisions of Accounting Principles Board Opinion No. 21, "Interest on Receivables and Payables," are not directly pertinent to this case.

Whether the stated understanding between New World and the partnership regarding use of the land sold for construction of a shopping center effectively places a restriction on the land in the hands of any third-party purchaser should be asked. The answer is that the restriction should be considered enforceable as a part of the overall plan for development of the property. The restriction should have no effect, however, on the accounting advice given for Alternatives 1, 2, or 3.

The case also may highlight the argument going on within the profession about the nature of interest and of interest expense, and the uncertainty that continues to surround the determination of losses on loans (both "good" and "troubled") and on foreclosed properties. Though the argument is not germane to this case, it is helpful to understand the controversy. At this moment, there is a conflict in the literature and that conflict has prevented the American Institute of Certified Public Accountants from publishing the new revision of the Bank Audit Guide. The Banking Committee of the AICPA wants to say that banks need not provide for the carrying cost of doubtful real estate loans, drawing on the theory of Statement of Financial Accounting Standards No. 15. But the Accounting Standards Executive Committee refuses to approve the Bank Audit Guide unless the banks' real estate loans are treated in the same way as loans by real estate investment trusts and savings and loan associations.

In REITs and S&Ls, the focus is on the valuation of the underlying real estate for the reason that the borrower seldom would be able or willing to repay a loan from other sources (and in some states deficiency judgments on real estate loans are virtually prohibited). In looking to the recoverability of individual loans and properties, estimated net realizable value of the real estate would be compared with the carrying amount of the loan (including accrued interest) or the carrying amount of real estate, if foreclosure had taken place. And, in determining estimated net realizable value, the estimated holding costs, including interest, are deducted from estimated future selling prices. As noted, the Bank Audit Guide would require no such provision for interest cost.

Though not a part of the case as presented, there is the broader question of the valuation of the real estate project as a whole. Presumably it is not in danger; management says it can wait out the hibernation period. Such a position undoubtedly is sufficient for purposes of management's evaluation of whether there are possible losses that should be recorded. But, management's statement is insufficient as a basis for an auditor's judgment regarding the possibility of losses in the project, and every student should recognize this fact.

Discussion

The business factors in this case are so significant that they tend to overshadow the accounting issues. Among many items, the final decision will depend on:

1. Management's assessment of the future profitability of the development in total, taking into account such factors as the general economic conditions, population growth in the area, competition, etc.
2. Management's desire and need for the immediate cash.
3. Management's approval of the risk connected with the restructured note and, in particular, the value of the additional collateral offered by the partners.
4. The opportunities and risks involved in repossessing and reselling the property, including:
    a. Management's appraisal of the overall suitability of the property for its current intended use.
    b. Increased materials and energy costs.
    c. Changes in environmental zoning regulations.
    d. Shortages of construction material, etc.
5. The accounting consequences of each of the three alternatives.

Case 19: Accounting for Doubtful Real Estate Loans

If Alternative 1 is selected, the students will know that the accounting is straightforward — settlement for $600,000 cash involves a loss to be recognized. If the second or third alternatives are selected by management, the assets involved will become the residuals of a troubled debt restructuring and the guidance of Statement of Financial Accounting Standards No. 15 will govern, subject to some further consideration in the instance of the second alternative: "A restructuring of a debt constitutes a troubled debt restructuring if the creditor for economic or legal reasons related to the debtor's financial difficulties grants a concession to the debtor that it would not otherwise consider." In the case of New World, the granting of a three-year moratorium could be considered a troubled debt restructuring since it is likely that the concession was granted due to the debtor's financial difficulties.

If Alternative 2 is selected, the three-year moratorium would be considered, under SFAS 2, a modification of terms. Where a modification of terms is involved and the total future cash receipts specified by the new terms of the receivable, including both receipts designated as interest and those designated as face amount, are greater than the recorded investment in the receivable before restructuring, no adjustment to the recorded investment in the receivable need be made.

The FASB seems to have taken a rather narrow position, and on form, not substance. The students may well share a view that the FASB is ignoring the more substantive issue of whether the receivable, however modified, is collectible. In fact, the FASB has specifically said that it is not presently prepared to deal with bad debt accounting. And, in the final analysis, that is the only issue — bad debt accounting, not the mechanics of restructuring a troubled loan.

The FASB does notice the issue of collectibility in footnote 18 in Statement on Financial Accounting Standards No. 15, but it neatly avoids facing that issue. In general terms it says that uncertainty of collection of noncontingent amounts specified by the new terms (such as the three-year moratorium in this case) is not a factor in applying provisions relating to modification of terms but should, "of course," be considered in accounting for allowances for uncollectible amounts. And there the Financial Accounting Standards Board drops the matter.

As a practical matter, a company acting in good faith would not be expected to grant a three-year moratorium if it expected to be unable to collect the face amount of the troubled receivable. The company would follow an alternative course if it recognized that its receivable was uncollectible. However, some companies, being less forthright, may use the moratorium or other modification tactics to forestall recognition of a known loss in the collection of a receivable.

The application of Statement 15 and its mechanistic accounting provisions would seem to answer the accounting requirements until one looks closely at the collectibility issue. In all cases of "modification of terms," the auditor is forced to assess collectibility because less forthright management will accept as fact a position that collectibility is not in question. If, indeed, after "modification of terms" the collectibility of the revised amount remains in doubt, most practitioners, and presumably most companies, except banks, would then apply the net-realizable-value test discussed earlier.

If Alternative 3 is selected by New World, the critical issue relates to the valuation of the real estate. For a number of years there has been little agreement as to the proper accounting. The Securities and Exchange Commission seems to take the position that generally profit on property sold and repossessed should be reversed or charged against earnings, and other adjustments should be made so as to record the foreclosed property essentially at its initial cost, unless lower valuations are indicated. Certain real estate company managements, and their auditors, said that foreclosed property should be recorded at estimated net realizable value, a term of art, defined somewhat uniformly in Statement of Position 75-2 (Accounting Practices of Real Estate Investment Trusts) and in the Audit and Accounting Guide for Savings and Loan Associations, and perhaps elsewhere; others said that current value or fair value should be used. Until the advent of Statement of Financial Accounting Standards No. 15 in 1977, the real estate industry and the savings and loan industry and their auditors tended to use estimated net realizable value for foreclosed properties in reliance on earlier guides. Now those industries and all others are required by Statement 15 to record foreclosed properties at fair value, defined thusly:

> The fair value of the assets transferred is the amount that the debtor could reasonably expect to receive for them in a current sale between a willing buyer and a willing seller, that is, other than in a forced or liquidation sale. Fair value of assets shall be measured by their market value if an active market for them exists. If no active market exists for the assets transferred but exists for similar assets, the selling prices in that market may be helpful in estimating the fair value of the assets transferred. If no market price is available, a forecast of expected cash flows may aid in estimating the fair value of assets transferred, provided the expected cash flows are discounted at a rate commensurate with the risk involved.

Factors that may be relevant in estimating the fair value of various kinds of assets are described in paragraphs 88 and 89 of Accounting Principles Board Opinion No. 16 [section 1091.88-.89], paragraphs 12-14 of Accounting Principles Board Opinion No. 21 [section 4111.11-.13], "Interest on Receivables and Payables," and paragraph 25 of Accounting Principles Board Opinion No. 29 [section 1041.25], "Accounting for Nonmonetary Transactions."

The Solution

If New World opts for Alternative No. 1 and accepts $600,000 cash as settlement of the note, a $150,000 loss will have been incurred and should be recognized in the current period.

If Alternative No. 2 is chosen, the three-year moratorium would be a troubled debt restructuring as defined by Statement of Financial Accounting Standards No. 15. Accordingly, since the total future cash receipts specified by the new agreement will exceed the recorded investment in the receivable before restructuring, no adjustment is required. Though the Statement deals with modification of terms in relation to the "total future cash receipts specified by the new [agreement]," an evaluation will still be necessary as to whether the amounts so specified are ultimately collectible. The evaluation should take into account the additional collateral to be pledged as well as the mortgaged property. If the evaluation indicates that less than $750,000 ultimately may be collectible, the provision of Statement of Financial Accounting Standards No. 5, "Accounting for Contingencies," would apply and a reduction of the carrying amount may be appropriate. Statement 15 does not cover accounting for allowances for estimated uncollectible amounts and does not prescribe or proscribe particular methods for estimating amounts of uncollectible receivables. However, as noted above, the real estate investment trust and savings and loan

Case 19: Accounting for Doubtful Real Estate Loans

pronouncements give guidance for the mortgaged property, and amounts so determined would be increased by the value of the additional collateral.

If Alternative No. 3 is chosen and New World forecloses, it would again be troubled debt restructuring under Statement 15. Fair value would be used as the basis for recording the foreclosed property. In this case, fair value probably would be more than the $600,000 supposedly offered by the other development company. If its offering price was considered fair value, a loss of $150,000 would seem to be the maximum loss that would need to be recorded. Presumably, if another position is taken, it would be used only if it showed a fair value greater than $600,000. Other valuations that may be appropriate would include comparable sales of similar property, appraisal of fair value, discounted future cash flows, or estimated fair values. Estimated net realizable value would not be a proper basis for recording the property. Were another basis used, the company should be advised that it would need convincing evidence or documentation to support a valuation greater than the $600,000 now offered.

Depreciation

The Pension Reform Act has been an opportunity and a challenge for your client, Comprehensive Financial Services (CFS). CFS operates a series of mutual funds, particularly designed for pension funds and similar fiduciary institutions. CFS's customers can pick and choose from a wide variety of funds with a wide variety of investment objectives. Under the Pension Reform Act, trustees are responsible to maintain a specified level of diversity in their funds' investment portfolio. And CFS's shopping list of diverse funds gives them an important marketing edge in the competition for pension business.

The pressure for diversification has stimulated the imagination of all the investment services. CFS, like many of its competitors, offers a mutual fund investing in real estate. The CFS real estate fund, which has purchased a number of apartment houses, hotels, and commercial buildings, is a little different from common stock funds, and CFS has asked all of the participants in the fund to leave their moneys invested for a specific period. But, the real estate fund is similar to the common stock funds in many important ways: participants expect to share in the cash flow from rentals, and they also expect to share in any appreciation. In fact, CFS promotes the real estate fund as an appropriate place to put long-term money where appreciation is a principal objective and promises to provide its financial statements on a "current value" basis, based on annual appraisals of all of the properties. The fund is a closed-end type, such that sales or purchases of units of ownership by the fund would be unlikely.

CFS's treasurer has called you in for advice. He stands looking at a mockup of the financial statement for the real estate fund, and he looks perplexed. He has thought through the balance sheet presentation — the real estate investments will be shown at their current value, with original cost shown parenthetically as a reference point. He also has an income statement roughed out, as follows:

Rental Revenues	xxx
Other Income	xxx
	xxx
Property Costs	xx
Administration Costs	xx
Operating Income	xxx
Gain in Current Value	xx
Net Income for the Year	xxx

Case 20-1

Case 20: Depreciation

The treasurer explains his question about the earnings statement: "Our people have conflicting ideas. Some say we should charge the rental operation with depreciation expense, picking the depreciation up as an increase or a decrease in the appreciation. The logic for that presentation is that it provides an income statement more comparable to other real estate entities. On the other hand, others in our group argue against a depreciation charge because depreciation is not relevant to an investor who is looking for appreciation. Some have even suggested that increasing the gain in current value for an arbitrary depreciation adjustment will confuse and maybe even mislead. I can see merits to both arguments." He asks, "What do you think?"

WHAT DO YOU THINK?

DISCUSSION LEADER'S GUIDE

Depreciation

Objectives of the Case

A number of objectives can be identified. Perhaps the broadest is to focus attention on who are the users of the financial statements and on their needs in those situations where doubt has been raised as to the availability of "garden variety" financial statements.

Other objectives that warrant discussion include:

1. Helping the students think through the nature of depreciation expense and how it fits into the determination of operating results. And related thereto are the issues of what is depreciation from an economic standpoint, as contrasted to an accounting standpoint, and what is the concept of depreciation in a current value environment, with subquestions such as:

   a. Whether depreciation on appreciation is an acceptable method of accounting; and

   b. Whether depreciation is appropriate in the context of a managed portfolio of real properties.

2. Understanding the objective of the earnings statement of a fund such as this, as well as how that objective relates to the meaning and determination of net income and "operating" income.

3. Illuminating the controversy between historical cost and current value as a basis of measurement in financial reporting, and also the subjective nature of estimates and their frequent lack of reliability even though used as a basis for buy/sell transactions, as in this case.

Applicable Professional Pronouncements

AICPA Professional Standards Vol. 3 - Accounting Current Text; Section 1026.26-28, "Effect of Initial Recording, Realization and Expense Recognition Principles" (APB Statement No. 4, Chapter 6)

Statement of Financial Accounting Standards No. 35, "Accounting and Reporting by Defined Benefit Pension Plans"

AICPA Statement of Position, "Accounting Practices by Real Estate Investment Trusts" (SOP 75-2)

Accounting Principles Board Opinion No. 6, "Depreciation on Appreciation," paragraph 17

Case 20: Depreciation

Accounting Principles Board Opinion No. 12, "Disclosure of Depreciable Assets and Depreciation"

Accounting Terminology Bulletin No. 1 - "Review and Resume," paragraph 56 re definition of depreciation

Statement of Financial Accounting Standards No. 33, "Financial Reporting and Changing Prices"

Business Assumptions and Other Data

Conflicting views of depreciation are held by businessmen, accountants, and tax authorities. Many businessmen feel that depreciation allowances should help provide funds necessary to replace fixed capital assets. Accountants generally believe that depreciation is simply an allocation of costs to the revenues which those costs produce. Engineers may be inclined toward a loss in value concept. And, tax authorities view depreciation as an allowable deduction, the manipulation of which will affect government revenues and macroeconomic capital investment stimulation. Given these discrepant views, it is difficult to achieve a consensus on the provision for depreciation on appreciated properties or properties whose replacement costs have increased, notwithstanding the requirements of APB Opinion No. 6 to provide depreciation on appreciation.

Since the case is silent on the point, it is assumed the company has not found any particular precedent to support either of the presentations.

Tax consequences related to the operation of the real estate fund are not being considered since they are not the key issues or objectives of the case.

The case was initially presented during an era of inflation — and inflation has continued unabated since. Were the economy in a downturn, with protracted deflation, it is fair to speculate that individual points of view might well differ from those now held.

The case does not deal with fair value financial statements as a whole, though properties are proposed to be carried at fair value. Were comprehensive fair value statements used, holding gains (or losses) on debt incurred also would need to be taken into account (to conform to SFAS No.33, "Financial Reporting and Changing Prices").

Discussion

Over the years financial statements that carry all or selected assets at fair value have become more commonplace; yet that method of accounting has not been found acceptable for the vast majority of reporting entities, such as commercial and industrial companies. The practice is mixed in the financial field, with some banks, savings and loan associations, and real estate investment trusts carrying their assets at cost, less appropriate allowances, while certain investment companies, including Small Business Investment Companies, for example, and others carry certain assets at fair values. The discussion should deal with the reasons why cost or value is more appropriate for a mutual fund investing almost exclusively in real estate.

SFAS No. 35, on defined benefit pension plans, requires real estate to be carried at fair values at the reporting date. The entity at hand, a mutual fund designed for pension plans and such, though not a pension plan, might follow the accounting for investments required in that SFAS. Article 6 of SEC Regulation S-X relates to investment companies, but might also furnish guidance in accounting for real estate investments at fair value. It does not require depreciation on real estate investments (on either cost or appreciated basis) but does require increases or decreases of unrealized appreciation or negative appreciation to be shown separate and apart from the income or earnings statement. On the other hand, SFAS No. 35 seems to require increases or decreases in unrealized appreciation or negative appreciation as an integral part of net income. And, as with Article 6 companies, the SFAS seems not to require depreciation of appreciated real estate investments.

A key factor in deciding whether cost or fair value should be used in accounting for the real estate investments of a mutual fund, since the issue is not covered explicitly in professional pronouncements, could be the purpose served by the financial statements. CFS has agreed to furnish financial statements on a current value basis, probably the only meaningful financial statements for fund participants. The valuation of their units of participation would be almost entirely related to the current value of the real estate and, most likely, not to earnings per unit (share) as may be true for commercial companies or to "book value" per unit based on historical cost less depreciation. Where the participants invest solely for appreciation in property values, the use of current values makes the most sense.

Regardless, were the case at hand a commercial company rather than a mutual fund, current or fair values would not be acceptable accounting in the present state of the art but, if used, depreciation on appreciation would be required. The students may want to discuss the apparent imponderables of the legal form of an entity dictating the use of less meaningful accounting methods.

In 1953 the Committee on Terminology of the American Institute of Certified Public Accountants, in Accounting Terminology Bulletin 1, defined "depreciation accounting" and "depreciation" thusly:

> *Depreciation accounting* is a system of accounting which aims to distribute the cost or other basic value of tangible capital assets, less salvage (if any), over the estimated useful life of the unit (which may be a group of assets) in a systematic and rational manner. It is a process of allocation, not of valuation. *Depreciation for the year* is the portion of the total charge under such a system that is allocated to the year. Although the allocation may properly take into account occurrences during the year, it is not intended to be a measurement of the effect of all such occurrences.

This accounting definition, hardly new, still applies. It simply does not fit the perception of the economist, the engineer, or others, of a "fall in value" or a means of evaluating present usefulness. And, where there is an increase in value rather than a fall in value, increasing the carrying amount of the real property (or negative depreciation) may be appropriate, as discussed above. Assuming that to be so, then the question before the students is whether depreciation (accounting type — not economic type) should be charged against earnings in arriving at net earnings.

To argue that historical depreciation expense should be included in the earnings statement, one must first argue that the company is investing for two kinds of income — capital appreciation and operating income (which would be net of depreciation expense), and that the components of the earnings statement should reflect the respective contributions of each of those types of income. In support of this argument, one would say operating income is important in evaluating operations, and generally accepted accounting principles normally require a provision for depreciation in determining operating income.

Case 20: Depreciation

On the premise that investors try to make informed decisions, one must determine whether depreciation expense is significant to the investors in evaluating whether operating income is important to assessing long-term earning ability.

It appears from the case that the investors probably would be more concerned with the net cash flow from the property rentals (i.e., for dividend payments) than with the measurement of periodic "operating" results. Since depreciation is not a source of funds and, for accounting purposes, only represents the systematic allocation of costs, these investors probably do not need this information to assess long-term earning ability or net cash flows.

Although it might be desirable to include depreciation expense for comparability to the operations of other real estate entities, a more significant consideration might be the comparison of performance to other common stock or investment funds. In reviewing the performance of common stock funds, the investor would normally have readily available information as to dividend payments and capital appreciation, based on current market values. In the case of common stock, the appreciation would be "pure," that is, it would represent the absolute increase in market values over a period. If, in the real estate fund, depreciation were included in operations, the "gain in current value" would represent a hybrid of recaptured depreciation expense and an increase in current value since the increase in current value (or decrease if that were the case) is measured from one fair-valued balance sheet (the real estate account) to the next. It would not properly reflect the true capital appreciation. The problem with including the recaptured depreciation in the capital appreciation is that it commingles two completely different accounting concepts which are totally unrelated to each other.

The area of confusion here is that depreciation accounting is merely the systematic allocation of costs over the estimated service lives. Both the method of allocation and the estimated service lives are essentially arbitrary determinations used to match costs with the expected period of benefit. Depreciation is a cost concept that does not, in any way, purport to provide for impaired serviceability or decrease in "value." Appreciation is a value concept and has no relationship to amortized cost. (A discussion of the term "value" [i.e., value to owner, value to investor] is not germane to this case.) Since the principal objective of the fund appears to be capital appreciation, the "gain in current value" would probably be most meaningful if the amount represents only the increase in fair market value (appraisal) over the period.

If depreciation expense is not charged to earnings, the students should discuss whether disclosure of that fact is required in the footnotes and whether pro forma amounts should be given if such disclosure is made.

An implicit part of the discussion as to whether fair values should be used and whether depreciation should be provided deals with the meaning of net earnings and of operating income in a real estate fund. The question of meaning is highlighted by analogy to the problem of administering a trust that has an income beneficiary and a remainderman. If the income of the trust is derived from rents on real property, a large amount will be distributed to the income beneficiary if no depreciation is deducted from net rent receipts than if depreciation is deducted. If the income beneficiary receives all of the cash flow then it is possible that the remainderman will receive a fully depreciated, worn-out property, with no income potential. However, real estate often has increased in value rather than depreciated, so that the remainderman may not be unfairly treated after all.

DLG 20-4

In the real estate fund situation, the income beneficiary and the remainderman are one entity, namely the investors; therefore, income and corpus distinctions are not as important.

It is clear that by distributing net cash flow and by calling this net income that, in the absence of capital appreciation, the capital investment of the fund will be depleted if the properties depreciate in an economic sense. Further, general price level adjustments would probably demonstrate that a portion of the cash flow-net income is actually liquidation of invested capital. Despite the problem of hidden liquidation, depreciation does not seem appropriate for the fund.

In fact, the question of whether to charge depreciation is unsettled for the determination of net earnings in CFS, and, as mentioned above, the question is also open as to whether any appreciation recorded is a part of net earnings. For investment companies, the SEC would say "no," and for pension funds the FASB would say "yes."

The discussion of the case also should cover the difficulty management will encounter in assigning fair values to the various rental properties. Such valuations are highly subjective; yet, those valuations will affect prices paid or received should the units of participation change hands.

The Solution

Sufficient precedent in other industries seems to support a decision that carrying the real properties at current or fair value is appropriate in the circumstances. Depreciation should not be charged and reflected in the income statement of the fund. Although that decision was purely pragmatic, it is heavily influenced by our concern that readers — even sophisticated investors — would misunderstand an income statement that includes both depreciation and appreciation and by our belief that present and potential investors and other users of the financials are more interested in net cash in-flows for purposes of their decision making. In addition, net income should be defined as what is shown in the case as "operating income" rather than "operating income" plus "gain in current value." Our basis is that operating income more properly reflects distributable net income of the fund for the period. This decision, too, could have gone either way.

Audit Planning

You are considering your audit plan for work on Together, Inc., a large multi-industry company that has been privately held but now is negotiating with an underwriter regarding a sale of securities to the public. You realize that segment information will be required for the first time, and based on guidelines in Statement on Financial Accounting Standards No. 14 (segment information), three segments with the following revenue percentages should be reported this year:

Ponderous (heavy equipment manufacturing)	60%
Speedy (transportation)	14
Solar Window (technology)	6
	80%

Solar Window sales were three percent of total sales last year, and one percent in the preceding year, with the corresponding percentage declines generally at the expense of Ponderous. The growth in sales in the technology unit has excited the prospective underwriter.

You have asked the manager on the job whether the disaggregation of information (initial reporting for Solar and Speedy) should affect the audit plan and personnel assigned this year.

You have been trying to keep up with current developments and you have read the two auditing standards: (1) Segment Information and (2) Planning and Supervision. Your initial reaction is that they will have an effect on this year's plan so you express the following concerns to your manager:

1. "Because about 60 percent of the company's business is in the heavy manufacturing segment, and because other segments have been acquired only in the last four or five years, most of our audit engagement personnel have gotten their experience in the heavy equipment manufacturing business. Do our people adequately understand the other elements of the company's business that must now be separately reported?"

2. "Based on a quick reading of the segment auditing standard, I am somewhat troubled by paragraph 8, which seemed to say that if a matter is important to an investor's understanding of a trend within a segment, it could be material to the financial statements taken as a whole, even though on a quantitative basis it would not appear to be so. And that's a change in the way we view materiality when reporting on financial statements."

WHAT ARE SOME OF THE CHANGES, IF ANY, RELATED TO SEGMENT INFORMATION, THAT YOU WOULD EXPECT TO SEE IN THE AUDIT PLAN FOR THIS YEAR?

Case 21-1

DISCUSSION LEADER'S GUIDE

Audit Planning

Objectives of the Case

Broadly, the objective is to get students to talk about the importance of planning in the audit process and about the impact of changes in conditions and circumstances on the audit planning process. The discussion should focus on the following issues: (1) The interplay between Statement on Auditing Standards No. 21 (Segment Information) and Statement on Auditing Standards No. 22 (Planning and Supervision); (2) the relationship between Statement of Financial Accounting Standards No. 14 (Segment Information) and Statement on Auditing Standards No. 21; (3) the need to reconsider and revise the audit plan and audit program to encompass new developments such as the segment information reporting requirements and to decide whether the information reported complies with Statement of Financial Accounting Standards No. 14 in all material respects; (4) the possibility that engagement personnel, including the partner in charge of the engagement, may lack sufficient industry knowledge as to the disaggregated industries to meet professional standards; (5) the probability that segment information, being "soft," is very much subject to the influence of management and thus less susceptible to audit support in the conventional sense; and (6) the attempt made by AICPA to define the concept of materiality, particularly as to qualitative characteristics, which further influences the approach to audits.

The case is not an exercise in developing an audit program to test the allocation of revenues, costs, and assets — so don't let the students get into that level of detail. Keep the focus on planning.

Applicable Professional Pronouncements

Statement on Auditing Standards No. 21, "Segment Information"

Statement on Auditing Standards No. 22, "Planning and Supervision"

Statement of Financial Accounting Standards No. 14, "Financial Reporting of Segments of a Business Enterprise"

Business Assumptions and Other Data

The relative size of the three reporting subsidiaries was chosen with care, in that the technology subsidiary accounts for only six percent of sales, while its trend information has "excited" the underwriter. Thus, an almost insignificant subsidiary has become important to users' evaluations of trends concerning the entire company. Additionally, the subsidiary is "high technology," apparently requiring some particular skills and consideration on behalf of the audit team. Furthermore, this is the first year of disaggregation, so last year's audit plan more than likely is not valid for this year's reporting issues.

Discussion

The disaggregation of segment information can have a significant effect on the audit plan, as illustrated by this simplified set of circumstances.

The standard on segments (SAS-21) requires that the auditor consider qualitative as well as quantitative factors in evaluating whether a matter is material to the financial statements taken as a whole. Qualitative concepts are not yet too well developed and thus should elicit considerable discussion as to how to apply them. This manner of viewing materiality linked with the need for industry knowledge and consideration and documentation of matters that, in the past, have been immaterial, should be sufficient to stimulate concern.

The planning and supervision standard (SAS-22) requires that the auditor's plan consider such matters:

- The entity's business and its industry.
- Preliminary estimates of materiality level for audit purposes; pertinent discussion says, "The significance of a matter to particular entity . . . and the impact of the matter (for example, whether it distorts the trends reflected in the segment information) should all be considered in judging whether a matter relating to segment information is material to the financial statements taken as a whole . . . "
- Conditions that may require extension or modification of audit tests; in this case, the conditions are disaggregation of segment information.

In addition, Paragraph 4 of the standard (SAS 22) necessitates items such as:

- Inquiring about current business developments affecting the entity (this could be extended to those that would affect the disaggregated segments and their trends).
- Considering the effects of applicable accounting and auditing pronouncements, particularly new ones (this would have to be assessed for previously immaterial subsidiaries that, this year, are being reported upon).

Paragraph 6 (which provides details concerning the level of auditor knowledge) states in part: " . . . that level of knowledge that should enable him to obtain an understanding of the events, transactions and practices that, in his judgment, may have a significant effect on the financial statements." This language makes it important to add:

- Identifying areas that need special consideration.
- Assessing conditions under which accounting data are produced, processed, reviewed, and accumulated within the organization.
- Evaluating the reasonableness of management's representations.
- Making judgments about the appropriateness of the accounting principles applied and the adequacy of the disclosures.

Paragraph 7 requires the auditor to "consider matters affecting the industry in which the entity operates," such as economic conditions, government regulations, and changes in technology as they relate to his examination. Other matters such as accounting practices common to the industry, competitive conditions and, if available, financial trends and ratios should also be considered. These probably should also be considered for each disaggregated segment, requiring some refinements to most audit plans.

The case specifically emphasizes the one-industry background present on the audit team to suggest the possibility the audit team may need more experience or knowledge to review adequately the new disaggregated segments.

The Solution

Some changes you would expect to see in the audit plan are the following:

The planning considerations should embrace the possibility, or even the likelihood, that the segment information, being "soft" information susceptible to the influences of management, may be unauditable in the conventional sense and may call for additional inquiries and analyses to obtain audit satisfaction. As a result, there should be:

- Inquiry and evaluation regarding the appropriateness of the designation of three lines of business as segments of a business enterprise.
- Review of accounting records to evaluate whether they are likely to provide data responsive to the designations of three segments.
- Evaluation of qualitative (in addition to quantitative) factors in determining materiality.
- A concentrated effort to obtain the level of knowledge (specified in Statement on Auditing Standards No. 22, "Planning and Supervision") that is required to plan and perform this examination as it relates to the two new reporting segments (new in the sense that they have not been disaggregated before).
- Increased partner involvement in the audit planning this year to ensure that the requirements for the disaggregation of previously consolidated information receive attention.
- Identification of possible problems early enough to avoid last-minute crises. For example, Statement on Financial Accounting Standards No. 14 requires that sales to any one customer of ten percent or more of consolidated revenue be separately identified. This may require special effort to assure that this information will be available when the company intends to issue its report.
- Understanding in the following areas:
  - Internal accounting control for each reporting segment and the degree of integration, centralization, and uniformity of the accounting records.
  - Bases of accounting for sales and transfers between segments.
  - Methods used for allocating common expenses and assets between the reporting segments.
  - Disclosure requirements, particularly those related to revenue, operating profit, and identifiable assets for reporting segments.

Case 21: Audit Planning

- Information necessary to perform an analytical review of the segment information, including a comparison of the current year segment information with the prior year and current year budgeted information. Also, a consideration of the interrelationships among elements that would be expected to conform to certain predictable patterns and investigation of any unusual variations. This latter requirement, in that this is the initial reporting year, may require the client to go back and do some work related to prior years. (Although prior years' financial statements do not need to be restated, because the company was private, the underwriters may be expected to require segment information for at least three years. In such case, the auditor will need to apply essentially the same procedures to the earlier two years or see that segment information for those years is marked "unaudited.") Also, the client may need to modify internal budgeting mechanisms so that the reportable segments can be isolated and compared.

- A redesign of tests to focus on the disaggregation of the entity's financial statements into segment information.
- A plan for the identification and documentation of accounting principles used in segments.
- A comparison of those accounting principles to other related industry norms.

Auditing — Confirmations

This is your first year as partner in charge of the audit of the All-American Bank. All-American is a publicly held bank in excellent condition; it has been a client of the firm for several years. Two years ago the bank installed a highly computerized system for processing transactions. The system and all related controls have been tested and relied upon in all audits since the installation. Generally, prior years' audit tests of both transactions and balances have revealed very few errors in the processing of transactions.

Audit planning has begun: the supervisor and senior on the engagement are designing the year-end audit program and specifically are trying to decide on the scope of confirmation of the demand deposit (checking) accounts. When you took over the audit you asked the staff to make the maximum effective use of statistical sampling. Tests of the system have been performed and indicate the proof and transit function is operating effectively as are other controls related to demand deposit accounts.

As of the confirmation date, there are 40,000 accounts totalling $100,000,000. Earnings before taxes for the year are expected to be about $500,000.

The senior presents the following plan for confirming the accounts:

Because the system is strong, he reasons that he need not look for specific errors, but instead he should look for a total dollar assurance. Variables estimation will be used to achieve a precision of $12,500. This amount represents one-half of the financial statement measure of materiality, where materiality is five percent of expected earnings before taxes. Since internal control can be relied upon, a low reliability level can be used — say 70 percent. However, sample size will still be large (he estimates 1,000) so negative confirmations should be used to reduce follow-up work.

The supervisor believes a different plan is appropriate; he argues that:

Since internal control is good, a low reliability level is appropriate. However, the objective should be to discover an error if one should exist, not to measure whether hypothetical errors could be material for adjustment purposes. On that basis, an attribute approach would be used and sample size would be based on a zero expected occurrence rate and an upper precision limit relating to the population being tested (say one percent). This would result in a small sample of about 120 items. Positive confirmations would be used to assure that a supportable conclusion is reached for each sample item. Only if an error requiring an adjustment is found would a variables estimate based on materiality be necessary.

WHICH APPROACH WILL YOU HAVE THEM USE?

Case 22-1

Case 22: Auditing — Confirmations

DISCUSSION LEADER'S GUIDE

Auditing — Confirmations

Objectives of the Case

The case will appeal to a statistically oriented student group. But that should not be the focus of the discussion. The real focus is on the importance of establishing the objectives for an audit procedure. The statistical question posed here is really rather mechanical. The substantive question is, "What is the objective of the confirmation procedure?" The case should draw attention to the choice between sampling for variables, attributes or some alternative and to the precision and reliability criteria to be used. It should also focus on the choice of type of confirmation to be used, be it positive or negative, and, in relation to all the foregoing, should touch on materiality.

Applicable Professional Pronouncements

Auditing Standards, Auditors Study of Internal Control, AU 320, and related Appendix A, Relationship of Statistical Sampling to Generally Accepted Auditing Standards, and Appendix B, Precision and Reliability

Handbook of Accounting and Auditing, Burton, Palmer, Kay - Chapter 14, Audit Sampling (nonauthoritative)

Montgomery's Auditing, Ninth Edition, Chapter 5, Auditing Procedures — Their Nature and Extent (nonauthoritative)

Business Assumptions and Other Data

The case does not tell whether All-American Bank has its own internal audit function. The size of the bank would seem to warrant an internal auditor or two and their activities could affect the external auditor's approach to the audit of demand deposits. In the case at hand the students can properly assume that an internal audit function has not been established but is under consideration by bank management.

The case does not give a profile of demand deposits by size of account. The homogeneity, or lack of it, in account size could affect the auditor's procedures. Assume a heavy concentration of accounts with small balances; and a number of accounts carry balances in five and six figures. The students may further assume that stratification by account size is regularly available from the bank's computer and that time-consuming manual stratification is not necessary.

Discussion

Objectives:

A number of objectives should come under discussion by the students. The broad audit objectives regarding demand deposits, followed by the narrower objectives of confirmation procedures and testing procedures, could be discussed.

The objective of the audit of demand deposits should be that the bank's liability for demand deposits is reasonably stated. That objective might be viewed as having two subheadings: (1) Whether recorded deposits are valid and (2) whether there are unrecorded deposits.

As the auditor cannot place complete reliance on internal control with respect to material amounts in financial statements, even though, as in this case, internal control at All-American has been stated to be "strong" and "effective," some audit procedures will need to be applied to the material demand deposit account. The case tells that the auditor, for at least one procedure, will send confirmations, supposedly using some statistical method, once that method can be agreed upon.

Confirmation is a favorite audit procedure for receivables because it is fast and efficient. The students might discuss, by way of background, the objective of receivable confirmation procedures, a subject that has been debated by accountants for years. Some view the procedure as a validation that can be extrapolated to support the total account — a view that was universal many years ago. Others view the procedure as a compliance test of the auditor's understanding of the way internal controls work. And, a third group would see the procedure meeting both the validation and the compliance objective. Students maintaining the latter view might be asked to discuss how confirmation procedures can reasonably validate an account unless the amounts confirmed are sufficiently material in relation to the total that the margin for error in the remainder is immaterial or unless the sample confirmed is sufficiently representative to permit valid conclusions to be drawn about the total account.

The discussion of the objective of confirmation in relation to receivables, is valid for receivables. But, is it equally valid for "payables" — in this case demand deposits? Audit guides of financial institutions, such as banks and savings and loan associations, require confirmation of customer deposits. Thus, confirmations must be sent. But, can the objective be the same? Accountants have long debated whether confirmation of "payables" (such as trade accounts) is necessary or desirable. Those taking the position that confirmation is not necessary say that receivables originate from internally generated documents which require acceptance of the customer to validate their legal bona fides (but not their collectibility). On the other hand, the vendor generates the documents for a trade payable, and acceptance and recording by the purchaser validates the legal bona fides of the purchase (but not the ability to pay). The students should be aware of the anomaly. In both cases the controlling document is generated externally (be it invoice or deposit slip) and in both cases the document is accepted and recorded by the other party as a validation of the transaction; yet for vendor payables confirmation procedures are often considered unnecessary but are required for customer (creditor) deposits.

Supporters of confirmation procedures for payables (demand deposits) hold that such procedures will disclose unrecorded invoices (deposit slips), and that position may be supportable. But, because of the strong, effective external controls in effect by way of collection department activity by vendors (and by way of bank account reconciliation activity by depositors), the students might suggest that confirmation aimed at finding unrecorded invoices or deposit slips is necessary only in instances where the control system is not effective or where management deception is suspected. For if management deception is susspected, extraordinary and extended procedures, involving extensive confirmation, would be in order.

DLG 22-2

Statistical procedures:

The students may, by way of background, want to discuss the evolution of statistical methods in the audit process and their status today. The discussion should cover when to use and when not to use. They should recognize, further, that audit decisions should not rest entirely on data obtained from statistical procedures which are alternatives for different procedures that could produce equally reliable results. For one view on the limited role of statistical sampling in auditing the students might refer to *Montgomery's Auditing*, pages 146-149.

The students should discuss the merits of the two sampling methods proposed for All-American and why one method has greater appeal for audit satisfaction than the other. In general, sampling for variables gives direct information in dollar amounts about an account total; it provides confidence interval estimates of total population dollar amounts. On the other hand, sampling for attributes gives direct information about error rates but not the dollars involved; it can be used to estimate the probable occurrence rates of one of two possible specified characteristics in a population. The *Handbook of Accounting and Auditing*, Chapter 14, gives a detailed discussion of the two sampling methods.

The *Handbook* also discusses another approach, unit-dollar sampling, which tends to combine characteristics of both variables and attribute sampling and should result in an estimate of maximum dollar error amount. The method was not suggested by the audit staff at All-American, though its use is bound to have appeal to some students as best suited in the circumstances.

Should the results obtained from whatever statistical method is used differ from expectations, that method may be unusable in achieving the audit objectives. The students should discuss fall-back plans for use in case of unexpected results. In a similar vein, what to do in case confirmations disclosed errors or in case positive confirmations were not returned seems an essential part of the discussion.

Irrespective of the method of sampling chosen, some students should suggest that the auditor supplement the statistical work with positive confirmation of selected accounts with large dollar balances, dormant accounts, and accounts with zero balances.

The students should discuss the relationship of reliability to internal control and to expected errors. Though reliability levels specified may vary inversely with the subjective reliance assigned to internal control and to anticipated errors, a level of 70 percent may seem too high or too low to various students.

Materiality:

The word "materiality," or derivatives, is used constantly in accounting and auditing literature; yet, its meaning remains elusive. Some general guidance in relation to auditing is offered by the American Institute of Certified Public Accountants (AU 150.04):

> The concept of materiality is inherent in the work of the independent auditor. There should be stronger grounds to sustain the independent auditor's opinion with respect to these items which are relatively more important and with respect to those in which the possibilities of material error are greater than with respect to those of lesser importance or those in which the possibility of material error is remote. For example, in an enterprise with few, but large, accounts receivable, the accounts individually are more important and the possibility of material error is greater than in another enterprise that has a great number of small accounts aggregating the same total. In industrial and merchandising enterprises, inventories are usually

of great importance to both financial position and results of operations and accordingly may require relatively more attention by the auditor than would the inventories of a public utility company. Similarly, accounts receivable usually will receive more attention than prepaid insurance.

Specifically related to statistical sampling, Appendix A (AU 320.13) remains equally vague with this observation:

> The auditor's decision as to the monetary amount or frequency of errors that would be considered materal should be based on his judgment in the circumstances in the particular case. In addition to the statistical evaluation, the auditor should also consider the nature and cause of errors revealed by the sample and their possible relation to other phases of his examination.

The students should be encouraged to discuss materiality in relation to auditing issues in the case study, but after the discussion is exhausted, it is unlikely that a great deal more will have crystalized than what is said above to the effect that what is considered a material dollar misstatement or a material error rate depends on the judgment of the auditor and can in no way be determined mathematically. The discussion could touch on such matters as:

- preliminary estimates of materiality;
- the relationship of materiality and sample precision;
- quantitative materiality;
- the control of auditing costs in relation to providing reasonable assurance about the financial statements; and
- the inapplicability of normal audit materiality guidelines to irregularities involving management deceit or misrepresentation.

In this case, no errors are expected and the population being sampled is very large in relation to the commonly used materiality base — earnings. If materiality is based on earnings, precision will be so small relative to demand deposits that required sample size will be very large. This seems illogical because all evidence to date indicates everything is all right and the remaining audit work in this area should be restricted. The supervisor recognized this aspect, but in suggesting an attribute approach, may be overlooking the substantive aspects of the test to some extent.

Positive versus negative confirmations:

The students should discuss the value of each of the above types of confirmation, a subject that has been long debated by auditors. Neither camp has been able to develop conclusive empirical data to sustain its argument, though efforts continue. Both sides, however, would seem to agree that negatives should not be used if the auditor believes they generally will be ignored by the recipient and that, if used, the number sent would normally be greater than the number of positives that would be sent.

Current theory says that consumers can be expected to respond reasonably and rationally to negative confirmations, and the same may be true of depositors. If so, one could argue that negatives would be appropriate for this situation. There has been little research to indicate whether negatives or positives are more effective, and that conventional wisdom may be mistaken. In any event, the decision (to use positives or negatives) should not be based on the volume of transactions to be tested. If the nature of the test here is a test to confirm the auditor's understanding that there will be no errors in the system, it seems appropriate to go for the maximum assurance and use the positive confirmations. Some auditors believe negatives should not be used where errors are expected because of the inaccuracy of estimates of total error that may result because of failure to respond. Some other auditors believe positives should be used for large balances and negatives for small balances.

The Solution

The solution in this case was to use the attribute sampling approach, biased toward the high dollar accounts. Positive confirmations were to be used and the relatively low reliability level, in the area of 70 percent, was accepted because of our appraisal of the system and our experience in the prior years. Naturally, if our test for attributes indicated that there were errors in the system, our initial conclusion about the system's strengths would be invalidated, and we would have to determine the nature and cause of the errors and go on with additional substantive work to determine the amount of the potential error. But our experience with this account in the past justified our taking a compliance approach initially. Of course, the answer in the case is not completely correct. The fact is that the confirmation procedures were considered to have a joint objective — it is a compliance test and it is a substantive test. There was a search for major dollar balances, for zero balances, dormant accounts, and the like, and separate confirmation procedures were applied.

It should be clear to the students that the answer is simply one auditor's judgment, and other auditors will form other judgments. For example, in the case involved, some in the firm considered the use of unit-dollar sampling, biased toward large balances, to be preferable to the attributes approach.

Prior Period Adjustments

Following successive loss years, the management of Universal Gloom determined that a retrenchment was absolutely necessary. Accordingly, they drew up plans to discontinue certain models, to close one of the plants, and to purchase rather than produce various component parts. The planned retrenchment did not qualify for accounting as a discontinued operation of a segment of the business (APB Opinion No. 30). Curtailment itself was to be costly: management estimated that the plant closing would cost $1,500,000; recognizing the now obsolete inventory would cost an additional $500,000. But, management also was confident that future reduced operations could be profitable.

The financial statements for the year ended December 31, 1978, included a $2,000,000 provision for the curtailment costs, and the annual report included a detailed description of management's plans.

Following the presentation of the retrenchment plan at the annual stockholders' meeting in April, 1979, a proxy fight unexpectedly ensued. As a result, old management was replaced by a new management group that promised to "turn the business around" by expanding rather than contracting the business.

During the remainder of 1979, new management undid all of prior management's retrenchment plans and went on an aggressive campaign to find new profitable markets for all of their products, and with some success. Universal still lost $1,800,000 during 1979 but the last quarter was profitable and the backlog was at an all-time high.

The new treasurer calls to ask your advice about the previously provided reserve. He explains that the marketing V.P. would like to keep the reserve around, "just in case." The president, however, would simply like to eliminate the reserve currently, because the reversal would give Universal its first profitable year for some time. But the treasurer has been arguing that the reversal should be treated as a prior period adjustment, or even as correction of an error. He would like to see the $2,000,000 provision eliminated from the 1978 statements. He reasons that the change in management nullified old management's plans, and that change should also nullify old management's reserves.

HOW SHOULD UNIVERSAL GLOOM ACCOUNT FOR THE $2,000,000 RESERVE AT DECEMBER 31, 1979?

Case 23-1

DISCUSSION LEADER'S GUIDE

Prior Period Adjustments

Objectives of the Case

This case raises several fundamental questions:

1. Are the financial statements the reflection of management (which can change completely from year to year) or the company (which has a perpetual life of its own)?

2. Do financial statements reflect the results of a discrete period or do they reflect a continuum?

3. Is it more important to preserve the integrity of the prior years' presentations or the integrity of the current year's income measurement?

Specifically, the case asks the following questions: How should the traditional financial statement techniques be used to report what has really happened to Universal Gloom? And, if traditional techniques seem inadequate, should an alternative be followed?

The case also can be viewed by the students as a classic case of "rule book" accounting, where answers are derived based on the book rather than on an analysis of what may be preferable. The students may discuss the types of evidential matter necessary to sustain a position that the reserves are no longer needed. The case should promote an understanding of the evolution of the concept of prior period adjustments and the fact that the FASB has virtually eliminated them except for specified corrections of errors and for retroactive adjustments. Further, the case should promote an understanding of what constitutes a correction of an error, an extraordinary item, and an unusual item which is not extraordinary.

The diverse points of view of management individuals regarding the reserve should lead to a discussion that touches on the motivations of each officer, and the students should be encouraged to explore their own motivations in formulating their answer.

Applicable Professional Pronouncements

Accounting Principles Board Opinion No. 20, "Accounting Changes," paragraphs 36-37

Accounting Principles Board Opinion No. 30, "Reporting the Results of Operations," paragraphs 19-26

Statement of Financial Accounting Standards No. 16, "Prior Period Adjustments"

Business Assumptions and Other Data

Many financial analysts feel that a current-operating-performance concept of income measurement provides a most useful bit of information for prediction of future stock prices. In years past, pursuit of the current operating concept seemed to occasion all kinds of prior period adjustments, which invariably were debit, or charge, adjustments. For some reason, always supportable in one fashion or another, most credit adjustments were not considered prior period adjustments at all, but rather current period income. The abuses of prior period adjustments, whether real or imagined, were of concern to the profession and presumably of greater concern to the SEC. Since the early 1950s, it has been advocating a "clean surplus account."

The abuses diminished after Accounting Principles Board Opinion No. 9 appeared in 1966, and there has been a gradual elimination of current operating performance as a generally accepted method of income statement presentation. The operating performance concept received a further setback upon issuance of Statement of Financial Accounting Standards No. 16 in 1977, largely at the instigation of the SEC. These pronouncements continue to cause dissatisfaction among certain users of financial statements and ultimately may result in further revisions of the rules regarding extraordinary items and prior period adjustments, particularly when the focus is swinging toward predictive reporting. At present, there is no accounting standard regarding matters presented in this case that adequately serves all valid user interests. The "clean surplus" interests are presently served, but less so the users who want to understand one year's operating results in relation to other years and in relation to prospects for future years.

The case study gives little in the way of facts to support the position that the reserve is no longer necessary. The change of plans regarding retrenchment and one profitable quarter followed by a record backlog of orders, while encouraging, may not be sufficiently strong evidence that indeed the reserve is needed no longer. What is the economic reality? Whether reversal of the reserve is appropriate is part of the case study, and it is probably the most difficult issue to resolve. Those discussing the case may come to the conclusion that the reserve should be retained in the accounts until some future operating results show that it is no longer needed. The facts cited are not convincing one way or the other. However, the discussion assumes that the correct conclusion is to reverse the reserve and that the management and the auditors have produced or seen documentation to support that conclusion.

Discussion

It appears that Universal became a completely new company in 1979, with totally new management and new plans. However, under current accounting rules, the advent of new management does not constitute justification for a new accountability. If new management had bought Universal Gloom, the company would have gotten a "fresh start" and its assets and liabilities possibly could have been stated at fair value, using concepts followed for business combinations accounted for as a purchase, and the reserve would have disappeared. (Controversy continues within the profession and elsewhere as to whether purchase-type accounting, often referred to as "push-down" accounting, can be applied in the separate financial statements of an acquired company. Nevertheless, "push-down" accounting has been used on a number of occasions.) But, no purchase was involved; that concept won't soon extend to those situations where the corporate share ownership continues unchanged. Though we might like to do so, we have not yet been able to say new management has "in effect" or "in substance" purchased the business and new accountabilities are required. Had such accounting been appropriate, it would have resolved the reserve issue.

DLG 23-2

Case 23: Prior Period Adjustments

The mixed motivations of the various parties involved (not uncommon) are of interest. One's motivations should not dictate the choice of accounting methods; yet, in practice, they often are found to be persuasive or influential. The vice president seems to want a "nest egg" that he can use in the future when earnings may not be up to par (the "hidden reserve" ploy, akin to the "new broom" ploy); the president seems bent on showing a profit in his first year at the helm; and the treasurer seems to be striving for objectivity in the current year's income, as he perceives objectivity, by keeping the extraneous $2,000,000 credit out of 1979 operating results. The case gives no clue as to the motivations of the auditor; yet, such motivations exist. A typical auditor will rebel against any position that gives a company a profitable year with an accidental bookkeeping entry. And, in the same way, a typical auditor will not want a "hidden reserve" to remain on the books, lest it lead back into future income statements to obscure unprofitable operations.

Because Statement on Financial Accounting Standards No. 16 effectively rules out the possibility of a prior period adjustment, except for correction of an error, four possible alternatives exist within the framework of generally accepted accounting principles. These are:

1. Correction of an error requiring prior period adjustment, restating the comparative 1978 financials, as discussed in paragraphs 13 and 36 of Accounting Principles Board Opinion No. 20.

2. Presentation as an extraordinary item in the 1979 financials, as discussed in paragraph 20 of Accounting Principles Board Opinion No. 30.

3. Presentation as a 1979 income item but disclosed as a separate component of income from continuing operations, as discussed in paragraph 26 of Accounting Principles Board Statement No. 30, relating to unusual or infrequently occurring items.

4. Presentation as a current income item in the 1979 statements resulting from a change in accounting estimate, as discussed in paragraphs 10, 11, 31, and 33 of Accounting Principles Board Opinion No. 20.

The reversal of the reserve would qualify as a correction of an error, and thus as a prior period adjustment, only if the reserve resulted from any of the following:

a. a computation error;

b. a mistake in the application of accounting principles;

c. an oversight or misuse of facts.

The establishment of the reserve may have been a management error, but given these three criteria as a definition, it cannot be considered to be an accounting error. Therefore, accounting for the reversal of the reserve as a correction of an error requiring prior period adjustment is inappropriate.

Since it has been determined that the reversal cannot affect 1978 statements, it must be a current year (1979) item. Because the item is unusual and has not been a continuing occurrence for the company, the question of accounting for the reversal as an extraordinary item should be considered. However, since a plant closing and inventory write-downs are not abnormal to a manufacturing business, the establishment of the reserve in 1978 was not an extraordinary item. Likewise, the reversal of the reserve in 1979 does not seem to meet the criteria for an extraordinary item, as upward and downward adjustments of reserves are commonplace.

The accounting choice would thus seem to reside between that of an "unusual or infrequently occurring item" (APB Opinion No. 30) or a "change in accounting estimate" (APB Opinion No. 20). The accounting result of either choice is the same; that is, a credit to 1979 income. However, if the choice is that Accounting Principles Board Opinion No. 30 applies, disclosure must be made of the facts on the income statement or in notes to the financial statements. If Accounting Principles Board Opinion No. 20 is considered applicable, no disclosure requirement exists, although disclosure is recommended if the effect of the change in estimate is material. In the latter case, the president, if he so chooses, could refuse to disclose the reversal of the reserve and remain in compliance with generally accepted accounting principles; a recommendation in an Opinion is just what it says. Arguments can be made to sustain either position; yet the ultimate selection will be of no importance if the company proposes to make full disclosure under any circumstances.

The accounting treatment in either case increases 1979 income by $2,000,000. The auditor should insist on thorough disclosure in the footnotes, should the company object to disclosure. Further, a recommendation to set out the provision and the reversal as a single line item in the 1978 and 1979 comparative income statements would be appropriate.

Even with disclosure, this technically correct answer is not totally satisfactory. The treasurer seems to have the correct answer — get the $2,000,000 credit out of 1979. But, the "rule book" does not allow for such an answer. Users of financial statements typically think of "net income" as operating income. The bottom line figure on the 1979 income statement (and the earnings per share figure) benefits from a significant nonoperating credit.

If management and the auditor conclude that, because of unusual circumstances, the inclusion of the $2,000,000 reversal of reserve in current 1979 income makes that year's income statement misleading, they could depart from GAAP and report the reserve reversal in a manner considered not misleading. What constitutes "unusual circumstances" is a matter of judgment and involves the ability to support the position that adherence to a promulgated principle would be regarded by reasonable people as producing a misleading result. In this case study, the judgment call could be considered close by many practitioners and their clients. If the decision is to depart from GAAP, the auditor's report would need to describe the departure, the approximate effects, and the reasons why compliance with the promulgated principle would result in a misleading statement. It is fair to state that most auditing firms and most client companies are quite reluctant to depart from GAAP and report with a so-called "Rule 203 Opinion."

The Solution

After considerable anguish — while looking for an alternative to the inevitable — the "rule book" answer was adopted, and the reversal of the reserve was included as a current period income item in the nature of a change in estimate. The so-called "Rule 203 Opinion" was not considered appropriate. The income statements for 1978 and 1979 should show the provision and the reversal in juxtaposition on the same line in the comparative financial statements, though we could not insist on it. Full disclosure of the reserve and its subsequent reversal, however, had to be made in the notes and in management's commentary.

DLG 23-4

Historical Cost Accounting

The President of East Coast Enterprises had been looking for a merger candidate that would give his company an entry into the lucrative California market. He was finally able to purchase the West Coast Corporation, an old, well-established company. East Coast paid a premium over book, although almost everyone was satisfied that the price was fair. East Coast's acquisition team reported that West Coast had used a relatively simple accounting system. Capitalization policies were very conservative; West Coast's financial statements understated the fair value of its assets. On the other hand, vacation pay had been expensed as paid and pension accruals were on the low side; they were based solely on the actuaries' computation of cash needed.

When the acquisition was consummated, East Coast's accounting people went through the West Coast balance sheet, item by item. They obtained appraisals on all of West Coast's tangible property and established values for various assets and liabilities in accordance with East Coast's accounting policies. They allocated East Coast's total purchase price over West Coast's individual assets and liabilities and produced a new opening balance sheet which effectively capitalized retained earnings and the premium paid over book value, on the theory that new West Coast represented a "fresh start." A summary of the balance sheet data for old West Coast (Column A) and new West Coast (Column B) is shown in the attachment.

Because West Coast still has bonds outstanding in public hands, separate financial statements of West Coast will be required. You meet with the controllers of East Coast and West Coast to discuss the preparation of those separate financials, and it is apparent that you have stepped into a buzz saw. The East Coast financial people have assumed that West Coast's financial statements would be prepared on the parent's cost basis, using the same asset and liability numbers as will be used when West Coast is consolidated with East Coast. However, the West Coast financial people believe that the West Coast financial statements should be presented using West Coast's original costs. They argue that, legally, West Coast is no different now than it ever was and that East Coast's costs and West Coast's costs are entirely different. You are a bit surprised, though not displeased, when your manager on the engagement speaks up amidst the hassle, adding a third view. He says, "Why not let the goodwill show only in consolidation and leave the retained earnings showing in the separate statements of West Coast but adjust assets and liabilities to East Coast's costs?" (Column C). East Coast's controller turns to you and says, "You'll have to issue an audit report on West Coast's separate statements. Which numbers present West's balance sheet in accordance with generally accepted accounting principles?"

**WHICH ALTERNATIVE FAIRLY PRESENTS WEST COAST —
IN ACCORDANCE WITH GENERALLY ACCEPTED
ACCOUNTING PRINCIPLES?**

Historical Cost Accounting

Financial Data Attachment

($000 omitted)

	(A) Old West	(B) New West	(C) New West
Current Assets	$ 40,000	$ 40,000	$ 40,000
Property, Plant & Equipment	100,000	150,000	150,000
Intangibles	15,000	—	—
Goodwill	—	10,000	—
	$155,000	$200,000	$190,000
Current Liabilities	$ 20,000	$ 30,000	$ 30,000
Pension Liabilities	—	10,000	10,000
Long-term Debt	80,000	80,000	80,000
Stockholders' Equity			
Common Stock	25,000	25,000	25,000
Retained Earnings	30,000	—	30,000
Additional Capital (comprising the portion of premium over book value paid by parent related to the company's tangible assets)	—	—	15,000
Additional Capital (comprising capitalized retained earnings and premium over book value paid by parent company)	—	55,000	—
	$155,000	$200,000	$190,000

(A) Historical cost basis

(B) Goodwill recorded by the acquired company; retained earnings not carried forward

(C) Goodwill not recorded; retained earnings carried forward

DISCUSSION LEADER'S GUIDE

Historical Cost Accounting

Objectives of the Case

In its most general sense, the case should raise the question of whether the entity concept of accounting is applicable for the life of the entity. Can events during an entity's lifetime destroy that concept in favor of others? The case should bring into focus a discussion of the business purposes served by financial statements of an acquired company and the needs of the various users of such statements.

This case demonstrates some of the many problems that develop in accounting for business combinations, and it should develop an understanding of the principles of purchase accounting as they relate to business combinations, namely, revaluation of assets and liabilities of the acquired entity to fair market values at the date of acquisition, and allocation to a goodwill account of the excess of the purchase price paid over the fair market value of the net assets acquired. Also, the discussion should demonstrate the unsettled state of the art in situations such as described, and should show that financial statements of components of a business enterprise prepared on a current value basis are in limited use. Further, it raises the question of whether simultaneous presentation of financial statements of the same entity on more than one measurement basis constitutes fair reporting and whether both presentations may be said to conform to generally accepted accounting principles.

Separate financial statements for West Coast are required in order to provide bondholders with information concerning their investment. The specific question is: Should West Coast's statements be based on historical costs as presented in previous financial statements issued prior to acquisition, or should the financial statements be based on the purchase price paid by East Coast, or on some other basis?

Applicable Professional Pronouncements

Accounting Principles Board Opinion No. 16, "Business Combinations," paragraphs 66-96

Financial Accounting Standards Board Discussion Memorandum, "Business Combinations and Purchased Intangibles," paragraphs 399-408

Burton, Palmer, Kay, *Handbook of Accounting and Auditing*, page 30-26

Defliese, Johnson, MacLeod, *Montgomery's Auditing*, Ninth Edition, pages 692, 696

Business Assumptions and Other Data

There are no authoritative professional pronouncements which deal directly with reporting on the separate financial statements of an acquired component as illustrated by this case study. Accounting Principles Board Opinion No. 16 is silent about whether a new accounting basis used for an acquired company's assets and liabilities recognized in a combined enterprise's financial statements should also be used for those assets and liabilities in separate financial statements of the acquired company. The *Handbook of Accounting and Auditing* and *Montgomery's Auditing* discuss the matter and point out the unsettled state of the art, as does a 1976 FASB Discussion Memorandum that presents arguments for both sides.

For a number of reasons (e.g., the existence of common or preferred minority interests or financial arrangements with others), an acquired company may need to issue separate financial statements at the time of, or subsequent to, a combination. In this case, the need for separate audited financial statements of West Coast derives from the public ownership of its bonds. Presumably, the need for separate statements would disappear if the bonds were retired, unless other outside interests, such as trade creditors, bankers, customers, or the like, have sufficient influence to compel continued issuance.

When preparing separate statements, management should have in mind the needs of the users — including users of concern. However, even if the managements of both companies were clairvoyant, they probably could not conceive of the alternative accounting best suited to the needs of the various users. The case is essentially silent as to why East Coast and West Coast maintain their positions on what is the appropriate accounting. The case is also silent as to whether the use of parent cost basis would be acceptable to the bondholders for purposes of testing compliance with the debt instrument. Typically, the debt instrument requires compliance within the framework of generally accepted accounting principles. And that gets back to the question of what is generally accepted in such situations.

Were the bondholders to accept any method so long as the auditor opined that the method conformed to GAAP, this case dramatizes the impact of one method versus another method where, as in this case, the bond indenture contained a number of restrictive covenants. For example, use of parent cost would result in up to $50,000,000 additional depreciation over time and thus reduce earnings by a corresponding amount, while at the same time reducing earnings available for dividends to the parent under a restrictive debt covenant. Or, were historical costs of the acquired company used, it would have $25,000,000 less cushion in complying with restrictive covenants based on stockholders' equity.

A number of complex tax considerations are usually inherent in acquisitions such as this and in subsequent reporting of operations. They are not discussed here because tax accounting is not the issue of the case study.

Both companies have shares registered with the Securities and Exchange Commission, so they and their auditors certainly should preclear the accounting treatment adopted, particularly in view of the indecisiveness of the Securities and Exchange Commission and the Financial Accounting Standards Board and of the mixed views within the profession.

Regulatory accounting deserves mention: in certain regulated industries, for example the savings and loan industry, recording any goodwill in a purchase transaction as described would probably be prohibited. Following the regulatory requirements would present a dilemma to any auditor who insists that generally accepted accounting principles require the use of parent cost in reporting on an acquired subsidiary. The auditor may be trapped and may have to take exception in the report because of the regulatory accounting followed.

DLG 24-2

Discussion

The students should spend some time discussing some of the anomalies in the entity and proprietary concepts present in today's practice. The word "entity" should focus the students on the two most frequently discussed concepts, the accounting (or reporting) entity and the legal entity; one may differ from the other in various respects. What we should be most interested in here is the accounting (reporting) entity. A legal entity typically is bound by close definition. An accounting or reporting entity tends to be more flexible, a fact that is duly recognized in Accounting Principles Board Opinion No. 20, Accounting Changes, which covers the subject of reporting a change in the entity.

The students also should discuss the conceptual differences in the proprietary theory and the entity theory. Consolidated statements in the present state of the art do not portray a legal entity; some would say they do, but indeed they portray an accounting or reporting entity (though subject to change in certain circumstances). Others would disagree, where minority interests are shown, and would contend a proprietary entity is portrayed — that is, the consolidation is from the viewpoint of the parent's shareholders alone, excluding the equity of shareholders of the subsidiaries.

If we assume the proprietary concept is valid — that, indeed, what is reported on stems from proprietary interests within the entity rather than the entity itself — the door is open to consideration of the main issue in this case; that is, are we dealing with a consolidation of entity interests or a consolidation of proprietary interests? And, if the latter, does a change in proprietorship establish new accountabilities?

This area is addressed in the AICPA's *Technical Practice Aids* (which provide nonauthoritative examples and commentaries on accounting issues), in the following reply to an inquiry regarding the proper accounting basis for properties of an acquired company in separate financial statements:

> Paragraph 17 of Accounting Principles Board Opinion No. 6 states, 'The Board is of the opinion that property, plant and equipment should not be written up by an entity to reflect appraisal, market, or current values which are above cost to the entity.' This statement is not intended to change accounting practice followed in connection with quasi-reorganizations or reorganizations. The acquisition of a company by another company would not by itself constitute a 'reorganization.' It would not be proper to restate the assets in the financial statements of the acquired corporation.
>
> If there was any likelihood that financial statements based on cost to the acquired company and financial statements of the same operation based on cost to the parent company were being prepared for distribution to others (and if an auditor's opinion is expressed, such distribution should be assumed), it would appear necessary to footnote one of the financial statements to indicate that other statements were being prepared on a different basis. It would be more appropriate to prepare such a footnote for the financial statements of the acquired company.

Assuming the students accept the above nonauthoritative answer as the appropriate one, would their position be the same if the assets and liabilities were transferred to another company, Subsidiary X, formed for the purpose of acquiring West Coast? In substance nothing has happened. The proprietary interests are the same in either subsidiary; only the legal entity has changed from West Coast to Subsidiary X. Yet, the students might be expected to favor new valuations in Subsidiary X and accounting convention would require such new valuations. The old valuations could not be carried through. So their discussion should center on why the accounting method chosen for West Coast should acknowledge the "paper" form of a subsidiary and not its substantive form.

Below are comments taken from the 1976 Financial Accounting Standards Board Discussion Memorandum. In support of retaining historical cost as long as the legal entity remains, some have contended that, in connection with a combination in which a new accounting basis is recognized in the combined enterprise's financial statements, any separate financial statements of an acquired company should retain the existing accounting basis. Their primary reason is that the acquisition of a company represents a change in its ownership but does not establish a new accounting basis in its financial statements under the historical cost accounting framework. The reporting entity did not acquire any assets or assume any liabilities as a result of the combination. According to this view, recognition of a new accounting basis based on a change in ownership, rather than on a transaction on the part of the company, is undesirable. Further, the acquired company may have entered into credit or other agreements with others, with terms related to financial statements or other financial data prepared on the existing accounting basis. Restatement of the financial statements to recognize a new accounting basis could create problems in determining or maintaining compliance with various financial restrictions under those agreements or in calculating amounts that are based on income before income taxes, net income, or other financial data. Also, restatement could cause difficulties in comparing that company's financial data with those for prior periods, though restatement of the company's financial statements of prior periods to give retroactive effect to the new accounting basis could help provide comparable data.

The same Discussion Memorandum also says some have contended that where a new accounting basis is determined to be appropriate in the combined enterprise's financial statements, any separate financial statements of an acquired company should also recognize that new accounting basis. Their primary reason is that such financial statements would provide information that is more relevant to users in making investment and credit decisions. According to them, as part of an exchange transaction — the combination — the acquired company's aggregate cost has been established and current values have been estimated for its assets and liabilities. Presentation of the assets and liabilities based on the resulting new accounting basis, rather than on their carrying amounts prior to the combination, enables financial statement users to estimate better the acquired company's future cash flows.

Also, an acquired company's financial statements that recognize the new accounting basis would be prepared on a consistent basis with the combined enterprise's financial statements. If the acquired company's financial statements were to retain the existing accounting basis, readers might be confused by the different accounting bases used in the two sets of statements. Some have indicated that recognition of a new accounting basis in the acquired company's financial statements would give rise to nominal, if any, incremental costs and may even provide a cost savings because the combined enterprise's financial statements, which include the acquired company, would be prepared on the new accounting basis in any event.

The controversy has not been resolved in the years since 1976. The Accounting Standards Executive Committee prepared an Issues Paper on the subject, but the Financial Accounting Standards Board did not take it under consideration. Earlier, in 1973, the SEC tentatively considered adopting rules for SEC-reporting companies, but the rules were never adopted.

Case 24: Historical Cost Accounting 155

Aside from the general arguments identified by the Financial Accounting Standards Board in its Discussion Memorandum, some further specific arguments are noted, first, as to those favoring retention of West Coast's old historical costs:

1. Fair value accounting is the ultimate answer to many accounting problems but it is not yet accepted. At present, generally accepted accounting principles are based on cost. To depart from West Coast's historical costs and use the values as allocated by East Coast is tantamount to booking appraisal values.

2. West Coast is a legal entity and its reported capital should not be affected by who owns it. The legal entity has capital stock and paid-in capital based on transactions between the company and its owners. Legal capital structure should not be changed by transactions among shareholders.

3. The price paid by East Coast is not cost to West Coast. The price simply represents East Coast's estimate of the potential earning power of East Coast and West Coast combined. The values in excess of West Coast's original net worth are East Coast's assets and should not be included with those of West Coast.

4. In defense of the old historical cost, some would argue that publicly traded companies change their stockholding makeup significantly during any one year. And yet, the values reflected by those stock market transactions are not integrated into the entity's basic financial statements.

5. The purpose of the separate financial statements on West Coast will be directed to a legal audience, the bondholders. Insofar as the bondholders are concerned, their rights have not changed and, therefore, it could be argued that the basis of the financial statements reported to them should not change.

As to those favoring a new accounting basis (often referred to as "push-down" accounting, complete or partial), some further arguments are:

1. If East Coast had purchased the net assets of West Coast, the assets would be stated at East Coast's acquisition price. Accounting Principles Board Opinion No. 16, paragraph 21, says that whenever there is a purchase, the acquirer should record the economic substance of the transaction, to wit:

    a. "The bargained costs of assets acquired less liabilities assumed, not the costs to the previous owner."

    b. "Expenses and net income after an acquisition computed on the bargained cost of acquired assets, not on the cost to the previous owner."

It is emphasis of form over substance to preserve historical costs simply because the legal shell continues to exist.

2. There should not be two sets of financial statements for a company, both of which "present fairly." It is illogical to have one set of financial statements which present fairly the separate operations and balance sheet of West Coast based on historical costs and one set of financial statements which present fairly the operations of West coast in combina-

tion with its parent, based on the parent's cost. And, in consolidation, no alternatives exist; parent cost must be used.

3. There may be a continuing legal entity known as West Coast, but when East Coast acquired the West Coast stock, the substance of West Coast disappeared, and a new economic reality was created. It clearly will be a different company as a part of the East Coast empire. No matter what basis is used for presenting the West Coast financial statements, the operations of West Coast after the acquisition will not be comparable with preacquisition operations. It would be misleading to include "old" West Coast and "new" West Coast in a five-year summary of earnings.

4. The nearest thing to a professional pronouncement on this issue is Accounting Principles Board Opinion No. 16 regarding accounting by the acquiring company (not the acquired company). The accounting procedures proposed by East Coast follow the provisions of Opinion No. 16 quite literally. The resulting proposed balance sheet would be appropriate for consolidation.

Auditing firms are split on the accounting to follow, with perhaps the larger number favoring continuance of historical cost in the separate financial statements of an acquired company. The use of historical cost has even greater support where a sizable minority-interest ownership remains in the acquired company. For example, no firm is known to be advocating a new accounting basis where only 51 percent of a component company was acquired.

On the assumption that a new accounting basis would be adopted, the students should discuss (a) whether retained earnings reported should include only earnings subsequent to acquisition, (b) the percentage ownership by the parent that would sustain the adjustment of asset and liability valuations, and (c) disclosures that should be provided in the separate financial statements as a consequence of the acquisition. If the new accounting basis is not adopted, the disclosure questions would still be present.

The two reference books noted above both seem to favor "push-down" accounting. However, neither takes a position on what to do with retained earnings of the acquired company at the date acquired. If one views the acquisition as a "fresh start," much as in a quasi-reorganization or reorganization, then, presumably, retained earnings would be closed out and become a part of additional capital. Or, if Subsidiary X were used in the acquisition, as discussed above, such retained earnings would disappear. Further, in favor of elimination, any retained earnings added in the future would be of a different character because of the new valuations in use. Those in favor of carrying such retained earnings forward could say that such earnings have some legal basis, that they are indicative of amounts that may be available for dividends, and that they show what earnings the company has accumulated over its corporate history.

In the present case, East Coast acquired 100 percent of West Coast so the question of minimum percentages never arose in the consideration of whether to use "push-down" accounting. Not all acquisitions are at 100 percent, and the students' discussion of where the break-off point should fall should be interesting. As noted above, no strong support seems to exist at the 51 percent level, at least not since the Securities and Exchange Commission withdrew its proposed rule generally requiring revaluation when 50 percent or more stock was acquired. But somewhere between 51 and 100 percent may lie a sensible breakpoint. *Montgomery's Auditing* states a preference for limiting the "push-down" to

100 percent acquisitions, or nearly so, such as 90 percent acquisitions, following somewhat the 90 percent pooling theory.

Also, not present in this case is any minority interest in the common or preferred stock of West Coast. Had there been any, the confusion as to what to do would be heightened still further, and a "what if" question on the subject could be posed to the students. They almost certainly will have differing views, and there is surely no authoritative literature to run to for an easy answer. The *Handbook of Accounting and Auditing* has this to say about the interesting problem facing those accountants supporting the "push-down" approach when the acquired subsidiary is not wholly owned:

> ... Because the parent company obviously didn't purchase it, the minority interest must be maintained on its previous historical cost basis. The minority shareholders do not share in the additional capital resulting from the restatement, nor do they share in the depreciation, amortization, or any other charges or credits based on the differences between restated amounts and historical cost. As a result, when the purchase cost is to be allocated to the net assets of the subsidiary, a question arises whether to allocate only a percentage of the fair value increment or decrement based on the parent's ownership percentage or to allocate 100 percent of it. Obviously, the allocation of 100 percent could result in a total fair value assignment in excess of the purchase price, since the parent acquired less than 100 percent ownership of the subsidiary . . . .

The Handbook goes on to say that the allocation should be done on a proportional basis, and in theory there are many variations possible where a minority interest remains. It says further that there are relatively few "push-down" examples available, and none with a large-majority interest percentage. On the other hand, *Montgomery's Auditing* would seem to suggest that the minority interest must also reflect the changed values.

An additional consideration the students should discuss is the treatment of goodwill in the separate financial statements. If the financial statements for West Coast are based on the price paid by East Coast, $10,000,000 of goodwill is created. Should the goodwill be included in the West Coast financial statements (Column B) or should it be included only in the consolidated financial statements of the parent and the acquired company (Column C)? Some professionals consider restricting goodwill to the consolidated statements somewhat on the basis that only purchased goodwill should appear on a balance sheet, and in this case West Coast did not purchase the resultant goodwill. These accountants would distinguish between revaluing existing assets and creating, as it were, a new asset. Accountants favoring inclusion of goodwill on the balance sheet of an acquired company believe that to be a natural consequence of substituting parent cost in the acquired subsidiaries' balance sheet.

The Solution

The profession has tried several times to deal with the questions posed by this case, but each time has backed away. The students will recognize that there can be no one answer and that GAAP, as the case shows, must be extrapolated from close analogies or judgment. And, as noted, auditors disagree among themselves as to the appropriate accounting. In the present case it was decided that the separate financial statements of West Coast should be based on the purchase price paid by East Coast (Column B).

GAAP lacks a definitive solution for the fact situation illustrated by the case, and other approaches probably would be acceptable to many auditors. Some auditors would insist on continuance of historical cost in the absence of authoritative pronouncements directing otherwise. Whatever basis is used, full disclosure should be made of cost and earnings differences if one basis is used for consolidation while a different basis is used for the separate financial statements of the acquired company.

Case 25: Letter of Representations

Letter of Representations

As partner in charge of the office, you have been consulted and asked to recommend a course of action in an unusual client situation. Here, briefly, are the facts you have obtained after interviewing the engagement partner, controller (chief accounting officer), and executive vice president (chief financial officer) of the company involved, Mighty Magic Widget Makers, an American Stock Exchange company:

- The controller has refused to sign the letter of representations.
- Because he believes the controller's knowledge of corporate activities is so important, the engagement partner intends to take a scope qualification in his report, citing the controller's refusal to sign the representations letter.
- The oil shortage is beginning to raise the cost of electric power, and there is even concern about possible brownouts.
- The controller is concerned about the effect of a possible power shortage on the sales of the company's main product, Mighty Widget Home Air Conditioners. He believes a larger inventory valuation allowance (an additional 10 percent) should be provided. By any measure, this is material.
- Other members of the company disagree. Significantly, the chief executive and chief financial officers reason that the oil shortage may keep people at home more, enhancing the salability of the Mighty Widget Home Air Conditioner. In fact, they believe that the inventory valuation allowances, if anything, are excessive this year.
- The engagement audit team believes that the valuation reserve is adequate.

Both your technical expertise and your skills with difficult clients are well known.

HOW WILL YOU ADVISE THE AUDIT PARTNER?

DISCUSSION LEADER'S GUIDE

Letters of Representation

Objectives of the Case

The objectives of the case are to promote the students' thinking on (1) the purpose and importance of clients' letters of representation, (2) the reliance auditors can place on them, and (3) the significance of differing views among client management as to the fairness of financial statements. Specifically, the case asks how best to resolve the issue presented by refusal of a management person to sign a company's letter of representation to its auditor. A broader objective is to illustrate the need for an auditor to do something when furnished with information, oral or otherwise, that the financial statements may be materially misleading — whether that information comes from a signatory to a letter of representations or from someone else. The case could also focus on who should have to sign a letter of representations.

Applicable Professional Pronouncements

Statement on Auditing Standards No. 19, "Client Representations"

Montgomery's Auditing, Ninth Edition, page 335 (nonauthoritative)

Business Assumptions and Other Data

Disagreements between members of a management team are commonplace. Corporate "infighting" at times seems to be the norm rather than the exception. However differences between management team views as to the reliability of the financial statements, as illustrated by this case, are not now commonplace. By the time the financials are ready to be issued and the letter of representations signed, differences regarding carrying amounts of assets and liabilities are usually resolved, or, as may happen in more cases than known, simply "swept under the rug" as an expedient or for some other reason. If the required representations are not obtained, Statement on Auditing Standards No. 19 is quite clear in requiring a qualified opinion, but that is the kind of opinion not likely to appear in practice.

The students might try drafting a qualified opinion covering the circumstances in this case. But, that draft is likely to be so ludicrous as to be unissuable. In one way or another the uncertainty should be resolved. Limited search for such a qualified opinion disclosed only one instance where a disagreement between members of management reached the reporting stage — and that was one more than was expected. In that case, the management team could not agree on the carrying value of certain assets. The accounting firm, one of the large ones, gave an initial report explaining the circumstances and categorically deny-

Case 25: Letter of Representations 161

ing any opinion until such time as management decided what the company's financial statements were to look like.

The company involved was an SEC reporting company. Thus, the disclaimer of opinion may have been no more than a ruse to force agreement among management people on the asset valuations; for a certainty, the Commission would not accept the disclaimed opinion in any 1933 Act filing and most likely would find it unacceptable in any 1934 Act filing.

In contrast, many members of management teams sign representation letters without giving them the least attention. How often perfunctory signatures are obtained by auditors is not known; in all probability the occurrences are extensive — and certainly more extensive than the auditors would prefer. An attitude exists in some companies that if this is what the auditors want, give it to them. Countless examples can be seen in practice to lead to a conclusion that management did not take the letter seriously. For example, the management group of a savings and loan association signed a letter that contained, in error of course, a representation that the association had made provision "for any material loss to be sustained as a result of purchase commitments for inventory quantities in excess of normal requirements or at prices in excess of prevailing market prices."

Statement on Auditing Standards No. 19 does not require controllers to sign letters of representation; it does suggest that normally the chief executive and the chief financial officer should sign the representations. The students need to know that, in this case, the auditors' firm policy, rather than professional literature, requires the controller to sign the representations. Such a policy requirement may exceed, but does not seem to exceed, professional requirements that state the representations "should be signed by members of management whom the auditor believes are responsible for and knowledgeable, directly or through others in the organization, about the matters covered by the representations." That professional pronouncement would seem sufficiently broad to let the auditor pick and choose the signatories on the basis of the auditor's perception of who is responsible and knowledgeable.

The case does not give the nature of the impairment causing the controller's concern for additional valuation allowances; nor does it give those data for allowances already on the books (believed excessive by the chief executive and chief financial officers). The students may assume that in each case the allowances proposed or recorded relate to impairment through change in price levels. In the case of the allowances booked, the change in price level was related to one specific model with less efficient output. In the case of the proposed additional allowances, the change in price level anticipated was generally "across the board," involving over 60 percent of the models.

Discussion

Any number of different views are observed as to the purpose of a letter of representations, and probably most can be considered appropriate. To understand how this case should be resolved, the students should have in mind the purpose of clients' representations. Some of the comments from Statement on Auditing Standards No. 19 that are pertinent to identification of the purpose are:

Written representations from management ordinarily confirm oral representations given to the auditor, indicate and document the continuing appropriateness of such representations, and reduce the possibility of misunderstanding concerning the matters that are subjects of the representations.

The auditor obtains written representations from management relating to its knowledge or intent when he believes they are necessary to complement his other auditing procedures. In many cases, the auditor applies auditing procedures specifically designed to obtain corroborating information concerning matters that are also the subject of written representations . . . the auditor should obtain a written representation to provide confirmation of management's intent. Unless the auditor's examination reveals evidential matter to the contrary, his reliance on the truthfulness of management's representations is reasonable.

Other comments from other sources say, for example, that the purposes of the letter are to impress upon management its responsibility for the financial statements, to show that the auditor has made proper inquiry of company officials as to various matters not otherwise determinable, or to document responses to inquiries directed by the auditor to the client.

Part of the "confusion" about the purpose of the letter of representations stems from the breadth of the matters covered, their lack of homogeneity and their varying degrees of audit corroboration and audit interest. Some matters relate to "intent," which is almost impossible to corroborate in an audit sense. Examples would be intent not to repatriate foreign earnings; intent to close down a product line or a business segment; or intent to refinance short-term debt as long-term. Some relate to physical presence or bulk and can seldom be corroborated in an audit sense. Examples would be availability of all books and records to the auditor; availability of all the board minutes and their completeness; or absence of communications from regulatory agencies. Some relate to accounts that have been extensively audited. Examples would be proper recording of material transactions or provision to reduce excess or obsolete inventories to net realizable value. And a great number falls somewhere between the extremes above, such that the extent of audit corroboration necessary is uncertain and, in practice, varied. Thus, the students should perceive that the purpose of the letter is manifold because of the characteristics attached to items covered. As to the air conditioner inventory, they should view the primary purpose as that necessary to complement the other auditing procedures, and the secondary purpose as being to confirm management's intent not to discount sales prices to amounts below cost.

The students should discuss the extent of reliance auditors can place on management representations. The extent of reliance is subject to the same homogeneity fact pattern as above. In some cases, reliance is essentially absolute, as in representations of management's intention. In other cases, the audit work is paramount, with the letter of representations serving as little more than "in-house" confirmation, as in representations regarding reduction of excess or obsolete inventories to net realizable value. And in a great number of cases, the extent of reliance is uncertain and varied.

The Securities and Exchange Commission takes the position that auditors should not rely on management representations but should corroborate them through auditing procedures. And auditing literature generally accords with that position. So the enigma the students should recognize is that auditors are told they should not rely on management representations or that such representations are not a substitute for the application of necessary auditing procedures; but the facts are that, in varying degrees, dependent on the

Case 25: Letter of Representations

subject matter, the auditor must rely on such representations because there exist no corroborating procedures, or only limited corroborating procedures.

While the students should understand this enigma, it is hardly present in the Mighty Magic case, because significant auditing procedures can be applied. The principal missing ingredient, that generally can be reached only by representation, is whether management intends to mark down its air conditioners to sell at below cost. Here the letter of representations is critically important — and unless the auditor's examination "reveals evidential matter to the contrary, his reliance on the truthfulness of management's representations is reasonable."

With regard to the inventory allowance question, the auditor should be satisfied that the products in inventory are moving satisfactorily in the post-balance-sheet period. And to that extent, any representation by management is simply corroborative. However, the auditor cannot know what management intends to do with its product prices or with its marketing programs and so must rely on the representations of management as to its intent to move the merchandise in inventory at a price that will recover the cost. That is an important theoretical distinction which the class should understand. And in the context of this case, the controller should be asked whether he has any evidence of management's intent to discount the merchandise in inventory, or whether he has any knowledge of marketing problems the company has encountered.

The students may ask what is meant by "management." No definition is given in Statement on Auditing Standards No. 19, and they should be able to come up with their own definitions. They could use as guidance the definitions given in Statement on Auditing Standards No. 6, "Related Party Transactions" (1975), or Statement on Auditing Standards No. 30, "Reporting on Internal Control" (1980), each of which differs to a degree from the other. The point of concern would be whether the controller is "management." Giving a person a title that sounds like management does not make a person part of management, if that term is adequately defined.

The Statement on Auditing Standards seems to say only that the representations letter should be signed by the chief executive officer and the chief financial officer. Some might be tempted to argue that a controller is not "management" but is a secondary officer, and that his signature is not really necessary on the letter of representations. It could be argued that the auditor should simply accept the letter signed by the president and the chief financial officer. Such was the position of the other two officers, and that position was not unreasonable in the context of the language of Statement on Auditing Standards No. 19. It might also be argued that the inventory reserve is not so much an accounting determination as it is a marketing strategy determination. Therefore, it might be argued that the auditors ought to have a separate letter from the marketing vice president expressing his views about the future of the questioned product.

The case should afford an opportunity for the students to discuss the basis for the positions taken by the controller and by the other two management people. They should also consider the motivations of the individuals as undoubtedly they will not be the same. Presumably the controller has more bullets in his belt than the one marked "oil shortage." To quantify that phrase alone into dollars of inventory write-down, as he seems to have done (because the amount is said to be material), seems improbable at best, unless he simply used a broad-brush approach and plucked ten percent off the wall. His position should not be capricious. By the same token, the other two executives must have more to support their position than is apparent from reading the case; that is, the oil shortage "may keep people at home more." The students may show some concern over the disparity in stated positions regarding the amount of the allowance:

Controller - low side by material amount

Other executives - excessive

Auditor - adequate

The students may sense that the auditor is a bit ahead of himself with a conclusion of "adequate" when the company seems unable to find an acceptable number.

The students might be inclined to explore whether the problem and solution would be different had the controller refused to sign based on a lack of information sufficient to decide the allowance rather than on a perceived misstatement. In comparison to auditors' reports, the first position would seem comparable to an "unaudited" disclaimer; the second, to an "adverse opinion." And the latter should seem more onerous to resolve.

Some of the alternative solutions to be explored include the following:

- Leave out the controller as a required signatory, as discussed above. The omission would require appropriate approval within the auditing firm, because omitting the controller would be a violation of firm policy.

- Encourage the controller to sign a letter he does not believe in. There is a question of principle at stake here. The auditor must stand up for the controller's right to express his views, and the auditor must avoid coercion, or apparent coercion.

- Modify the letter to put in the controller's belief. In this way the controller can record what he honestly believes regarding the inadequacy of the reserves and include such a statement in the letter of representations as his personal qualification of the fairness of the financial statements.

- Attempt to convince the controller the reserves are adequate. The auditor would need very strong audit documentation to take this stance. In effect that would be saying the auditor is better informed as to the reasonableness of the inventory than is the controller.

- Attempt to convince the two senior executives that some upward adjustment of the allowance is required. The above admonition also applies here — very strong audit documentation would be needed.

- Stay out of the conflict until it is resolved. The auditor should figuratively lock the three executives in a room until they reach an accord, which is a good theoretical answer because it emphasizes management's responsibility for a fair presentation of the company's financial position.

- Refer the matter to the Board of Directors and ask that they commission such investigation as is necessary to resolve the disagreement. Such an investigation could include the use of independent market researchers or other outsiders.

- Conclude that the action of the controller is capricious. The controller may be carrying a large-sized grudge — he may have been bypassed for a promotion; he may have been bypassed for salary increase and bonus; he may have been told he should start "looking" as the company is looking for a replacement; or he may have other real or imagined grievances. He may be trying to "get even." The case does not suggest capriciousness (and in this case it was not suspected), but the students should be aware that employee grievances have affected, and will continue to affect, responses furnished to auditors.

Some students may suggest that the case study is really an inventory valuation problem and less so a letter of representations problem. Having been told by a responsible employee that something is wrong with the inventory valuation, the auditor has little choice but to audit until satisfied — irrespective of who signs the letter of representations. For example, had the plant manager, instead of the controller, expressed the same concerns, the auditor would be confronted with essentially the same problem, the difference being the plant manager is not a signatory to the letter.

Each officer signing the letter of representations has a heavy responsibility for fair presentation. If in good faith, as opposed to capriciousness, an officer is contending that the financials are misstated, the auditor would be well advised to obtain concurrence of all signatories before signing his own name to a certificate. *Montgomery's Auditing* takes a somewhat similar position (page 335), though perhaps from a somewhat different viewpoint.

Some students may want to discuss the apparent economic distress facing this company if the controller is right, or even close, and the company cannot recover the cost of producing its principal product. Though not a part of the case study, the students should realize that auditors should be mindful of the economic environment that surrounds specific accounting and auditing issues.

The Solution

The auditors took the position that they would not issue, in this circumstance and most likely in any other circumstance, their unqualified opinion so long as a necessary signatory to the letter of representations contended in good faith that the financials were materially misstated. Nor were the auditors interested in issuing some peculiar qualification running to failure to sign the letter of representations. If the three executives could not come to agreement, the matter should go before the Board of Directors for further investigation and action and until all parties were in agreement, the audit opinion would be withheld. If the company demanded an opinion before agreement, the opinion would probably be a denial, or perhaps a qualification, but running to uncertainty in the inventory valuation and not to failure to sign a letter. The client was advised that both of the latter opinions would probably be unacceptable to the Securities and Exchange Commission, so the company should get on with the business of preparing statements acceptable to the three executives and the Board and, if they want a clean opinion, to the auditors as well.

The alternative of having the controller express an adverse opinion on the inventory valuations in the letter of representations was not acceptable. To proceed with a clean audit opinion in face of the controller's adverse opinion would expose the auditors and others to unacceptable professional and legal risks, and especially so if sales of the Widget Air Conditioner fell through the floor.

The additional allowance required by the controller may or may not have been necessary; but officers responsible for companies' financial statements had better make themselves heard if they believe the financials to be materially misleading, just as the controller did here. The Securities and Exchange Commission is looking more and more to financial and accounting officers to stand up and be counted in spite of top management pressure (as witness, for example, ASR 267). So disagreements between company management personnel, such as shown here, may become more commonplace and, though a bit sticky from the audit side, should further the progress toward reliability of financial statements submitted for audit.

New Client Acceptance

A recently promoted partner, Mr. Atlast, was appointed Treasurer of Community Fund Raising Foundation. There he worked closely with Mr. Pillar, the President of the foundation. Mr. Pillar is sole owner of a mini-conglomerate engaged in franchising laundries and developing real estate. Mr. Atlast was quite excited when Mr. Pillar suggested that they get together to discuss the possibility of an audit since Mr. Pillar was planning on "going public."

Mr. Pillar said he was familiar with the work of Mr. Atlast's audit firm from an association many years ago in another city when Mr. Pillar was involved with another company. After further discussion and a cursory review, Mr. Atlast learned that Mr. Pillar's present company was successful and profitable and that its audit fees should be substantial. Mr. Atlast told Mr. Pillar, with appropriate words of thanks, that indeed his firm wanted the work and he casually mentioned that his firm required approval of all new clients by at least one other partner in the firm, but that it should be of no concern to anyone.

Mr. Atlast began his new client investigation which would be submitted for approval to a partner in the executive office. Mr. Pillar was found to be a highly respected member of the community, active and highly placed in a number of charitable and civic organizations. His company was highly regarded by his banker and his attorney (who was a member of one of the more prestigious legal firms in town). The Dun & Bradstreet contained no negative information about his company or about him.

To round out the investigation, Mr. Atlast called up Mr. Post, the partner in the Haddit, Mississippi, office who had handled the firm's previous audit work. Mr. Post, now retired, had a number of things to say:

> His last audit of the Mississippi company, Realee, Inc., occurred some 12 years ago. Realee was a publicly held company engaged in real estate activities. Mr. Pillar, the chief executive officer, owned some ten to twenty percent of the stock. Post described Pillar as having been a "real little hot shot, maybe 28 or 29."
>
> During the firm's next to last audit of Realee, Mr. Post insisted, over strong objection by Mr. Pillar, that the company reduce the carrying amount of an apartment house held for sale from $600,000 to $200,000, based on appraisals obtained by Mr. Post. This adjustment was made. But, in the first quarter of the following year, the apartment house was sold for $600,000 to a trust and a profit of $400,000 was reported. Mr. Post and his audit team pressed for identification of the purchaser. Mr. Pillar said he did not know and could not find out the names of the principals of the trust.

The audit was at an impasse. The matter was about to be taken up with the Board of Directors when search of the County Recorder's records showed the property recorded in the name of Mr. Pillar himself. Stamps affixed to the deed indicated a purchase price of $50,000.

Without power of subpoena, Mr. Post was unable to prove that the property had been sold, using the trust as a "strawman," directly to Mr. Pillar, who had lied about it to the auditors. Nor was Mr. Post able to identify the source of the $600,000 cash paid Realee by the trust, but he believed it was the same $600,000 Realee paid for consulting services to a company that had engaged in reciprocal sales with Realee in the past. But, as he told the Board, he was confident that his analysis of the available data was correct.

Following the meeting of the Board, Mr. Pillar resigned, and within a year Realee was out of business.

Further, during the years of Mr. Pillar's management, Realee had engaged in other questionable transactions, primarily "parking" transactions and reciprocal sales, which had been appropriately adjusted in the audit process.

Disturbed by Mr. Post's story, Mr. Atlast spent the next few days weighing the pros and cons of taking on this engagement. He finally concluded that after 12 years Mr. Pillar must have matured to a point where he would no longer lie to auditors or engage in shady deals as he had in Haddit. The fact that he wanted to come back to the firm seemed proof enough that he would not pull the Haddit tricks again. Mr. Atlast packaged all the new client investigation data and shipped it off to an executive office partner requesting his approval.

You are the partner in the executive office.

**SHOULD YOU APPROVE ACCEPTANCE OF
MR. PILLAR'S COMPANY AS A NEW CLIENT?**

Case 26-2

Case 26: New Client Acceptance

DISCUSSION LEADER'S GUIDE

New Client Acceptance

Objectives of the Case

The objectives of this case are to introduce (1) the conflict of economic and ethical considerations inherent in the acceptance of some companies as new clients (or the retention of others), and (2) the difficulty in determining at what point of time, if ever, one's past transgressions or improprieties can be dismissed, leaving room for a fresh start. As a by-product, the case should suggest the impossibility, in the state of the art today, of auditing real estate transactions in which management and apparently unrelated outsiders conspire to falsify those transactions and the related record keeping.

The students' discussion should focus on the following issues:

1. The judgments involved in weighing the advantages and disadvantages of accepting the engagement.
2. The likelihood that the apparent misrepresentations (or lies) will not be repeated.
3. The likelihood that sham transactions will be eschewed in the future.
4. The consideration to be given to the apparent misappropriation of an apartment house from a publicly held company.
5. The possibility that additional audit procedures and additional partner reviews could nullify any future misrepresentations or attempts at sham transactions.
6. The difficulty or the impossibility of obtaining audit satisfaction regarding certain transactions without power of subpoena or other audit tools not now available.
7. The probability that regulations under the Foreign Corrupt Practices Act now will inhibit attempts at falsification of records.

Applicable Professional Pronouncements

Statement of Quality Control Standards No. 1 - Acceptance and Continuance of Clients

Regulation 13b-2 of the Exchange Act (relating to the Foreign Corrupt Practices Act)

Statement on Auditing Standards No. 16 - The Independent Auditor's Responsibility for the Detection of Errors or Irregularities

Statement on Auditing Standards No. 17 - Illegal Acts of Clients

Statement on Auditing Standards No. 19 - Client Representations

Statement on Auditing Standards No. 31 - Evidential Matter

Business Assumptions and Other Data

The students should have an understanding of the accounting environment in the mid to late '60s, when the Haddit, Mississippi office was involved with Mr. Pillar. The real estate industry was well known for "front ending" earnings in those days. And to an extent, the reputation earned in the earlier days has carried through the '70s and into the '80s. The extent of "parking," "strawmen," and "sham" transactions will never be known, as many were never discovered that ultimately were perfected through subsequent bona fide sales. However, the amount that surfaced, one way or the other, was truly sizable and indicated a practice not limited to just a handful of real estate operators.

When Mr. Atlast questioned the chief executive officer (Mr. Pillar) about the activities described by Mr. Post, Mr. Pillar replied that he had not understood the seriousness and possible ramifications of those transactions. Whether or not this was the case, it should be kept in mind that such practices had been commonplace during the 1950s and 1960s. The young Mr. Pillar was under substantial pressure from shareholders, and from his own sense of pride, to show good earnings.

The students should be aware further that while both the franchising and real estate industries showed uncanny ability at "front ending" earnings, the practice has waned, though not disappeared, in the more recent years. Bankruptcies, understandably, have taken a huge toll in "front enders." Great assistance has been furnished by the Securities and Exchange Commission in slowing the timing of income recognition. And, too, the profession has made its mark by writing ever tighter rules to thwart early, untimely recognition of earnings.

The case does not mention whether Mr. Pillar currently uses auditors for his mini-conglomerate. If the students pursue the auditing standard requiring communication with predecessor auditors, they can assume properly that indeed Mr. Pillar did use an auditor, whose practice, aside from Mr. Pillar's work, was quite small. Inquiry of this auditor by Mr. Atlast revealed nothing negative.

Discussion

The Statement on Quality Control Standards regarding acceptance and continuance of clients provides as follows:

> Policies and procedures should be established for deciding whether to accept or continue a client in order to minimize the likelihood of association with a client whose management lacks integrity. Suggesting that there should be procedures for this purpose does not imply that a firm vouches for the integrity or reliability of a client, nor does it imply that a firm has a duty to anyone but itself with respect to the acceptance, rejection, or retention of clients. However, prudence suggests that a firm be selective in determining its professional relationships.

Professional literature offers little more in the way of guidance to an auditor that would assist in arriving at a decision to accept or reject a prospective client. The decisions being made today are highly subjective and fraught with the possibility of error. Over the years, instances have occurred where one firm gladly accepted a client who was rejected by another firm. In some known cases the accepting auditors came to regret their decision; in others, no problems arose and the clients matured into profitable clients of integrity.

The livelihood of any CPA firm is to a great extent dependent upon its ability to attract new clients, for present clients have a way of dying, going out of business, being acquired, or changing auditors. Thus, auditors must be constantly alert to opportunities and seize them when they can. The competition for any available prospective client is usually keen and on occasion results in audit fees that leave no profit for the auditor. Thus, the prospect, faced here, of obtaining a profitable and successful client without engaging in competition is particularly appealing.

Case 26: New Client Acceptance

Over the years, many auditors have taken on new clients whose businesses have failed subsequent to issuance of their audit reports. Proceedings before the Securities and Exchange Commission or courts gave every indication, in some of these cases, that the auditors had been dealing with "crooked," or at least deceptive, managements whom they had not investigated prior to acceptance as clients. The impact of these proceedings, in part, was to focus on the quality controls within a CPA firm. One of the controls imposed was intended to minimize the likelihood of association with a client whose management lacked integrity. The control systems will differ between audit firms, and the acceptability of clients will also vary. As stated, however, an auditor has a responsibility to no one but himself as to whom he audits.

Students will sense early on that the case has no right or wrong answer at the time an answer must be given. But, without any doubt, events of the future will support or deny the validity of the decision— be it "yes" or "no." Though the correctness of either a "yes" or a "no" answer must await future events, the students nevertheless should be encouraged to discuss their views and the rationale that supports such views.

In deciding whether or not to accept Mr. Pillar's new firm as a client, the executive office partner has to be careful not to make moral judgments about practices that may have been acceptable business behavior at the time. This partner also has to ask himself whether his judgment about Mr. Pillar would be different if it were another firm that Mr. Pillar had lied to 12 or 13 years ago. What, say, if it had been a local firm with three partners? A Big Eight firm?

Yet another variable to be considered here is the passage of time. Mr. Pillar's recent business behavior would appear to be exemplary. Whatever he did back in Haddit, Mississippi, he did it when he was young and, apparently, unsophisticated about acceptable accounting practices. Furthermore, Mr. Pillar now wishes to come back to the same audit firm which virtually accused him of fraud 12 years ago.

One fact which could offset all of these favorable indications about Mr. Pillar: Nowadays, as sole owner of his business, Mr. Pillar has enjoyed much greater latitude in business dealings than he had 12 or more years ago when he was involved with a publicly held company. Mr. Pillar simply has not been scrutinized as thoroughly as he would be if he were to go public again. If spurious transactions have continued, could his company be unauditable, notwithstanding the fact that he is audited? Might not one auditor perceive as unauditable what another perceives as auditable?

If nefarious entries to the accounts have continued in the present company, the students should recognize that their character has likely changed. As a sole stockholder Mr. Pillar should have no compulsion to record income on "sham" sales — the company would have to pay income tax on those. Rather the dubious transactions, if still practiced, would most likely be aimed toward reduction of income — and more importantly, reduction of income taxes.

The students appropriately should raise questions regarding why Mr. Atlast's firm continued with Mr. Pillar in years past. Was not the fact that he entered into "parking transactions" and "reciprocal sales" at Realee sufficient to warrant dropping that client? There can be any number of explanations — perhaps none too satisfying in the final analysis. (Though Realee went bankrupt, the auditors were never sued — something one should not count on happening too often where public shareholders are involved.) Regardless of reasons the auditors may piece together today for having continued to serve the client years ago, one can safely assume that the amount of fees and the confidence in

DLG 26-3

one's auditing ability, and the interaction of those two, played a major role. Fees were good — and even better because of the greatly increased time spent in ferreting out the flaky transactions and arguing about them.

Students should recognize that 12 years later, fees are still important; acceptance and retention of existing clients continues to bear a high priority, and confidence of auditors in their ability to find these dubious transactions remains high. Yet the students also should recognize an air of great skepticism and concern where management's integrity may be under question. The Commission on Auditors' Responsibilities (the Cohen Commission) reinforced the need for skepticism in its report (1978) by stating " . . . when management is untrustworthy, there is a significant chance that a valid independent audit cannot be performed." To this, some auditors would say, "Amen!" Others would hold to a belief that extended auditing procedures, assignment of super partners and super staff, top level reviews, and the like can adequately compensate for an untrustworthy management. The latter position may be supportable, but would seem so only if the auditor had subpoena powers, unlimited time, and no restriction on fees — three things that just do not exist in today's audit environment.

Since the time of the Realee audits the American Institute of Certified Public Accountants has issued a number of helpful Statements on Auditing Standards: No. 16 and No. 17, issued in 1977, offer some guidance regarding irregularities and illegal acts of clients, and No. 19 (1977) brings into sharper focus the reliability that should be placed on management's representations. No. 31 (1980) gives guidance for use in evaluating evidential matter. Further, Securities and Exchange Commission Regulation 13b-2 of the Exchange Act (1979) prohibits reporting companies from falsifying books and records, from making false or misleading statements to auditors, and from omitting a statement of fact essential to the integrity of the financial statements.

Thus, since the days of Realee, the SEC has adopted regulations prohibiting the behavior that was troublesome in the past, and the AICPA has issued a number of Statements on Auditing Standards that add insight for coping with such behavior. Recognizing that the SEC and the profession are facing up to the reality of Realee-type transactions, and recognizing that Mr. Atlast now knows enough to invoke a high level of due diligence on his part in performing the audit, we still have the question — should the executive office partner approve acceptance?

The students probably should discuss whether any auditing firm has a moral obligation to society to serve the Mr. Pillars of the world. That is: Is the public entitled to demand that a CPA must audit any given company requiring an audit, no matter how lacking in integrity? (This would be the equivalent of the auditors' Hippocratic oath, and certainly contrary to the position expressed in Statement of Quality Control Standards No. 1.) Since the firm in question knows the past foibles of the man that other firms likely would not know, does the knowledgeable firm have a responsibility to the public to carry on? And, if not to carry on, does that firm have a responsibility to come forward and tell the auditing firm ultimately engaged, or the public, what it knows? Most likely the other firm engaged will not know of the association 12 years ago with the firm that declined acceptance, and even if aware of the association, most likely would never think of communicating with a 12-year-old vintage "predecessor."

The state of the art is completely unsettled on these morality-type issues. In practice, most firms today probably would feel no obligation or responsibility either (1) to continue with a client they knew lacked integrity 12 years ago even though they were the only ones with that knowledge, or (2) to share that knowledge on any basis with the public or on any basis with the auditor ultimately engaged, other than through direct inquiry by that auditor.

The Solution

The decision of the executive office partner was that he would not approve acceptance of the new client.

It is fair to say that had the firm not been privy to Mr. Pillar's actions 12 years ago the necessary approval by the executive office partner would have been more or less automatic on the strength of the favorable current findings. This point is borne out by the fact that the engagement was accepted by one of the largest firms in the country, which presumably conducted an investigation according to its own standards, which apparently did not include contact with the firm that rejected the client. (In passing, it is well to note that some firms' investigation standards provide for inquiry of the prospective client as to whether it has been turned down by any other firm and, if so, that firm must be contacted.)

In due time Mr. Atlast's firm will know whether it turned down a good client or dodged a speeding bullet.

Attorney/Auditor Responsibility

As a member of the corporate law department in a major New York law firm, you have frequent occasion to work with your clients' auditors. In particular, the auditors send letters every year asking you to tell them about any contingencies or uncertainties hanging over mutual clients. Their letters of request conform generally to the model letter that seems to satisfy the requirements of the American Bar Association and the American Institute of Certified Public Accountants. Your firm, as a matter of policy, has always tried to cooperate with the auditors' requests. However, you know that some attorneys remain reluctant to answer those letters because of their concern that it may increase their own liability — and because it may jeopardize the client-attorney privilege.

In an attempt to dispel some of that reluctance and to better identify the various responsibilities, the accountants and the attorneys agreed some years ago (1976) to a compromise procedure. That procedure, in substance, may be summarized as follows: The client will list and evaluate all of the legal contingencies facing the company; the auditor will review files, minutes, and other documents in an attempt to corroborate that listing; and, as a final step, the auditor will ask the attorney to confirm that listing and to add any other information that the attorney thinks should be mentioned. Based on that listing, a decision to disclose or accrue a contingency will be made. Both the AICPA and the ABA agreed that the attorneys have some kind of a professional obligation to advise their clients regarding disclosure of material contingencies in their financial statements and if a client refuses to comply with that advice, the Bar has agreed that the attorney should consider resigning from the engagement.

Lawyers' responsibilities regarding their clients' disclosure obligations have been the subject of considerable discussion, and in time there may be further clarification and guidance on this sensitive matter. The 1976 compromise between the Bar Association and the Institute helps a bit, but you wish there were more and better professional guidance — particularly as you sit in your office staring vacantly at the standard form of legal letter just received from the auditors of National Consumer Products requesting your reply regarding that company's litigation, claims, and assessments. You say to yourself, "It's decision time again."

Answering the letter would be a snap were it not for one minor — or perhaps not so minor — item. You remember clearly what you have in your files on that item. It concerns a possible Federal Trade Commission (FTC) action against National, and it goes something like this:

Case 27-1

Case 27: Attorney/Auditor Responsibility

Earlier this year a young FTC investigator visited the company and asked routine questions about pricing policies. He was particularly interested in several of the company's more profitable products where there had been very little price competition. After the investigator left, you and the treasurer talked to several people in the marketing department. After some emotional discussion, the group vice president admitted that he and his peers in the competition met several times each winter at a ski resort to discuss product pricing. He denied fixing prices, but admitted that prices for all comparable products are very much the same. You advised him to steer clear of any such meetings in the future, and it was agreed that the company would simply wait to see what happened next. According to your records, very little has happened. The FTC investigator visited the other companies in the industry, but there have been no new developments in the last 90 days.

And, with equal clarity, you recall the treasurer's admonition, on more than one occasion, not to disclose the visit by the FTC to the auditors. The gist of his comments was to the effect that "all we'll do is run up a lot of expensive time, and waste a lot of my time, arguing with the auditors about whether we should disclose in our annual report the possibility of a lawsuit that may never be filed — after all, our man says he did not fix any prices."

It is not clear that this matter is enough of a "material contingency" to require disclosure in the financial statements. Still, you have never had to worry this much about the disclosures in a client's financial statements before. In other situations, all the relevant data had been "on the table," and you had been able to discuss the accounting side of the question with the auditor to add perspective to the legal side. But now you seem to be on your own and you are not comfortable with that responsibility; but it is beginning to look as though you will have no alternative but to accept it.

You sit there in your office torn between your time-honored responsibility to accommodate your client's request for attorney-client privilege and your nagging feeling that this investigation by the FTC might well be something that you have a responsibility to see disclosed to the investing public and others. One thing is clear, if you do not disclose the matter to the auditors, the chances of it being disclosed this year in the annual report are almost nil.

AS AN ATTORNEY, WHAT WILL YOU DO WITH YOUR KNOWLEDGE OF THE FEDERAL TRADE COMMISSION INVESTIGATION?

DISCUSSION LEADER'S GUIDE

Attorney/Auditor Responsibility

Objectives of the Case

Clearly, the objective of the case is not to educate auditors and accountants in the practice of law. Nor is the case intended to imply that auditors and accountants can solve legal questions, such as the one faced here. Students may properly question, then, "Why stick us with this case? That is for lawyers to solve." And, that is true. But, this case is designed to illustrate the amount of responsibility attorneys assume for the public reporting of their clients and to demonstrate the heightened dilemma faced by attorneys whose clients would withhold from their auditors information that may be essential to a fair presentation of financial position. General counsel have presumably had some responsibilities for adequacy of disclosure all along, but their responsibilities have come more and more into focus as experience is gained in applying the compromise procedures between the Bar and the accounting profession, which culminated in Statement on Auditing Standards No. 12. Also, there is an increasing public concern about the responsibilities of practicing attorneys as evidenced in the Securities and Exchange Commission's action against White and Case in the National Student Marketing matter. The fact is that practicing attorneys are under increasing pressure to acknowledge an obligation to the public which is beyond their advocacy obligation to their immediate corporate clients.

The case also illustrates how much the auditors have delegated to the attorneys as a result of the provisions of Statement on Auditing Standards No. 12. Auditors may always be dependent on attorneys, but the Statement on Auditing Standards and the formal position papers from the Bar Association highlight that dependence. The auditors consider themselves responsible for the adequacy of the disclosures in clients' financial statements; however, when it comes to disclosure of potential legal problems, auditors may not even have an opportunity to exercise that judgment — the judgment may be exercised for them by the clients' attorneys.

Discussion of the case should give the students some of the auditor's insight into the nature and import of inquiries and investigations by administrative agencies.

Applicable Professional Pronouncements

Statement on Auditing Standards No. 12, "Inquiry of Client's Lawyer Concerning Litigation, Claims, and Assessments," particularly Exhibit II — American Bar Association Statement of Policy Regarding Lawyers' Responses to Auditors' Requests for Information

Statement on Auditing Standards No. 19, "Client Representations"

Handbook of Accounting and Auditing, Burton, Palmer, and Kay, Chapters 29, 44, and 46 (nonauthoritative)

DLG 27-1

Case 27: Attorney/Auditor Responsibility

Business Assumptions and Other Data

In this case a major concern of the attorney seemed to be preservation of the attorney-client privilege, and the Statement of Policy of the Bar Association identifies the protection of that privilege as "fundamental." A bit of background regarding privilege taken from the *Handbook of Accounting and Auditing* and other sources should add perspective for nonlawyer students. The *Handbook* (Chapter 44) indicates that the attorney-client privilege is the only privilege derived from common law but goes on to say that a common-law privilege may be modified or abolished by statute. As privileges of any kind act as a derogation of a court's search for truth, they remain under careful scrutiny. The day of judge-created privileges is said to be probably past in federal courts or administrative proceedings. While that development may or may not have a bearing on the privilege of the attorney in this case to withhold information on the FTC investigation from the auditor, it may suggest a gradual erosion of the time-honored privilege enjoyed by attorneys and their clients.

Some of that erosion of the sanctity of the attorney-client privilege is evident in SEC matters. Commissioner Sommer, in a speech in January 1974, said that in securities matters, other than where advocacy is clearly proper, the attorney will have to function in a manner more akin to that of an auditor than that of an advocate. In some Securities and Exchange cases attorney-client privilege could not be invoked. In others, it seemed to hold.

A brief comment about the nature of investigations may also be helpful to the nonlawyer in considering the case. In a nutshell, an investigation leaves little maneuvering room for the one being investigated. The *Handbook* (Chapter 44) says:

> Investigations are perhaps most readily analogized to the discovery phase of civil litigation. There are, of course, important distinctions; an investigation is discovery that occurs in advance of the initiation of proceedings, and it is a decidedly one-sided form of discovery, with the subject of the investigation having only a very limited right, if any, to adduce evidence in his defense. And the scope of permissible inquiry during an investigation is subject to even fewer restrictions than the discovery that occurs in litigation between private parties.

The disclosure of investigations in financial statements is unsettled. Not too many years ago the SEC frowned on disclosure of their private investigations. Not so today. According to the *Handbook* (Chapter 46), the Securities and Exchange Commission now takes the position that a company and its auditors must judge materiality of an SEC investigation as in actual and threatened litigation. And, perhaps for this reason, there has been a substantial increase in the number of disclosures of SEC investigations. Would not the same approach seem valid for an FTC investigation?

Before the advent of Statement on Auditing Standards No. 19, Client Representations (1977), auditors frequently asked clients to represent whether any governmental agency had made inquiries or conducted investigations during the year under audit. Had such representation been requested of National Consumer Products, the dilemma of the attorney would be automatically resolved — assuming a truthful answer were given. However, since the issuance of Statement on Auditing Standards No. 19, auditors tend to follow the model letter in that Statement and the representations now sought probably can be answered truthfully by management without having to disclose the likes of the FTC investigation.

Representations from the model letter that might have exposed the investigation, if answered truthfully, could be interpreted — and probably are being interpreted — so as not to require disclosure of the investigation. Some of the tangential representations would be:

No. 3 - There have been no -
    c. Communications from regulatory agencies concerning noncompliance with, or deficiencies in, financial reporting practices that could have a material effect on the financial statements.

No. 6 - There are no -

    a. Violations or possible violations of laws or regulations whose effects should be considered for disclosure in the financial statements or as a basis for recording a loss contingency.

    b. Other material liabilities or gain or loss contingencies that are required to be accrued or disclosed by Statement of Financial Accounting Standards No. 5.

No. 7 - There are no unasserted claims that our lawyer has advised us are probable of assertion and must be disclosed in accordance with Statement of Financial Accounting Standards No. 5.

The case does not state whether the attorney is an officer or a director of the company. If such were the case, the attorney in the role of officer or director would be subject to the Foreign Corrupt Practices Act and, more particularly, Regulation 13b2 of the Exchange Act; he would then be required to state any material fact necessary to make the financial statements not misleading to an accountant in connection with an audit. In this case the attorney was neither an officer nor a director.

Discussion

The attorney's responsibility for maintaining attorney-client privilege seems rather clear. The attorney's responsibility regarding financial statement disclosure of unasserted claims and the like is less clear. The inquiry or investigation would seem to be in the nature of an unasserted claim; the following discussion, taken largely from the *Handbook* (Chapter 29) and from other sources about lawyers and unasserted claims, may be useful to the students in their appreciation of the attorney's dilemma.

Disclosure of an unasserted claim or assessment is not required unless it is probable that the claim will be asserted and there is a *reasonable possibility* that the outcome will be unfavorable. Unasserted claims or assessments are given special consideration in SFAS 5. Unasserted claims have been given this special treatment because (attorneys have argued) disclosure could cause the injured party to recognize the injury and assert the claim; in other words, the disclosure tends to be self-fulfilling. Attorneys were also concerned with the loss of attorney-client privilege if certain disclosures were made regarding unasserted claims.

Case 27: Attorney/Auditor Responsibility

The problem between auditors and attorneys centered around the auditors using the attorney letters to *discover* unasserted claims and the attorneys' reluctance to jeopardize privilege. Many attorneys who previously responded to auditors' requests became reluctant to respond to general requests, because they were aware of the increasing amount of litigation and believed that the less information available to outsiders, including auditors, from whom information could be "discovered" by a potential plaintiff, the better they could protect their clients from adverse consequences of litigation. The attorney-client privilege does not extend to information disclosed to an auditor, because the auditor legally does not have such privileged communication with his clients. Attorneys were adamant about giving potentially damaging information to auditors that could then be caught by "fishing" plaintiffs.

The lawyer's responsibilities are to consider an unasserted possible claim if he realizes one exists and to recognize there may be a requirement for financial statement disclosure; he does not commit to devoting substantive attention to searching for such claims. Because a lawyer is not considered an expert as to detailed disclosure requirements under SFAS 5, he should notify a responsible client officer or employee of an unasserted possible claim that the lawyer has concluded must be considered for disclosure to the auditor and should satisfy himself that the officer or employee understands the requirements of SFAS 5. Having done this, the lawyer has fulfilled his commitments unless he has concluded that the unasserted possible claim is probable of assertion; such a claim, if material, must be disclosed in the financial statements. The ABA Statement of Policy, in referring to disclosure, applies to whether or not the unasserted claim or assessment must be brought to the auditor's attention, and does not refer to the requirements of disclosure under SFAS 5. It is the client's responsibility to evaluate whether financial statement disclosure is required, and the auditor's responsibility to evaluate the appropriateness of that disclosure.

Some, however, believe that the lawyer's responsibility runs to disclosure in the financial statements and is not limited to "disclosure to the auditors." That such differing views exist is understandable. The Statement of Policy of the American Bar Association (paragraph 6) seems to suggest the responsibility runs to financial statement disclosure wherein it states:

> Independent of the scope of his response to the auditor's request for information, the lawyer, depending upon the nature of the matters as to which he is engaged, may have as part of his professional responsibility to his client an obligation to advise the client concerning the need for or advisability of public disclosure of a wide range of events and circumstances. The lawyer has an obligation not knowingly to participate in any violation by the client of the disclosure requirements of the securities laws. In appropriate circumstances, the lawyer also may be required under the Code of Professional Responsibility to resign his engagement if his advice concerning disclosures is disregarded by the client. The auditor may properly assume that whenever, in the course of performing legal services for the client with respect to a matter recognized to involve an unasserted possible claim or assessment which may call for financial statement disclosure, the lawyer has formed a professional conclusion that the client must disclose or consider disclosure concerning such possible claim or assessment, the lawyer, as a matter of professional responsibility to the client, will so advise the client and will consult with the client concerning the question of such disclosure and the applicable requirements of SFAS 5.

However, it is well to note the word "may" is used above in addressing the subject of the attorney's responsibility, which would seem to leave considerable room for interpretation. The possibility that the "disclosure" in question means disclosure to the auditor only, as noted above, is reinforced by the Commentary (paragraph 6) to the Statement of Policy, which states:

> ... In any event, where in the lawyer's view it is clear that (i) the matter is of material importance and seriousness, and (ii) there can be no reasonable doubt that its nondisclosure in the client's financial statements would be a violation of law giving rise to material claims, rejection by the client of his advice to call the matter to the attention of the auditor would almost certainly require the lawyer's withdrawal from employment in accordance with the Code of Professional Responsibility....

However, the legal profession's policy statement is not binding on a lawyer. Some attorneys may specifically dissociate themselves from the ABA Statement.

In the discussion, the group ought to deal with questions such as the following:

1. If the client insists that the attorney say nothing about the matter, what alternatives does the attorney have under the arrangements between the Bar Association and the accounting profession? The answer to the question is that the attorney may not violate the client's confidences — but the attorney may resign from the engagement. Or, the attorney may try to persuade the client to volunteer the matter to the auditors.

2. Does the attorney have an obligation to advise the auditor of the attorney's concerns, particularly if the disclosure question is borderline? No one really knows the answer to that question just yet. Probably, attorneys will conclude that they have no obligation to anyone other than themselves and their clients and will make this decision solely on their own. They will not involve the auditors in their decision-making until an attorney is sued for lack of disclosure. And, history shows that attorneys are seldom sued.

3. If the disclosure question were borderline, should an attorney retain another accountant as a consultant or adviser? The group might consider the implications of such a development.

4. Should attorneys go to the Securities and Exchange Commission on their own if they feel strongly an investigation should be disclosed in the financial statements? That was tried in one case:

A practicing attorney helped a client put together a prospectus to sell $25 million in bonds. The prospectus went effective, and the offering was successful. A short time later the attorney reviewed the firm's files on that client and noticed that there was a potential lawsuit which had been discussed by one of the other attorneys in the firm with the client's financial vice president. The suit had not been disclosed in the prospectus even though it could have been a material fact in any investment decision. The attorney asked the client to amend the prospectus and notify all purchasers of the securities. The client refused, reasoning that the offering was successful and that the lawsuit was a remote contingency. After some agonizing, the attorney reported the

Case 27: Attorney/Auditor Responsibility

matter to the Securities and Exchange Commission which required a recision of the offering. As a result of that attorney's actions the client fired the law firm; the law firm separated the partner; and the State Bar Association began proceedings for violating a client's confidences.

The group should not get into a discussion of the need to disclose this specific problem on this specific engagement. The discussion ought to focus on the responsibilities, in general, which attorneys may now carry in the disclosure arena.

The students may recognize or recall that where public offerings of securities are involved, attorneys for underwriters typically do a superb job in bringing forth disclosures of unasserted claims and other relevant data to a purchaser of securities. As the company selling securities is not their client, and thus not entitled to the same privileged communication, these attorneys tend to insist on disclosure of potential legal matters that may even seem remote. The list is endless of disclosures required by attorneys for underwriters that were not required by general counsel of the issuing company. A recent illustration goes something like this:

A company sold to the government approximately 80 percent of its products on a non-bid basis that generally provided for cost reimbursement and profit. The government discovered that the company was "padding" its costs through use of "shell" companies and fictitious invoices and through other means. The government notified the company by letter that it would honor the existing contracts, but when a new source of supply was established it would no longer buy the company's products. General counsel for the company advised that the government letter need not be disclosed to the auditors; the "padding" was not discovered in the audit process; and, thus, the financial statements and auditors' report gave no hint of past wrongdoings and of near-term loss of substantial business. Needless to say, lawsuits followed, including litigation against the attorney whose hands, it was alleged, were not clean on other counts as well.

In a somewhat similar case, the auditors were in a stronger role, but the attorney, as in the illustration above, opted for "cover-up." A summary of this case is:

A company was in the process of making a new tax shelter offering. It had made similar offerings in the past, and in each case had thereafter acted in the role of manager of the shelter. The president of the management company had used substantial funds for his personal benefit that by terms of trust agreements were restricted to specific uses for the benefit of the shelters. The auditors said that this misapplication of funds must be disclosed in the prospectus of the new shelter — that is, potential buyers should have knowledge of misapplication of funds in earlier shelters. The management and its general counsel were adamant that no such disclosure would be permitted nor would the company or its counsel permit the auditors to tell the underwriters and their attorneys what had happened. Contrary to the facts in the National Consumer Products case, the auditors knew of the matter and simply refused to sign their report until the underwriters were informed. Within five minutes after being informed, the underwriters withdrew from the offering, leaving for their office with a sobering comment

DLG 27-6

that should some other house go through with the offering they would surely expect to see the appropriate disclosure regarding management's misuse of trust funds.

What these illustrations seem to point out is that attorneys know what should be disclosed to the investing public even though attorneys are not trained in financial accounting and disclosure requirements. What gets in the way of doing what is right is often the desire to do what is "best" for the client. The adversary role on behalf of a client and the privilege of communication between attorney and client conspire at times to thwart fair and necessary disclosures in financial statements.

Regulation S-K of the Securities and Exchange Commission might suggest to the students that the inquiry or investigation should be included at least in the nonfinancial portion of reports required by the Securities and Exchange Commission. Under the caption "Item 5 — Legal Proceedings," the Regulation says, "In the case of proceedings by governmental agencies, disclosure is required even though the proceedings have not yet been instituted, provided it is known that the proceedings are contemplated." Of course that leaves a lot of room for contemplating what is meant by "contemplated" and by "known."

The Solution

The students will recognize that no correct or incorrect answer, from the lawyer's point of view, can be given by a layman — perhaps not even by a lawyer. Some lawyers would insist that the matter be exposed to the auditors for consideration; others would insist that there is no room for consideration — the facts must be disclosed in the financials; and still others would agree there is no room for consideration — the client's privilege must be respected and nothing said to the auditors or in footnotes. Lawyers in the first two groups presumably would need to resign, or at least "consider" resigning, should their clients ignore their advice — that is, if they are following the Statement of Policy of the Bar Association.

Presumably, until the courts or the statutes better define the responsibilites of attorneys to the public generally on financial disclosure matters, attorneys can remain silent on any number of grounds, including:

- They have not given substantive time to the issue nor has their client requested they do so.
- Amounts involved, if any, may not be material.
- Factors influencing the likelihood of an unfavorable outcome may not be within a lawyer's competence or ability to judge.
- Lawyers may lack sufficient information to conclude that it is probable a claim will ever be filed.
- If a claim were filed, lawyers may lack sufficient information to conclude that an unfavorable outcome is either probable or reasonably possible.

Auditing Commission Payments

Powerco manufactures and installs hydroelectric equipment used in power generating plants throughout the world. Each system is custom-built to the customer's specifications and each sale requires substantial engineering for design and installation.

Powerco's shares are traded on the New York, Montreal, and London stock exchanges. The company is headquartered in New York and your New York office issues an audit report on the consolidated financial statements. A significant portion of the audit work is referred to other offices, both domestic and outside the United States. As partner in charge of the job in New York, you will specify the scope of the work to be performed by each of the referral offices.

During your visit to plan the year-end work, you find that the company's international business is booming. During the year, the company got into the Middle Eastern countries for the first time, writing 13 contracts with an aggregate sales value of $300,000,000. From your discussions with management and from scanning the documentation supporting the sales contracts, you are surprised to learn that the company used local sales agents in each case. In all of the company's domestic and European business, contracts are negotiated by a salaried sales staff, all of whom are skilled engineers. Management explained that it was necessary to work through local commission agents in the Middle East in order to establish a feeling of trust with the buyers. The contracts were arranged through five different commission agents who were paid from 10 to 20 percent in commissions (totaling $40,000,000).

You review the contracts, and the names of two of the commission agents are familiar. You happen to remember that some years ago their names appeared in a *Wall Street Journal* article summarizing arguments between the Securities and Exchange Commission and various multinational corporations, including Ashland, Northrop, and Lockheed. You recall that, according to that article, the Securities and Exchange Commission was concerned that these commission agents, among others named in those investigations, used some of the proceeds of their commission payments to influence officials in the purchasing countries, and that later developments bore out the concern that, indeed, some of the commission payments of those agents turned out to be bribes of foreign officials.

You realize that the Foreign Corrupt Practices Act has been around since 1977 and, as a consequence of that Act, many, perhaps most, bribes of foreign officials have fallen by the wayside. You would like to think that no bribes are involved in the $40,000,000 of commissions, but you get a sinking feeling every time you reflect on the names of two of those commission agents, on the size of the commissions, and on the Middle Eastern countries involved.

HOW WILL YOUR PLANNED AUDIT PROCEDURES BE AFFECTED BY THIS INFORMATION?

DISCUSSION LEADER'S GUIDE

Auditing Commission Payments

Objectives of the Case

The broad objective is consideration of the economic substance of the commissions. If they are what their legal form purports, much of the auditing concern will evaporate. If, however, in substance they are in part a commission to a commission agent and in part a payment to a foreign official to influence a favorable purchase decision, the issues become significantly magnified.

The question raised in the case focuses upon "planned audit procedures," and a discussion of the appropriate extended procedures to apply should be a major consideration for the students. Such procedures, of course, would be directed toward substantiating that the economic substance of the commissions accords with their legal form. Discussion should develop understanding of the difficulty, and at times the impossibility, of proving in an audit sense, one way or the other, whether substance and legal form are in accord.

Another objective of the case is to focus on the reporting issues facing the auditor, if it is established — or there is significant unresolved concern — that the commission included, in part, payments in the nature of bribes that presumably were illegal or were in violation of the Foreign Corrupt Practices Act or some other law or regulation. The students should focus on the separate reporting issues involved when the client (1) refuses to make adequate disclosure of the facts or (2) agrees to footnote disclosures satisfactory to the auditor.

As a side objective, the case may bring out a discussion of the business morality of bribes or, if softer language is preferred, payments to officials to influence a decision to assist a company in obtaining or retaining business. Not all business people in the world agree that bribery is wrong. In some countries, it may be the acceptable way of life, and, even in the U.S.A., which has legislated against bribery, many business heads contend such a law significantly and improperly places them in an inferior competitive position as compared to similar foreign suppliers whose country of domicile has no such law. Will the students say the answer is to get the other countries to change their law, or will they say our country should not be so moralistic? (A Research Report from The Conference Board, "Unusual Foreign Payments," conducted before passage of the Foreign Corrupt Practices Act, showed that 48 percent of the respondents believed U.S. companies should adopt the standards of countries in which they are operating. The report quoted the chairman of an electrical component manufacturer as saying, "In our business of selling components around the world, we adopt the commercial modes and standards of the countries in which we do business, and we intend to continue that policy in spite of national publicity." Now, however, so long as the Foreign Corrupt Practices Act remains, the choice of standards is substantially eliminated, at least for that portion of foreign business involving foreign officials.)

Applicable Professional Pronouncements

Foreign Corrupt Practices Act of 1977

Statement of Financial Accounting Standards No. 5, "Accounting for Contingencies," paragraph 9

Statement on Auditing Standards No. 1, "Statement on Auditing Standards" (AU 430.06)

Statement on Auditing Standards No. 12, "Inquiry of Client's Lawyers Concerning Litigation Claims and Assessments"

Statement on Auditing Standards No. 17, "Illegal Acts by Clients"

Statement on Auditing Standards No. 20, "Required Communication of Material Weaknesses in Internal Control"

Business Assumptions and Other Data

The case did not state whether the business in the Middle East was done by the domestic parent or a foreign subsidiary. For this case, assume that no foreign subsidiary is involved. Points of view differ as to whether interposing a foreign subsidiary will remove the taint of a bribe, should one occur, and the complete answer on that issue is not in yet. Nor does the case indicate whether Powerco has adopted, and is enforcing, rules of conduct for its executives and employees that would prohibit use of bribes in obtaining business. Such a set of rules did not exist; however, the matter was taken under consideration following the company's entry into the Middle Eastern markets.

The Securities and Exchange Commission has alleged illegal acts (that is, bribes) by some of Powerco's competitors; and bribes and kickbacks in the past have typified that industry's behavior. (Also, there have been some price-fixing problems in the industry, but Powerco seems not to have been involved in any pricing conspiracy.)

The case gives the total commissions paid and percentage range. No further insight would be gained by listing the commission percentage of each of the 13 contracts. The commissions of the two agents whose names were recognized were in the 15 to 17 percent range.

In certain Middle Eastern countries, the use of bribes, kickbacks, and other forms of payoff has been commonplace for hundreds of years — some would say for thousands of years. And, the practice is not likely to change overnight; possibly never. The students should be aware of this business phenomenon as they formulate their extended audit procedures.

The case does not specify whether the 13 contracts were with foreign governments or with foreign private corporations. Some would say it does not matter — the answer would be the same. Others contend that payments of bribes abroad are not considered to be illegal under American law, except to the extent any bribes are covered by the Foreign Corrupt Practices Act. In general terms, a portion of that Act makes it unlawful for a domestic concern to make use of interstate commerce corruptly in furtherance of an offer or payment of anything of value to a foreign official or a foreign political party or its official to assist the domestic concern in obtaining or retaining business. It is difficult to imagine today that any domestic company would knowingly get itself involved in bribery of a foreign official or political party official. The penalties are stiff: not more than $1,000,000 for the company, presumably for each violation, and not more than $10,000 and/or imprisonment up to five years for the individual. The students would be correct in assuming that the business in question principally was with foreign governments.

Another portion of that Act requires publicly held companies, such as Powerco, to keep books and records which in reasonable detail, accurately and fairly reflect the company's transactions; it further requires such companies to maintain a system of internal accounting controls that achieve stated objectives. Regulations of the Securities and Exchange Commission issued under the Act tighten the screws a bit further and make it illegal for any person to falsify records and for any officer or director to misrepresent or fail to represent information to an auditor that is necessary for fair financial presentation. Some would say, probably aptly, that this is a Catch-22 situation — even if bribes are not paid to government or political party officials, but to corporate officials only, a company could still be in violation of the Act unless it records the payments as "bribes" (surely not that exact word, but something much nearer to the truth than "commissions paid") and so informs the auditor of the payola. It is fair to state that the penalties for violation of this portion of the Act are less severe; history to date has shown some Securities and Exchange Commission actions that focus on the accounting issue. In a speech in early 1981 (Release No. 34-17500), Chairman Williams focused on the interrelationship of the accounting and corrupt payments section when he said, " . . . clearly, Congress went further than determining whether the payments which gave the new law its name were ethically and commercially justifiable. It also chose to consider the corporate accounting and control deficiencies which had been breeding grounds for these practices . . . . " A predecessor, Chairman Hills, got to the same point in 1976 in testimony before Congress on the question of whether the then existing laws and regulations were adequate. He said, " . . . in my view an effective system of corporate accountability requires that facts pertaining to illegal payments not be concealed from a corporation's independent accountants or its board of directors. This is a key point. Nothing else in the system will work unless the books and records are kept in good faith . . . . "

Discussion

The facts presented in this case are insufficient; the students cannot decide whether the commissions paid involved illegal payments; that is a conclusion reserved for lawyers only. Nor is that the question asked, though the answer to it would seem to be the ultimate result of any extension of audit procedures undertaken because of the concern over the information obtained. The case does provide however, information to permit the students to identify the issues that have to be resolved and to outline the proposed action steps to provide answers or to furnish further data on the identified issues.

The students will probably look to Statement on Auditing Standards No. 17, "Illegal Acts by Clients," as their principal source of guidance. The Statement is very general and offers limited guidance as to specific procedures to apply to suspected illegal acts, such as the suspicion in this case. It makes a good point that auditors, when an illegal act comes to their attention, should make certain that the board of directors, audit committee, or others give appropriate attention to the matter. Though Statement on Auditing Standards No. 17 is silent on the question, it seems logical that the same attention would be required when an illegal act is suspected as when it is known.

Auditors cannot run to the board or audit committee with every suspicion on any subject; yet after they have applied extended procedures appropriate in the circumstances, including consultation with the client's legal counsel, and still are not able to obtain an opinion or reach a layman's presumption whether an act is illegal or determine the dollar

Case 28: Auditing Commission Payments

amounts if indeed illegal acts are involved, they should expect appropriate action by the board or audit committee to resolve the dilemma.

But what extended procedures are appropriate in the circumstance at hand? The students should be filled with ideas. They should, however, recognize that procedures are apt to be applied sequentially. If procedure A settles the issues either as legal or illegal — then there is no need for procedures B through Z. And the same is true all along the line — auditors may get to a point where their decision is "we have an answer" or "we are never likely to have an answer," and in either case they would undoubtedly stop.

Another thing the students should recognize is that the timing of the extended procedures is crucial. Since they tend to be sequential, if they are commenced late and if the whole string must be run out before a conclusion is reached, the lapsed time to complete could destroy any hopes of finishing the audit in sufficient time to meet Securities and Exchange Commission deadlines, annual shareholders' meeting dates, and the like. For example, if one of the procedures is to require a full-scale investigation by the board of directors and its legal counsel before a "clean" opinion will be given, such investigation would take 60 to 90 days. If the auditors do not make known their requirement for an investigation by the board until 30 days before the Form 10-K filing date, they have done themselves and their client a grave disservice. And the demand for a full-scale investigation may come far, far down on the list of things to be done. Any presumption of concern on the auditors' part that they may be looking at illegal payments, as in this case, should evoke early on a program of procedures that will give all parties a fair chance of discharging their reporting responsibilities within the prescribed deadlines.

The students' discussion of appropriate extended procedures is likely to focus on those that will accumulate sufficient competent evidential matter to enable client's counsel to opine as to legality, although in practice auditors often use such accumulated evidential matter in arriving at their laymen's conclusion of whether an act, or a payment, was "illegal." (After all, they passed "Business Law" in their CPA exam.) The discussion of procedures aimed at whether the payments are "legal," "illegal," or "uncertain as to legality" (regardless of who makes that conclusion), should lead the students into a discussion of internal control and attendant record keeping. Since Powerco has no corporate policy statement designed to prevent or limit the occurrence of illegal payments, the principal emphasis in the discussion will probably center around contract approvals, payment approvals, and management override. Other points of discussion, beyond the identification procedures and the internal control procedures, that should be encouraged would include:

- Materiality — As nebulous as the concept of materiality is, many practitioners and many others would say that what is material in relation to a financial statement becomes much smaller when applied to illegal acts, particularly where top management is involved. The Securities and Exchange Commission would seem to hold a similar view.

- Misappropriation — The possibility exists that a portion of the commission paid could have been paid out by the commission agent to one or more officials of Powerco.

- Presentation and disclosure — The discussion of these subjects will probably go in two directions — what is to be shown and said (1) if illegal payments are established and (2) if a resolution one way or the other cannot be reached. In the case of the former, the students would be guided rather specifically by Statement of Financial Accounting Standards No. 5, "Contingencies," as to what to record, how to present it, and what to disclose. Further, as noted above, the Foreign Corrupt Practices Act itself requires proper accounting for all transactions, including such payments, if the accounting provisions of that law are not to be violated. In case of the second possibility, the same Statement would probably furnish the guidance needed by the students. In both cases, income taxes (as discussed further below) would be a consideration as to the appropriate recording, presentation, and disclosure.

• Reporting — Statement on Auditing Standards No. 17 furnishes some guidance on how auditors should report on known or suspected illegal payments (acts). A discussion of variations in the report based on the numerous possibilities at Powerco could be extensive; such discussions should be limited, however, as no determination can be made as to whether Powerco did violate the Foreign Corrupt Practices Act or any other domestic or foreign law. The students could be asked, however, to discuss whether their reporting or other action steps would be different if the payments were illegal and had been made by top management, such as the chief executive officer, rather than some lesser official, such as the sales manager of the Middle Eastern branch office.

Of the numerous extended procedures that will be advanced by students, two are discussed in more detail below.

• Confirmation with recipient — Most likely, students will suggest confirmation with the recipient of the dollar amount of commissions received by the commission agent, together with pertinent facts surrounding the receipt. The wording of the confirmation will differ by company, but the overall thrust is to elicit information as to whether the commission agent was required to pay or paid any part of it to other people and, if so, to whom. The students should recognize that responses may be expected, generally, from such agents, though some refuse to reply. Of those replying, some deny further payouts — which may or may not be true; but, perhaps the greatest number replying are evasive on the subject of further payouts, or say their records lack sufficient information to reply, or say in substance, "it's none of your business." While confirmation with an "unrelated party" is definitely considered a good source of competent evidential matter in the "garden variety" audit, the students should understand that responses to confirmation requests from commission agents in certain parts of the world may be significantly lacking in candor. If people engage in bribery schemes to put millions in their pockets for little or no work (here some or all of $40,000,000), they may be less than candid in responses to auditors if they suspect for a minute that the truth might precipitate big trouble: as a minimum, say, loss of future commissions; as a maximum, say, loss of head.

• Income taxes — The Internal Revenue Code provides that no deductions shall be allowed as an ordinary and necessary business expense for amounts paid or incurred, directly or indirectly, to officials or employees of a foreign government, if such payment to a U.S. official or employee would be illegal under U.S. law. Further interpretations of the Code state that the place where the expenses are paid or incurred is immaterial and that lawfulness under the laws of the foreign country is also immaterial. The regulations take a fairly broad view of what constitutes an indirect payment, which inures to the taxpayer's benefit or promotes his interest, regardless of how paid and who actually receives or makes the payment. The Internal Revenue Service could disallow the deduction of commission payments to foreign agents for lack of substantiation if the recipient is not identified. On the other hand, if the recipient is identified, the Internal Revenue Service could challenge the legality of the ultimate payment. Because of "suspicious circumstances" the Internal Revenue Service may argue that it is reasonable to assume that the payment to the agent is, at least in part, an indirect payment to an official or an employee of the foreign government. This, in turn, would impose on the taxpayer (corporation) the exceptional burden of proving that no such payment had been made by their agents. To prove such may border on the impossible at times, and thus the possibility of another contingency arises, subject to the considerations of Statement of Financial Accounting Standards No. 5, and such contingency could include possible tax fraud penalties as well as the shortfall in the income tax liability and related interest.

The students should be aware that the Internal Revenue Service, Securities and Exchange Commission, and other agencies exchange information on such transactions, which may reduce the chance of "escape" by a client even where illegal payments have been unknown to top management.

The Solution

The list below of extended procedures is illustrative only. Additional procedures could be added almost without limit. Findings through use of one procedure could trigger ten other procedures, for example. In fact, audit pursuit of illegal payments typically results in a blurring of what may be thought of as audit procedures in the conventional sense and what by any standards would be thought of as special investigation procedures. On the other hand, only one or two of the procedures below, or some other procedure, may be applied, followed by a conclusion that renders further procedures unnecessary.

As noted previously, Statement on Auditing Standards No. 17 has little in the way of specifics, and only a few generalities, listed as "Procedures that May Identify Illegal Acts." Some of the numerous, possible, appropriate procedures are:

- Obtain from the chief executive officer and other appropriate top management their written understanding of the nature of the commission payments.
- Obtain the same from house counsel and corporate general counsel.

  Such representations may be requested to be reduced to opinion as to legality of the payments under the Foreign Corrupt Practices Act, other U.S.A. laws (including federal income tax laws), state and local laws, and laws of the country of the purchasers and purchasing agents.

- Discuss with those client personnel who negotiated with commission agents the details of the negotiations; get their understanding of the substance of the commission payment, the extent of services performed, the means by which the agents could "establish a feeling of trust with the buyers," the agents' knowledge of the products being handled (which will tie back to the "trust" issue) and other data bearing on the role of the agent.
- Review for reasonableness of amounts paid in relation to services rendered.
- Confirm amount and substance of commissions with commission agents.
- Obtain information regarding commission agents as to their bona fides, their business reputation, their staff, the size of their business, their customers, and other data bearing on their operations in relation to the client and the Middle Eastern countries.

- Compare product pricing with that for other customers in other countries.
- Discuss findings with auditors' own legal counsel.
- Request approval of board of directors of each commission payment.
- Request full-scale investigation by board of directors and company legal counsel.
- Request meeting of client and auditor with Securities and Exchange Commission.

If at any point along the line the auditor is stopped from pursuing the auditing/investigative procedures considered necessary (or if the company refuses to record, classify, or disclose or accept a modified report as the auditor considers appropriate), the auditor should consult his/her counsel and consider the appropriate course to follow, including the possibility of withdrawing from the engagement.

Appendices

American Accounting Association
Representatives Attending Trueblood Professors' Seminars

Professor	American Accounting Association Role	Year(s) Attended
Samuel Frumer	Seminar Board Committee Member	1983
Yuji Ijiri	President	1983
Harold Q. Lagenderfer	President-Elect	1983
Jay Smith	Seminar Board Committee Member	1983
Loudell Ellis Robinson	Seminar Board Committee Member	1981/82
Robert W. Rouse	Seminar Board Committee Member	1982/83
John Tracy	Seminar Board Committee Member	1982
Jerry Weygandt	Seminar Board Committee Member	1980/81
James Fremgen	Director of Education	1981
Joseph Silvoso	President	1981
Donald H. Skadden	President	1980
Wanda A. Wallace	Seminar Board Committee Member	1980
Maurice Moonitz	President	1979
Frank Rayburn	Seminar Board Committee Member	1979
Jack Robertson	Seminar Board Committee Member	1979
Rene P. Manes	Seminar Board Committee Member	1978/79
David Solomons	President	1978
Leon Hay	Director of Education	1978
E. Dee Hubbard	Director of Continuing Education	1977/78
Charles Horngren	President	1977
Robert L. Grinaker	Director of Education	1977
Gary L. Holstrum	Seminar Board Committee Member	1977
Wilton T. Anderson	President	1976
Lee Brummet	President	1975
Elba Baskin	Seminar Board Committee Member	1975

Trueblood Professors' Seminars
Touche Ross & Co. Faculty
(1966 - 1983)

Bevis, Donald	Ostlund, Clayton
Bintinger, Thomas	Padwe, Gerald
Bloom, Raymond	Perry, Raymond
Bohan, Michael	Polansky, Gerald
Brown, Michael	Presby, Thomas
Burns, Joseph	Puglisi, Joseph
Cropsey, Jeffrey	Robinson, Christopher
Domingues, Robert	Rothermel, Robert
Fairman, Robert	Sack, Robert
Fuchs, Frederick	Shepherd, Helen
Gale, Andrew	Sherman, Len
Gallagher, Richard	Shield, Hans
Georgen, W. Donald	Shuma, Richard
Henderson, Alan	Tang, Palmer
Higgins, Paul	Taper, Eugene
Kay, Robert	Trueblood, Robert
Konkel, James	Van Camp, John
Lavin, Norman	Wall, Tom
Loebbecke, James	Walters, Ralph
Mayer, Jerry	Ward, Bart
Miller, Robert	Waxman, Robert
Mullarkey, John	Wood, Donald
Murray, Richard	Yarnall, Kent

Others

Roger Eickhoff
Carol Galante
Richard Jensen
Robert Knox
Henry Korff